MAKING GARDENS

MAKING GARDENS

PATRICK TAYLOR'S
Essential Guide to Planning and Planting

Photographs by Patrick Taylor
Garden plans painted by Charlotte Molesworth

WEIDENFELD & NICOLSON

London

First published 1998 by
Weidenfeld & Nicolson
The Orion Publishing Group, Orion House,
5 Upper St Martin's Lane, London WC2H 9EA

This book was devised and produced by Open Books Publishing Ltd,
Beaumont House, Wells BA5 2LD, Somerset, UK

Designer: Andrew Barron and Collis Clements Associates

Garden plans: Charlotte Molesworth

A CIP catalogue record for this book is available from the British Library.

ISBN: 0 297 82394 9

Typeset by Wandsworth Typesetting Ltd
Printed and bound in Hong Kong

CONTENTS

FOREWORD *7*

ACKNOWLEDGEMENTS *9*

INTRODUCTION *11*

THE GARDENS *20*

PLANT DIRECTORY *180*

INDEX *223*

Alexander — with all
my love for Christmas 1999
from Granny.

FOREWORD

To design and create your own garden takes courage and assurance, whether it is to fill an open space or radically change an existing garden. You do not want to risk making mistakes that will be expensive to alter: a pond, pergola or path in the wrong place, or a flowerbed badly designed.

How do we acquire this courage? Today there are plenty of short gardening courses which can help you learn about the rudiments of design, the colour and flowering time of plants, and how to draw a plan that looks good on paper. Patrick Taylor's book is not only an excellent follow-on from one of these courses, but it is more: it is an indispensable tool for the many people who are too occupied by their own work or their growing family to attend such classes. It is both a pleasure to read and brim full of ideas to consider and absorb.

We all have our own ways of learning – and with gardening we go on learning all through our lives. My way is to take a notebook with me when I visit gardens, and star things which catch my imagination: sometimes this is a good plant association, sometimes an idea that I might incorporate into my own garden or use in one I am helping to design.

Gardeners who are young both in age and in experience will not have old notebooks to turn to in this way. Fortunately, Patrick has now provided this material for them, in his own engaging style. His extensive knowledge of Europe and North America allows him to look at the way gardens are planned and planted with an appreciative and critical eye, assessing how and why they succeed.

Gardening has become such an important aspect of the life of many of us – town dwellers as well as country people – yet it is an art form few of us can excel at without help. We need to be fed with ideas we can visualise and then implement – and this is where Patrick's book will be an inspiration.

You, too, will be able to greet your guests on a summer day, encourage them to enjoy the view from your drawing-room, find a place to sit and paths to wander along, and admire your well laid-out and productive vegetable garden. The plans of herb gardens will enable you to provide those essential summer tastes, freshly picked moments before they are tossed into the salad.

I admire the choice of gardens that Patrick has made, and by describing and analysing in detail a wide range of gardens, he helps us to transfer this information for use in our own gardens. Follow Patrick around on his travels, then back to Britain, and you will discover many out-of-the-way places. He describes, for example, walled gardens in Holland, Britain and California, and covers a broad spectrum of features, from front gardens (first seen from a gate off the road), to swimming pools (how can you deal with a swimming pool if it cannot be hidden away?), to borders. There are many excellent books about borders (perhaps too many?), but they can leave us with a feeling of despair: will we ever get it right? In Patrick's book the border plans, like the others drawn by Charlotte Molesworth, are consistently easy to follow.

Beth Chatto's writing, her garden, and her exhibits at the Chelsea Flower Show have surely done more than those of any other designer to make us aware of the necessity of providing plants with the correct habitat. Here, we see her gravel garden full of drought-resistant plants which not only survive but flourish without irrigation. Beth's planting is always appropriate to the site, with marvellous combinations of leaf form and flower colour.

Christopher Lloyd's influence also affects us all. Both he and Beth are so original in their thinking, and so generous in offering ideas to us gardeners. Beth's gravel garden is designed for year-long interest in an important site, but Christopher's hidden-away tropical garden at Great Dixter concentrates on plants which give a firework of colour from May until the first frost. If you have an appropriate site in your garden – perhaps part of your driveway or a 6m × 1m strip between a townhouse and the pavement for a garden like Beth's, or a hidden sunny corner for one like Christopher's – you will find plenty of inspiration here. Allow all these possibilities to filter through your mind as you consider your own garden.

"Do not be daunted!" is an important theme in this book. Turn to the plans which marry so well with the photographs. Study the chapters on flower gardens, and you will find how to provide interest from spring to winter. Why not install a miniature orchard, a box parterre, arches or a pergola? Highlight ideas that are appropriate for your own garden. Be bold, sit down with pencil and paper and create your own designs and patterns. You will be surprised how much fun you will have, and how your imagination grows, and your understanding of plants increases, after studying the ideas in the book.

Start to keep your own 'Garden Book': a record of visits, reading, reactions. A crucial record, too, of plants you have ordered or bought, where they have been planted and – after a few years – how well they have done.

We live in an age of computers, but to me there is nothing so useful as the hand-written notes in my garden books. They transport me back to the vivid moments when I turned a corner in a garden and saw a breathtaking sight: a statue, a clematis, a waterfall, or a vista.

Patrick's book is a wonderful starting-off point for a beginner gardener and can also be turned to as a refresher course for a seasoned gardener looking for ideas.

Rosemary Verey

ACKNOWLEDGEMENTS

My first, enormous, debt is to the garden owners and Head Gardeners who so kindly welcomed me and gave their time so generously. Not only did they take me round their gardens and give me much precious knowledge but they also read and corrected my descriptions. They could not have been kinder and I am profoundly grateful to them all: Sir Hardy Amies (The School House), Louisa and James Arbuthnott (Stone House Cottage*), Kate and Reggie Askew (Carters Cottage), Barbara Brooker and Kees van de Wekering (Holdenby House*), Beth Chatto (Beth Chatto Gardens*), A.R. Cleaver (Mallory Court), The Hon. Mrs Peter Healing (The Priory*, Kemerton), Lesley and John Jenkins (Wollerton Old Hall*), Judy and Hugh Johnson (Saling Hall*), Martin Lane Fox (Hazelby House), Wendy Lauderdale (Ashtree Cottage), Frank and Marjorie Lawley (Herterton House*), Christopher Lloyd and Fergus Garrett (Great Dixter*), Cynthia and Chapin Nolen, Margaret Ogilvie (House of Pitmuies*), Wendy and Michael Perry (Bosvigo House*), Sandra and Nori Pope (Hadspen Gardens*), the late Lady Anne Rasch and Gwyn Perry (Heale House*), Patricia van Roosmalen, Lord and Lady Saye and Sele, and Chris Hopkins (Broughton Castle*), Martin Summers (London Roof Garden), Caroline Todhunter (Old Rectory, Farnborough), Elizabeth MacLeod Matthews (Chenies Manor*), Anthony Noel, Kathy Sayer (Kellie Castle*), Geoffrey Smith (Warwick Town Garden), Richard Staples (York Gate*), Carol Valentine, Keith and Ros Wiley (The Garden House*). All those marked with an asterisk are regularly open to the public.

I am most grateful to Anne Askwith and James Bennett for their detailed editorial help. The text also received an expert wash and brush up from my wife, Caroline, to whom I am deeply indebted. Andrew Barron designed the book with his habitual skill and efficiency. It was a particular pleasure to work with the artist, Charlotte Molesworth, who painted the beautiful plans. It was a great honour that Rosemary Verey should have agreed to write a Foreword which she did with her usual perceptiveness and generosity.

INTRODUCTION

All garden visitors must have experienced the pleasure of being in a well-designed garden without consciously reflecting on the reasons for their delight. In the end, two qualities seem to matter   the garden feels right and all its ingredients, planting and 'hard' landscaping, are in harmony. But what is right and what is harmony? Many garden owners know these things by instinct and make fine gardens without reflecting at all on abstract ideas of gardening aesthetics. This book does not deal with ideas but with the actuality of gardens, although I have tried to show some of the principles that lie behind the actuality.

The purpose of this book is to encourage gardeners to think about the design and planting of their gardens. The text, photographs and garden plans will, I hope, give inspiration to help solve particular problems and inspire gardeners to have the confidence to plan their own designs. Instead of starting from the basis of principles, I start with examples of gardens and garden features which I consider have been successfully designed. I have chosen them to reflect a wide range of different features and various styles of gardening. This is, however, a book about *gardens* not about barbecues, tennis courts, children's playing fields and all the paraphernalia which people understandably desire to include in their gardens.

The great American gardener Thomas Church wrote in his book *Gardens are for People*, 'There are no mysterious "musts", no set rules, no finger of shame pointed at the gardener who doesn't follow an accepted pattern.' While there is much truth in that, it is far from the whole truth. By looking at well-made gardens and analysing the nature of their design, any gardener can learn from other people's experience. Only the most arrogant or foolhardy writer would assume that there is nothing to learn from Homer's poetry or the plays of Shakespeare and the work of much less eminent authors, too, has exemplary value.

For most gardeners the chief object is to create a place that is agreeable to be in. This book shows how this aim has been achieved and I hope the examples will help you to make the garden you want. A very few of the examples chosen are the work of professional garden designers or landscape architects, such as Rosemary Verey or Isabelle Greene. But most have been

Martin Summers's roof garden, high above the streets of London, scorns the limitations of its site and deploys an immense range of floriferous plants. Planted in pots closely packed together, they have all the impact of densely planted country borders.

created by amateurs for their own enjoyment. It is a curious fact that whereas virtually all successful artists have had some sort of training, some of the most accomplished gardens of the day have been made by people with no academic knowledge of garden design – some lucky gardeners seem to have an instinct for what works.

Those who design their own gardens always have one immense advantage over the professional garden designer working on other people's plots. They are able to know their own site far more intimately, in every season, than any visiting professional ever can. Vita Sackville-West, who had no professional horticultural training whatsoever, lived at Sissinghurst Castle for thirty years during which she and her husband, Harold Nicolson, made their great garden. It was the subject of endless refinement – and changes of mind – and depended as much on their own sensitive, and cumulative, understanding of the site in all its aspects as on their horticultural and artistic skills. We cannot have their extraordinary gifts but we can all get to know and understand our own plots in greater detail than anyone else.

The gardens I have chosen are, on the whole, conservative because that is my own taste and I believe that this largely corresponds to the taste of the time. The avant-garde in gardening has made little impact. Excellent modern designs exist, of which Carol Valentine's garden in southern California shown on pages 132–5 is a brilliant example. But even here it is easy to see the strong influence of the past, for it conforms strictly to Renaissance ideas about harmony between house and site. With its hillside views of the Pacific Ocean, and its 'Delight of Gardens' in the foreground, it would have pleased the Renaissance scholar Leon Battista Alberti who codified the essential principles of garden design in the 15th century.

A garden designed by Isabelle Greene at Santa Barbara in southern California is strikingly modern and yet honours ancient principles of garden design. It is in harmony with house and site.

At Herterton House herbaceous plants are allowed to grow naturally, usually unsupported, to assume their natural bushy shapes. Clipped shapes of hedges and topiary give solid structure amidst the softer planting.

Garden design, like many another art, is on the whole a cumulative process, with certain ideas going back a very long way indeed. I know this is a source of regret to some professional garden designers who think such fondness for the past is unhealthy and want to propel their clients firmly into the future. On the other hand, if there is continuing vitality in old traditions, why not draw on them for inspiration? Many of the gardens shown here plainly demonstrate the potency of the past. Frank and Marjorie Lawley's brilliant flower garden (pages 68–71) is rooted in tradition but, nonetheless, it is a thoroughly modern garden. The exotic new garden made by Christopher Lloyd (pages 100–3) uses the framework of a design by Sir Edwin Lutyens as the setting for a radically new style of planting to create a dazzling vision for the late 20th century. There has been much talk recently of naturalistic planting, copying the abundance and irregularity of nature's methods. Beth Chatto's gravel garden (pages 112–15) is a bewitching very recent example. Yet this, too, lies firmly in the tradition of the 19th-century gardener/writer William Robinson who preached the use of hardy exotics in a wild setting.

In order to make the book as immediately relevant as possible to most gardeners I have chosen examples from smaller gardens, or features that may be adapted to a smaller garden. For this reason two major categories are omitted – the woodland garden and the landscape garden. Although some of the techniques of the first, such as planting shade-loving subjects under deciduous trees, are entirely relevant to smaller gardens, the full effect of the deployment of great trees and shrubs in a naturalistic setting is something few private gardeners may do. The same is true of landscape gardens although these, too, will always contain lessons applicable to any garden. The positioning of an ornament, the effect of surprise, or the juxtaposition of

At Ashtree Cottage (*right*) the pool garden is rich in shade- and moisture-loving plants – hostas, ferns, irises, Solomon's seal and the giant leaves of *Rheum palmatum*.

different ingredients (a bench among flowers, a statue in a glade, a glint of water among shadows) are all relevant to gardeners.

Too much garden design is a bad thing. The gardens that are most pleasurable to be in are hard to analyse and have an air of mysterious inevitably. Visitors may sometimes be able to point at a few details not exactly to their own tastes but that will not detract from the success of the whole. Overdesigned gardens, on the other hand, trumpet the skills of the designer rather than addressing the merits of the site. In the most successful gardens there is almost always a quality of directness and simplicity. These sound like quiet virtues but they can often be the basis for gardens of explosive excitement, such as Wendy and Michael Perry's 'hot borders' (pages 120–3). Directness and simplicity are often the source, too, of magical atmosphere. The Lawleys' shining silver totem of clipped pear in the physic garden at Herterton (pages 168–71) is as simple, and as magical, as could be.

The single most important element in any garden is the spirit of the place. By this I mean the whole setting and circumstances of the plot. The vegetable garden at Heale House (pages 148–51) is an exceptional example of this. Its openness to its surroundings, the use of traditional materials in its walls, the delightful mixture of ornamental and productive gardening, and the boldly simple layout allow it to fit into its setting with perfect ease. In a small town garden, on the other hand, such as Anthony Noel's jewel-like patch (pages 92–5) the diminutive scale and undisguisable urban setting are the essential facts which form the starting point of the design. It responds to the challenge by pretending that the limitations are not there. The little front garden of Carters Cottage (pages 28–31) honours the spirit of the place in a quite different way. Here, the garden has simultaneously to fit in with its ancient,

The hot borders at Bosvigo House (*left*) illuminate a woodland setting. In the foreground *Arctotis* × *hybrida* 'Flame' with the scarlet dahlia 'Bishop of Llandaff', blood-red bergamot and yellow ligularia in the background.

On a raised bed at The Garden House, Keith Wiley has arranged naturalistic planting of brilliant simplicity. Swathes of white, pink or red rhodohypoxis are interspersed with rock roses, sedums and creeping thymes.

In Beth Chatto's gravel garden the plants are chosen to survive without irrigation in one of the driest parts of England. Planted in bold clumps, and allowed to self-seed, they have a convincingly natural appearance. The harmony of their effect comes from their similar drought-loving habitats.

unspoilt rural surroundings, to provide a sympathetic entrance to the house and to make a harmonious setting for it. All these things are achieved with an ease and straightforwardness which many a show-off television garden designer could learn from. The spirit of the place includes the climate and the soil. Nothing is sadder than the sight of some chlorotic camellia struggling to live in thin alkaline soil. Beth Chatto's gravel garden (pages 112–15) shows the effect, on a large scale, of choosing plants specifically for their site and climate. An apparently purely scientific/environmental approach has resulted in a garden of lovely magic.

The way in which a garden is enclosed and divided within is a vital part of its character. It is often said that the perimeter, especially of a small garden, should be concealed. However, if it is attractive – fine walls or a distinguished hedge – this seems to me absurd. On the other hand, in a garden in the country, the point at which the garden stops and the countryside starts is a critical moment, well worth thinking about carefully. This is no place for overwrought topiary – a simple hedge of holly, beech or hornbeam, or a mixture of plants, looks best. In an orchard or wild garden that abuts onto countryside nothing looks better than a field hedge containing the sort of plants used for such things locally. In my part of England it includes plants such as hawthorn (*Crataegus laevigata*), blackthorn (*Prunus spinosa*), field maple (*Acer campestre*), dog roses (*Rosa canina*) and elder (*Sambucus nigra*) woven together and forming a stock-proof hedge of unbeatable beauty.

The major divisions within a garden are essential to its nature. The pattern of beds, paths, paving, lawns, walls and hedges is the dominant visual ingredient. Two evergreen plants are by far the most valuable for internal

Fastidious but
simple use of local
stone marks the
garden at York Gate.
The path is made of
old granite sets laid
in a criss-cross
pattern.

garden hedges – box and yew. I am tempted to say that they are the two most valuable of all garden plants. Although evergreen, their foliage changes subtly with the seasons, a source of endless pleasure. Low hedges of box – either common box, *Buxus sempervirens* or dwarf box, *B. s.* 'Suffruticosa' – will fit in anywhere, harmonizing equally well with strict formality and with cottage-garden blowsiness. Dwarf box is for very low hedges, no more than 9in/23cm in height, and common box should be used for taller hedges. It is also admirable for topiary and simple geometric shapes. Common box is usually used to make hedges no more than 24–36in/60–90cm high – but much taller hedges are possible. I have seen a box hedge 18ft/5.5m high forming giant billowing shapes – magnificent, but of an entirely different character from the crisply cut hedge that marks out a parterre. There are gold and silver variegated forms of box, and many cultivars of curious foliage, all of which have their decorative uses. Neatly clipped common box makes wonderful edging for borders, adding a crisp boundary to profuse planting. Yew (*Taxus baccata*) is the best plant for substantial hedges within the garden but it should never be used for boundary hedges in the country for parts of it are poisonous to livestock. It is long-lived, needs clipping only once a year and forms a marvellous background to planting of all kinds.

I always think that local materials, or convincing imitations of them, are best for paths and garden buildings. The garden at York Gate (pages 52–5) is near Leeds in West Yorkshire, a part of England rich in fine quality building stone which is used throughout the garden for beautifully judged paths, walls, ornaments and buildings. The conservatory at Saling Hall (pages 172–5), in a part of eastern England where virtually all houses are made of brick, has walls of exactly the same type of slender 17th-century bricks of which the house and old paths in the garden are made.

Much of this book describes planting schemes showing a huge variety of styles. It is a defect of much British gardening in recent times that the deployment of colour has been too timid. That is changing, and pioneer gardens such as the Priory at Kemerton (pages 108–11) and, more recently, Hadspen Gardens (pages 128–31), show that harmony need not be insipidly soporific and can produce thrilling drama. Many of the ideas used in these plantings hark back to the colour theory of 19th-century painters on which Gertrude Jekyll drew. If colour can be exciting, so can its absence. Furthermore, no amount of brilliantly executed colour scheming, however seductive it may be, can remedy the defects of weak design. Patricia van Roosmalen's avenue of evergreens leading to a summerhouse of pleached dogwood (pages 88–91) and her exquisite largely green formal orchard (pages 160–3) show the essential power of a strong underlying layout.

There is no advice in this book about the construction of gardens. Many books are available which are full of valuable information of that kind. All the plants mentioned in the planting plans are included, alphabetically by plant name, in the Plant Directory (pages 180–222) at the end of the book. This gives information about size, hardiness and cultivation. The gardens themselves are arranged broadly in groups: entrances (pages 20–31), pools and water gardens (pages 32–47), sitting places and terraces (pages 48–67), town and walled gardens (pages 68–99), flower gardens and borders (pages 100–47), productive gardens (pages 148–71), a conservatory (pages 172–5) and a roof garden (pages 176–9).

Patricia van Roosmalen's miniature orchard in Belgium vividly displays the attractions of green geometry. Old local varieties of apples and pears are espaliered in little box-edged beds.

A PERGOLA FORMS A DECORATIVE ENTRANCE TO A COUNTRY COTTAGE

A wooden pergola straddles a gravel entrance path, from which the front door of the house is only revealed at the last moment.

A pergola is a precious garden feature, creating structural emphasis and providing a sturdy frame on which to train climbing and twining plants. Even in winter, unadorned with leaf or flower, its shape will give pleasure. The placing of a pergola in a garden is important – if it is set down in some arbitrary place, leading nowhere, it always looks uneasy. It is most effective when incorporated into some logical passage, as in the example here.

When the owner first came to this cottage, an unattractive tarmac path led from the road to the front door. The road entrance and the front door were not on the same axis; straight for most of its length, the path turned quite sharply towards the end to meet the door. However, this potential awkwardness has been turned to good advantage. You now enter the pergola from the road, where a single window of the house presents itself as a focal point; the front door is revealed only when the end of the pergola is reached.

This country cottage garden is in a rather exposed, windy site which has been much improved by planting windbreaks. The pergola itself is protected by plantings of trees and shrubs – an important consideration because many climbing plants are particularly vulnerable to the blast of cold winds when held aloft on the unprotected framework.

The planting of the pergola is so lavish that in high summer it is a tunnel of flower and foliage and you must brush aside the sprawling growth of catmint (*Nepeta* 'Six Hills Giant') which is planted in regular pairs down its entire length. There is plenty of plant interest earlier in the season, too, when tulips – the tall single pink 'Rosy Wings' – ornament the beds that run along either side of the pergola path. These are followed by *Viola cornuta* and its white-flowered variety, as well as the grey-leafed daisy, *Anthemis punctata* sbsp. *cupaniana*. Unnamed seedling delphiniums rise up on either side, providing in June a wall of soft blues. Honeysuckles give their irresistible scent, both the old *Lonicera × italica* (formerly *Lonicera × americana*) and an unnamed seedling of the European native *L. caprifolium*. Apart from the beauty of the flowers, the fresh green foliage of both plants is ornamental.

The pergola runs for 80ft/25m and is made of tanalised softwood with round supporting posts spaced at intervals of 9ft/2.75m. The path, now surfaced with fine gravel, is 4ft/1.2m wide and edged with stone. This is wide enough for only one person but the relative narrowness emphasises the tunnel effect and the atmosphere of mystery and enclosure when the planting is in full flow. The section shown in the plan is about one quarter of the whole and shows its characteristic planting style. Roses are dominant, intermingling with clematis to form the pergola's 'roof'. Scented plants add an essential ingredient to its pleasures. The Rambler rose 'Wedding Day', with lustrous foliage and generous

In high June the shade of the pergola is enlivened by the glowing colours of roses, clematis and catmint sprawling across the path. Enticing glimpses are seen of the cottage at the end of the tunnel, and, on either side, of planting in beds flanking the pergola.

trusses of sweetly scented white flowers, is immensely vigorous. It makes an excellent pergola plant but does need much work to keep it in order. Planted on the other side, but intertwining with it, is another Rambler rose, 'Violette', whose small cupped violet flowers have a rich scent. Scrambling over the 'roof' of the pergola is 'Sanders' White Rambler' which, although very thorny, is comparatively easy to keep in control. Its double white flowers – appearing rather later in the season than most roses – are marvellously scented, and it has attractive gleaming foliage. It is, incidentally, best grown on a pergola; it is prone to mildew, and when trained on a wall is especially susceptible. Another Rambler rose, 'Bleu Magenta', has miniature double flowers of a striking deep purple and is also excellently scented. It has the further attraction of being virtually thornless. Here, it intermingles with the summer-flowering clematis 'Comtesse de Bouchaud' whose flamboyant large flowers of a warm mauve-pink start before the rose has finished flowering, in late June or early July. On the north side of the pergola is a modern Climbing rose, 'Bantry Bay', whose blowsy pink flowers are well scented and produced throughout the season. Among the bush roses planted in the beds alongside the uprights are two outstanding old Gallicas: the crimson 'Duc de Guiche' and the dusty purple 'Cardinal de Richelieu', both of which are sweetly scented. Late in the summer, waves of Japanese anemones take over from the catmint and the delphiniums.

A pergola planting such as this needs careful maintenance. The climbing roses are pruned in late autumn, with old growth being removed and new growth, on which the following season's flowers will be borne, tied in. They are fed with bonemeal, or other organic fertiliser in the winter, with a mulch of used mushroom compost. In the summer regular foliar feeds and an occasional dose of proprietary rose fertiliser are given. A pergola provides a healthy

The pink rose 'Bantry Bay' festoons the uprights of the pergola, with delphiniums and the trailing fronds of *Nepeta* 'Six Hills Giant' rising from among the handsome foliage of Japanese anemones.

setting for plants and no use is made of sprays against pests and diseases. The catmint and violas are cut back in July when they have become leggy, to produce further flowers in the late summer and autumn.

This simple pergola is perfectly in keeping with the unpretentious style of the rest of the garden – the plain woodwork and gravel path in character with the thatched stone-built cottage. The pergola charmingly fulfils its primary purpose of leading you – in the most attractive possible way – deeper into the garden and towards the house. As you walk along, shifting views of other parts of the garden are framed by the uprights.

In late summer the sprawling shoots of catmint drag against your feet as an encouragement to walk slowly and savour both the the pergola itself and the views that open out on either side. And from other parts of the garden the pergola is an important decorative feature, its framework all but hidden by the profusion of flowering plants that cover its surface. Thus it plays several roles and at the same time fulfils its primary function as an entrance.

ASHTREE COTTAGE PERGOLA

1 *Anthemis punctata* sbsp. *cupaniana*
2 *Nepeta* 'Six Hills Giant'
3 *Anemone × hybrida* 'Honorine Jobert'
4 *Anemone × hybrida* 'Superba'
5 *Iris* seedling
6 *Rosa* 'Wedding Day'
7 *Rosa* 'Violette'
8 *Rosa* 'Bantry Bay'
9 *Rosa* 'Ballerina'
10 *Clematis*, unnamed, blue
11 *Rosa* 'Cardinal de Richelieu'
12 *Rosa* 'Duc de Guiche'
13 *Rosa* 'Bleu Magenta'
14 *Clematis* 'Comtesse de Bouchaud'
15 *Rosa* 'Sanders' White Rambler'

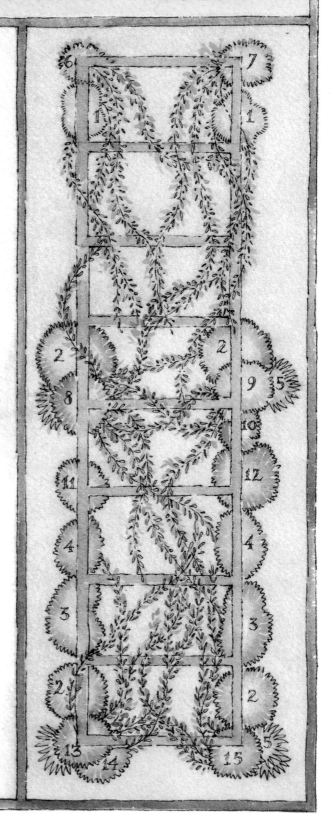

A FORMAL FRONT GARDEN FOR A COUNTRY HOUSE

Designed to solve the problem of an awkward entrance, this front garden provides a model that could be adapted for many different settings.

Front gardens are too often ignored in favour of their larger brethren at the back. Their unique design problems should always be addressed independently of the rest of the garden, in order to give the house a decorative and logical entrance. A successful solution, as here, breathes an air of inevitability so strong that it is difficult to see how it could have been solved in any other way.

In this case the garden is that of a self-contained dower house attached to the main building. The approach to the front door is from the side, making the most direct route from the entrance an unsatisfactory oblique line. A curved path would have been a possibility but this would have created awkwardly shaped areas on either side of it. In the event, the owners contrived a satisfyingly simple solution which also provided logical spaces for planting.

The area to the front of the house is roughly square, 40ft × 40ft/12m × 12m, enclosed by walls and hedges of holly (*Ilex aquifolium*) and *Lonicera nitida*. It has been divided into four parts with a cruciform pattern of paths which closely matches in spirit the gentlemanly formality of the four-square 18th-century house. The entrance path thus continues to the centre of the garden, where the visitor turns at ninety degrees in order to reach the front door.

Four square beds each have a square notch taken out of the inside corner, and the square area formed in the centre of the garden is marked with a brick plinth and a block of stone surmounted by an urn – filled in spring with the double

white daisy *Bellis perennis* 'Alba Plena', and in summer with white verbena. Standing inside each 'notch' is a terracotta pot planted with box (*Buxus sempervirens*) clipped into the shape of a cone. The paths are surfaced in fine sea pebbles of a warm pale grey colour and the beds are edged with slightly raised bricks.

The whole area is low-lying, with the house, walls and hedges casting much of it into shade. This has restricted the choice of plants – although it certainly does not give the air of having been a limitation. At the centre of each bed a 6ft/1.8m broadly-based cone of clipped golden privet (*Ligustrum ovalifolium* 'Aureum') provides a firm punctuation mark. The planting of each of the four beds is similar but not identical, and a colour scheme of white, blue and gold predominates. The planting scheme shown on page 27, described here, illustrates the planting in just one of the beds.

Lapping at the feet of the golden privet is a wave of variegated hosta (*Hosta crispula*) with sprightly white undulating margins, and behind it, in the corner, a bold clump of *Ligularia* 'The Rocket' which in high summer throws out 6ft/1.8m slender spires of crisp lemon-yellow flowers. Even when not in flower its shield-shaped boldly toothed leaves and dark stems are strikingly ornamental. To one side rise the equally tall spires of the delphinium 'Alice Artindale', with very double chalky blue flowers, and at its feet the sea holly *Eryngium* × *zabelii*, with intense electric-blue flowers and

Even on an overcast day the golden foliage of the evergreen privet (*Ligustrum ovalifolium* 'Aureum') gives a glow of light. The edges of the strong four-part pattern of beds facing the front door are hidden by planting, but they still impart harmony.

Within the beds much of the planting is strikingly bold in form and colour. Yellow spires of *Ligularia* 'The Rocket' rise up in the background with, in the front, the metallic blue flowers of *Eryngium* × *zabelii*, the chalk blue *Delphinium* 'Alice Artindale' and white mophead flowers of *Leucanthemum* × *superbum* 'Shaggy'.

intricately cut petals. Other substantial herbaceous plants make shapely contributions to the centre of the bed: Japanese anemones (*Anemone* × *hybrida* 'Honorine Jobert'), an elegant white agapanthus (*A. campanulatus* var. *albidus*), and the Shasta daisy *Leucanthemum* × *superbum* 'Shaggy' with large white shaggy flowers, so heavy that they bow down the tips of their stems. In summer, *Gladiolus* 'The Bride' makes a valuable ornamental plant with its emphatic sword-like leaves and shapely white trumpet-flowers.

The planting along the edge of the bed, occasionally flopping over onto the paths, repeats on a smaller scale the colour scheme at the centre. Here are golden marjoram (*Origanum vulgare* 'Aureum'), variegated box (*Buxus sempervirens* 'Aureovariegata'), *Lamium maculatum* 'White Nancy', *Alchemilla mollis*, the curious coffee-coloured *Viola* 'Irish Molly', and various annuals which vary from year to year but might include white *Cosmos bipinnatus* and a pretty, pale cream form of the Californian poppy (*Eschscholzia californica*).

These beds are planted chiefly for summer display – almost all the plants are either herbaceous or deciduous. But in winter the simple geometry of beds

and paths, privet cones and square hedges of box forms a decorative pattern, and in spring there is a dazzling display of the lily-flowered tulip 'White Triumphator' which erupts from the emerging herbaceous foliage – especially that of the self-seeding columbine *Aquilegia vulgaris* whose glaucous rounded leaves make a distinguished background.

The chief maintenance, apart from keeping the gravel paths free of weeds, is the removal of dead herbaceous top growth in the autumn and winter. After that, before the new season's growth stirs into life, there is a heavy top-dressing of mushroom compost. As the hosta foliage unfurls a remorseless battle against slugs is fought, with scatterings of slug pellets put down on a weekly basis – 'few and often' is the principle. By June the planting in the centre of the borders is so dense as to suppress almost any weed, and the only weeding subsequently needed is among the lower-growing plants at the very edges of the borders.

These beds are full of valuable lessons for decorative planting. There is little permanent woody planting apart from box and the tall cones of privet. The remainder of the planting is

THE VEAN ENTRANCE GARDEN

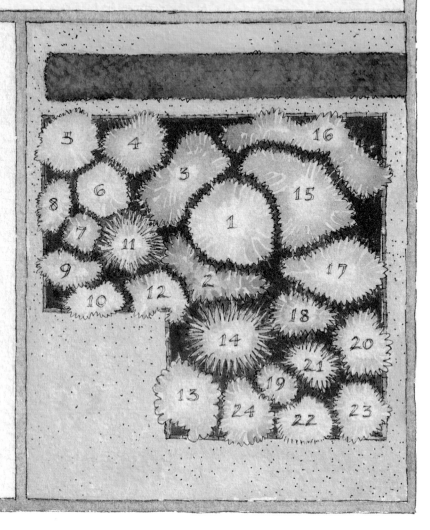

1 *Ligustrum ovalifolium* 'Aureum'
2 *Hosta crispula*
3 *Phlox* 'Fujiyama'
4 *Cosmos bipinnatus* 'Purity'
5 *Origanum vulgare* 'Aureum'
6 *Buxus sempervirens* 'Aureovariegata'
7 *Viola* 'Irish Molly'
8 *Potentilla* unnamed
9 *Geranium* 'Johnson's Blue'
10 *Lamium maculatum* 'White Nancy'
11 *Gladiolus* 'The Bride'
12 *Eschscholzia californica* cream form
13 *Alchemilla mollis*
14 *Agapanthus campanulatus* var. *albidus*
15 *Anemone* × *hybrida* 'Honorine Jobert'
16 *Ligularia* 'The Rocket'
17 *Delphinium* 'Alice Artindale'
18 *Eryngium* × *zabelii*
19 *Viola* 'Little David'
20 *Leucanthemum* × *superbum* 'Shaggy'
21 *Sisyrinchium striatum* 'Aunt May'
22 *Artemisia alba* 'Canescens'
23 *Thalictrum aquilegiifolium* var. *album*
24 *Calamintha grandiflora* 'Alba'

herbaceous and provides a striking example of the variety of flower and foliage and, above all, of the firm structural presence of many herbaceous plants. Each bed has veils of tall ligularia rising at the back, and bold planting at the centre about the golden privet. The harmony of the cool colour scheme is actually based on a considerable range of flower colours – omitting only reds and purples.

The starting point for the design of this front garden is the house itself and the approach to it. The garden serves two purposes – it provides a decorative and logical entrance and makes a self-contained garden in its own right; it is not a mere passage leading to the house. The views of patterns and planting seen from within the house – especially from its upstairs windows – are particularly attractive, and from handsome wooden benches at the end of two of the paths there are views both of the house and of the beds.

This garden epitomises the principle that once a good layout is established many different sorts of plants may be harmoniously deployed. The firmness of the plan allows flexibility of planting. Here, restricted colours and repetition of plants give additional harmony.

A FRONT GARDEN FOR A COUNTRY COTTAGE

Lively planting, touches of formality and an unpretentious sense of design create a front garden that is the perfect prelude to an attractive old stone house.

The front garden is an opportunity to create a first impression that may well dominate the mood of the whole place. It makes a statement about the owner's way of life; it can create a sympathetic setting for the house; and it provides a foretaste of the rest of the garden. But, just as it is an opportunity for displaying garden virtues it is, just as obviously, a chance to go horribly wrong.

Front gardens often bring out the worst in garden designers, who seize upon them to create a trumpet blast of ostentation in the most public part of the garden. The approach to the front door of the house is always best treated as simply as possible. The finest garden designers, from Humphry Repton to Russell Page, are very firm on the matter of paths – their route should be dictated by reason rather than by whim. In the front garden of the cottage shown here, a gate in a low stone wall leads to a path which proceeds straight to the front door. This is the obvious, and natural, way of linking the two entrances. Dramatic designs can result from ignoring the obvious but in this case simplicity is called for.

The character of the house and its immediate setting are the two most important points of reference in any garden design. The house shown here is a typical English country house of the early 19th century, still showing the straightforward symmetry of its classical origins. It fronts onto a little road on the edge of a village where, although there are other houses nearby, the atmosphere is wholly rural.

The front garden here is 15ft/4.5m deep, fronted by a stone wall 36in/90cm high. A hedge of *Lonicera nitida* planted along the back of the wall has been trained and clipped so that it now forms a green coping to the top of the wall. Together they form a boundary that neither blocks views of the garden nor obscures the windows of the house. Lonicera, universally used in cottage gardens, is usually disdained in more formal gardens, and dismissed as 'poor man's box'. But it makes an admirable evergreen hedge and also lends itself well to topiary. The small leaves take clipping well, create an attractive surface, and are a good mid-green in colour, while in spring the new foliage has a sparkling freshness. However, to achieve the impeccable effect seen here does involve frequent clipping. This hedge, decorated at one end with a clipped bird sitting on a sphere, and with a second bird in progress, is given a trim every ten days from mid-April to the autumn. The garden path is surfaced with stone flags, with beds on either side. By the gate a honeysuckle (*Lonicera periclymenum*) trained on a lollipop frame is the first among several scented plants which contribute to the atmosphere of the place. A bush of rosemary (*Rosmarinus officinalis*) and a clump of pinks (*Dianthus* cultivars) also give fragrance. In the bed to the left of the path are two bushes of Mexican orange (*Choisya ternata*) whose glistening evergreen leaves give off an attractive scent of varnish in the sun. These, if left to their own devices, would be too big

The front garden presents a welcoming appearance to visitors and is also wholly in keeping with the cottage and its surroundings. A cheerful topiary bird of clipped *Lonicera nitida* greets visitors, and enticing plants are glimpsed through the opening.

A sweeping hedge, of box at one end and *Lonicera nitida* at the other, echoes the ancient sculpted landscape which rises in front of the cottage. The old shrub rose 'Ispahan' is girdled by lavender, and a standard rose, 'Iceberg', provides perpetual summer ornament.

for the area, and are pruned back after their spring flowering to keep them small and shapely. Individual branches are cut back with secateurs so that no cut stems or mutilated leaves are visible. Too much evergreen foliage, especially if it is dark in colour, can give rise to claustrophobia but the glossy leaves of the choisya reflect the light, giving a cheerful air. It also makes an excellent background to other plants, which in spring include the splendid yellow flowers of crown imperials (*Fritillaria imperialis* 'Maxima Lutea'). Rising like a fanfare above the two bushes of choisya are standard trained 'Iceberg' roses. The slightly scented double flowers are produced perpetually throughout the summer, and the slight creaminess in their colour avoids harsh chalk-white. To one side the perpetual-flowering Polyantha rose 'Gruss an Aachen' has sweetly-scented creamy pink flowers. The almost tropical scent of the white perennial stock (*Matthiola*) adds an exotic note.

Trained against the walls of the house are two deciduous fruit trees. To the right of the front door is that most decorative of quince cultivars – *Cydonia oblonga* 'Portugal'. This has particularly large pale pink flowers and fruits well on this sunny wall, the golden fruit looking especially beautiful against the pale stone. At its feet is a clump of the Algerian iris (*Iris unguicularis*), relishing a dry, sunny position and providing dazzling flowers in mid-winter. On the other side of the door a fig (*Ficus carica* 'Brown Turkey') is meticulously trained round windows and tied to wires. Although vigorous, and needing much pruning and training, this makes an admirable wall plant. In high summer it provides shade but, being deciduous, does not obscure precious winter light, while the orderly framework of branches, revealed after the leaves have fallen, makes a handsome ornament. The fruit, too, is marvellously decorative. Fruiting is improved by the wholesale cutting back of extension shoots on fruiting branches in June.

This front garden strikes a harmonious note of unpretentious ornament in a setting where anything too contrived would be false. A garden's first impression is always important. The mood is set by the cheerful formality of the topiary bird which greets visitors at the entrance gate. Just as the house is not symmetrical, so there is no strict symmetry of planting in the garden, but there is balance: the

CARTERS COTTAGE FRONT GARDEN

1 *Lonicera periclymenum*	**14** *Agapanthus* Headbourne	**25** *Geranium phaeum* 'Album'
2 *Hydrangea macrophylla*	Hybrid	**26** *Iris* unnamed
3 *Rosmarinus officinalis*	**15** *Rosa* 'Iceberg'	**27** *Anaphalis triplinervis*
4 *Weigela* 'Newport Red'	**16** *Lunaria annua alba*	**28** *Thymus vulgaris*
5 *Dianthus* unnamed	**17** *Salvia officinalis*	**29** *Omphalodes verna*
6 *Phlox subulata*	Purpurascens Group	**30** *Iberis saxatilis*
7 *Daphne* × *burkwoodii*	**18** *Heuchera sanguinea*	**31** *Daphne acutiloba*
'Somerset'	**19** *Choisya ternata*	**32** *Acanthus spinosus*
8 *Iris unguicularis*	**20** *Rosa* 'Gruss an Aachen'	**33** *Matthiola* White Perennial
9 *Cydonia oblonga* 'Portugal'	**21** *Osmanthus delavayi*	**34** *Hebe topiaria*
10 *Ficus carica* 'Brown Turkey'	**22** *Tiarella polyphylla*	**35** *Campanula latifolia alba*
11 *Viola cornuta*	**23** *Anemone hupehensis*	**36** *Centranthus ruber*
12 *Primula auricula*	**24** *Fritillaria imperialis*	**37** *Buxus sempervirens*
13 *Erysimum* 'Wenlock Beauty'	'Maxima Lutea'	**38** *Lonicera nitida*

standard honeysuckle on one side of the path is matched by the topiary bird on the other, and the two bushes of *Choisya ternata* make strong evergreen shapes at the centre of the bed, with the standard 'Iceberg' roses on either side. Other evergreen shrubs – purple sage, hebe, rosemary and osmanthus – give shapely winter ornament. The many scented plants also have a vital contribution to make, their fragrance wafting up as you walk from the gate to the door. It is the kind of successful garden that depends on the spontaneous judgement of its makers rather than on the calculated application of principles of design. It makes an example for others, not to be copied slavishly but for inspiration.

AN INFORMAL POOL AT THE HEART OF A GARDEN

A lively selection of shade- and moisture-loving plants gives the edges of this little pool sparkling character.

Few gardens are lucky enough to have natural water in the form of either a pool or a stream, but the addition of a water feature will add an extra dimension that no other garden feature can provide. In small gardens a formal geometric pool will fit easily with many different garden designs, and its reflective surface will give the welcome illusion of greater space. Water will also add a note of calm to even the busiest area. Irregularly shaped pools are always more difficult to use successfully, and the supposedly naturalistic shapes of mass-produced plastic or fibre-glass pools invariably add a false note to a garden unless their outline is concealed.

This little irregularly oval pool, however, is used with great success in a country garden. Its edges are concealed by lavish planting and by rough pieces of local limestone on which moss grows easily, providing an informal setting for a well-chosen range of plants. In summer the surface of the pool itself is almost invisible because of the planting crowding all about. It is tucked away, hidden from other parts of the garden by a group of wild plums (*Prunus cerasifera*) whose white blossom is ornamental in spring. Later in the season their foliage gives the shade that provides the best environment for many of the herbaceous plants used.

The only touch of formality in the pool area is a little composition-stone figure of 'The Water Bearer'. Its chief functions are to give a vertical contrast to the horizontal pool and provide a crisply delineated shape among the foliage that almost submerges it. I do not care for this figure but its purely decorative qualities are of much less significance than the strong part it plays in the shape of the whole scheme.

The success of the planting that edges the pool lies in the skilfully deployed variety and contrast of leaf shapes, many of which have striking architectural form. The largest of them is the species of rhubarb, *Rheum palmatum*, with magnificent deeply cut spreading leaves flushed with red and as much as 36in/90cm in length. This strongly horizontal shape is planted to one side of the statue, and behind it is a spreading mass of Solomon's Seal (*Polygonatum* × *hybridum*). The blade-like foliage of the larger kinds of iris make striking vertical emphases – among them the variegated flag (*Iris pseudacorus* 'Variegata'), with the palest gold striations on leaves as high as 4ft/1.2m; the magnificent, slightly tender *I. orientalis* with wonderfully refined white flowers carried on 5ft/1.5m stems; and *I. sibirica*, that most valuable of moisture-loving plants, with narrow upright leaves and exquisitely formed purple-blue flowers. Hostas, usually best in the shade in a moist position, also make a powerful contribution. The boldly ribbed glaucous leaves of *Hosta sieboldiana* var. *elegans* rise above the lime-green variegated foliage of *H. fortunei* var. *albopicta*. Ferns, too, relish similar conditions and their unfolding leaves make marvellous ornaments. The feathery fronds of *Polystichum setiferum* are tipped with silver as they open, and next to it the curving leaves on dark

By late spring the water of the pool has all but disappeared in the luxuriant surrounding foliage. The emphatic striped foliage of *Iris pseudacorus* 'Variegata' contrasts with the spreading leaves of *Rheum palmatum,* and the orange of *Euphorbia griffithii* and red of candelabra primulas give sprightly notes amid the green.

brown stems of the deciduous Japanese painted fern (*Athyrium niponicum* var. *pictum*) are almost white.

The edges of the pool are fringed with *Alchemilla mollis*, astilbes, the pink *Dicentra spectabilis*, and seedlings of the Lenten hellebore (*Helleborus orientalis*) and of lungwort (*Pulmonaria saccharata*), with its attractively marked leaves.

Scattered about among the exciting foliage are various herbaceous plants whose chief contribution is their flowers. The candelabra primula (*P. florindae*), provides splashes of yellow and purple-red. *Brunnera macrophylla*, which flowers well in shade, creates a haze of blue flowers hovering above other plants. Several aquatic or marginal plants are planted in the water or at its marshy edge. *Alisma plantago-aquatica* has decorative fleshy leaves and throws out veils of gypsophila-like flowers in summer. The wild marsh marigold or kingcup (*Caltha palustris*) finds a place in the water where its golden yellow flowers glow in the shade. It is curious how even a small informal patch of water makes wild plants seem more naturally at home than they ever would in the more contrived setting of a border. The rounded leaves of *Scrophularia auriculata* 'Variegata' – another shade-lover – are splashed with cream.

The plants used in this pool garden have been carefully chosen for the site but they also show the subtle value of striking foliage. In this small area is concentrated a range of plants that gives interest from early spring right through into winter. Although some are unusual, most are not – careful choice not rarity makes a successful garden. The effect here is one of naturalistic profusion, with rare plants jostling with less rare. However, a scheme of this kind needs much work; nature must be allowed a certain amount of freedom – but not too much. Left to their own devices, the thugs would quickly elbow out the more reticent plants. That lovely thug, *Alchemilla mollis*, seeds itself vigorously, and it is wise to cut off the flowerheads

as the seeds form and the flowers turn brown. Slugs and snails thrive in the moist soil and relish the foliage of hostas. They are kept at bay with a proprietary liquid poison applied in late winter before the foliage emerges. Over the winter the water of the pond gathers leaves and other garden rubbish, and is always cleared out before the end of February.

This is an area of very strong atmosphere. In the context of the whole garden it is rather concealed, its presence unmarked by any very obvious route, and you come upon it almost by surprise; it is not an area to hurry through on the way to somewhere else. The trees that rise above it, giving it much of its seclusion, mean that in summer the only direct light comes in the early morning or late afternoon when the sun is low. The light then throws into relief the various leaf forms, bringing out their distinctive character most strongly and giving an air of excitement. In the middle of the day, when the sun is high and the planting is submerged in shade, the atmosphere is delightfully subdued and contemplative.

Strong contrasts of the shapes and colours of foliage mark the pool-side planting: the curving heart-shaped leaves of pale gold variegated hostas, palm-shaped leaves of *Helleborus orientalis* and the more exotic silver filigree foliage of *Athyrium niponicum* var. *pictum*.

ASHTREE COTTAGE POOL GARDEN

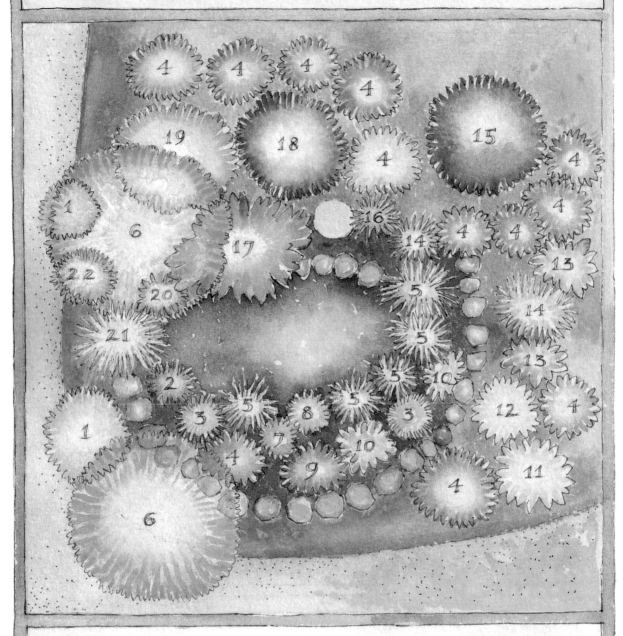

1 *Epimedium grandiflorum*
2 *Filipendula rubra*
3 *Astilbe × arendsii*
4 *Helleborus orientalis*
5 *Iris ensata*
6 *Prunus cerasifera*
7 *Alisma plantago-aquatica*
8 *Caltha palustris*
9 *Filipendula purpurea*

10 *Scrophularia auriculata* 'Variegata'
11 *Hosta fortunei* var. *albopicta*
12 *Trollius superbum*
13 *Hosta sieboldiana* var. *elegans*
14 *Iris orientalis*
15 *Camellia* 'Lady Clare'
16 *Iris sibirica*
17 *Rheum palmatum*

18 *Rhododendron* unnamed
19 *Polygonatum × hybridum*
20 *Primula florindae*
21 *Iris pseudacorus* 'Variegata'
22 *Asplenium scolopendrium*

A POOL ADDS AN EXTRA DIMENSION TO A SECLUDED SITTING AREA

In a town garden a well-designed pool adds a note of calm to an intensively planted area.

A formal pool of crisp geometric shape always seems best in the restricted area of a town garden. Informal pools demand an informal setting which few town gardens are large or wild enough to provide. An expanse of water, even when space is very limited – as it is here – gives an exciting new dimension, reflecting planting and other features and providing a still, peaceful centre. In this garden the pool is part of a sitting area which is surrounded by richly planted walls and beds.

The whole area of this pool garden is only 45ft × 45ft/14m × 14m and yet, despite this severely limited space, it is packed with interest. Forming a separate compartment within the garden, it lies at the end of a passage linking it to the house. To one side there is an attractively framed view through an archway in an old brick wall of the second part of the garden. In a small garden these glimpses are important – they prevent the feeling of claustrophobia that can all too easily grip an intensively planted small area.

The pool is square and unashamedly modernistic, with mysterious square stepping stones forming a geometric pattern across the surface of the water and supported invisibly from below; they appear to float on the water.

Above the pool, to one side and at a higher level, is a second one, originally built as a dipping pool to fill watering cans. From it water flows over a channelled lip into the main pool, making a soothing sound as it falls.

Water lilies (*Nymphaea* cultivars) grow in the main pool, and goldfish swirl in its dark waters. Classic features of the garden pool, water lilies are indeed very decorative; do not, however, allow them to become too dominant, as they may easily do. One of the main attractions of a pool is its mirror-like surface, creating illusions of space and reflecting light into shadowy places; water lilies may quickly obliterate a pool's surface and conceal one of its chief virtues.

The narrow path down one side, and the surroundings of the pool, are paved with composition slabs with courses of dark grey bricks. The style of planting contrasts with this formality, for it is boldly naturalistic. The bed on the near side of the pool faces north and is planted with substantial shrubs which do well in a shady position – among them, *Viburnum burkwoodii* 'Park Farm Hybrid', *Mahonia japonica* and *Hydrangea macrophylla* 'Veitchii'. At their feet are the sweetly scented false spikenard, *Smilacina racemosa*, and the low-growing shrub *Sarcococca hookeriana* var. *humilis* whose gleaming foliage lights up the shade.

To one side, making an emphatic ornament in the corner, the pink winter-flowering cherry (*Prunus × subhirtella* 'Autumnalis Rosea') spreads its canopy wide over other plants. Among these is a mound of the tender grey-leafed shrub *Brachyglottis greyi* whose rounded shape makes an attractive contrast to the crisp lines of the pool. In one corner of the pool a pot of *Gunnera*

The crisp white garden furniture and sharp edges of the pool are softened by lavish planting. *Brachyglottis greyi* forms a shapely mound and the foliage of bergenias, water-lilies and *Alchemilla mollis* give structural interest.

manicata is suspended in the water. Unconstrained, this great South American plant produces vast rhubarb-like leaves, at least 6ft/1.8m across, but with its roots crowded into a pot its growth is severely restricted. Behind the pool at this point the height of the wall has been increased by adding a pergola-like wooden framework. Here are trained the yellow Banksian rose (*Rosa banksiae* 'Lutea') and a wisteria (*Wisteria sinensis* 'Alba'). In the shade at the feet of these climbing plants are various herbaceous perennials – among them a clump of *Kirengeshoma palmata*, a Japanese plant with very handsome lobed and pointed leaves which produces pale lemon-yellow trumpet-shaped flowers on dark stems in August. Other shade-loving plants have naturalised themselves round about, among them Welsh poppies (*Meconopsis cambrica*), the lovely fumitory *Corydalis lutea*, with ferny glaucous foliage and sharp yellow flowers, and the white-flowered form of the spreading cranesbill *Geranium macrorrhizum* 'Album'.

A west-facing border has a lead figure of 'The Water Bearer' which forms an eyecatcher visible through the linking archway in the neighbouring garden compartment. The border is edged in dwarf box (*Buxus sempervirens* 'Suffruticosa') and has lively late-summer planting. Here are the blood-red dahlia 'Arabian Night', the tall tiger-lily *Lilium pardalinum*, *Penstemon* 'Garnet' and waves of the pale pink Japanese anemone (*Anemone* × *hybrida* 'Königin Charlotte').

Many books on the design of small gardens emphasise the importance of concealing boundaries by planting lavishly about the perimeter. However, the wisdom of that advice depends on the nature of the perimeter and the choice of plants to conceal it. I would much rather admire an impeccable hedge of yew or a fine brick wall than a horrible tangle of Russian vine (*Polygonum baldschuanicum*). Certainly, few things make a small garden so

A lead figure of 'The Water Bearer' rises up among lively planting. The grey foliage of *Rosa glauca* makes a good background for the deep crimson dahlia 'Arabian Nights' and the pale pink *Anemone* × *hybrida* 'Königin Charlotte'.

unsatisfactory as an unremitting jumble. In this garden of limited space, with its great range of plants of strikingly varied character, the contrasting hard materials – the bricks of the wall, the paving slabs, the wood of the 'pergola' – give a structural framework. Some of the planting such as the clipped box edging and the shapely mound of brachyglottis serve the same purpose. A white table and chairs in a sitting area at the back also gives structural focus, with the bold foliage of mahonias in the background.

Although the whole area of this town garden is quite small, the pool garden forms a separate compartment within it, and it is the geometry of the pool itself which gives it its character. Large plants, such as the *Gunnera manicata*, the mahonias and winter-flowering cherry are used in naturalistic contrast, while shade-loving plants such as the *Smilacina racemosa* are given appropriate sites, and scatterings of self-sown plants (like the Welsh poppies) are allowed to ruffle the designed scene. It makes a setting which is both a soothing place in which to sit, and yet provides plenty of plant interest for the keen gardener.

WARWICK TOWN GARDEN

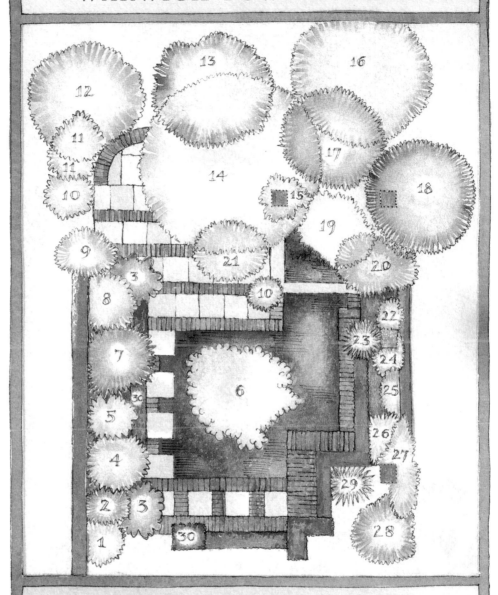

1 *Jasminum nudiflorum*
2 *Sarcococca hookeriana* var. *humilis*
3 *Bergenia cordifolia*
4 *Viburnum burkwoodii* 'Park Farm Hybrid'
5 *Smilacina racemosa*
6 *Nymphaea* cultivars
7 *Mahonia japonica*
8 *Hydrangea macrophylla* 'Veitchii'
9 *Clematis tangutica*
10 *Anemone japonica*
11 *Clematis* 'Jackmanii Superba'
12 *Viburnum bodnantense*
13 *Mahonia × media* 'Charity'
14 *Prunus × subhirtella* 'Autumnalis Rosea'
15 *Clematis victoria*
16 *Betula ermanii*
17 *Prunus lusitanica*
18 *Ilex aquifolium*
19 *Acer japonicum* 'Aconitifolium'
20 *Fallopia japonica*
21 *Brachyglottis greyi*
22 *Rosa* 'Constance Spry'
23 *Iris foetidissima*
24 *Rosa banksiae* 'Lutea'
25 *Chaenomeles* 'Crimson and Gold'
26 *Weigela florida*
27 *Wisteria sinensis*
28 *Rosa glauca*
29 *Agapanthus* Headbourne Hybrid
30 *Buxus sempervirens*

'Spectablis'

A RICHLY PLANTED SWIMMING-POOL GARDEN WITH MARVELLOUS VIEWS

This swimming-pool garden is concealed behind high walls, while lavish planting brings the garden in from the outside.

Few garden features are more difficult to accommodate than a swimming pool. The usually garish colour of the pool lining and the paraphernalia that accompanies it are more often than not uncongenial to the spirit of a garden. The only hope is either to disguise it as a garden feature – a canal or a formal pool – and give it a lining of subdued colour, or to conceal it. The solution triumphantly adopted here is to conceal the pool within an enclosure and then to blur sharp lines and pale surfaces with abundant planting.

The pool is in a country garden with marvellous views. It is tucked away from the garden proper, hidden behind painted breeze-block walls, a high hedge and dense planting, and its entrance is quite inconspicuous. But the owner, a keen gardener, wanted to keep up the high degree of plant interest found in the rest of the garden, and has planted the interior of the pool's enclosure, using bold flowering shrubs and climbers, to give the agreeable illusion of swimming or sunbathing in a floriferous jungle. The planting is very bold, with shrubs and climbing roses billowing away from walls that are almost entirely concealed. Since this is a place used almost exclusively in the summer, the planting gets into its stride in June but continues until late in the season, with many tender exotics in pots remaining decorative well into the autumn.

A white-painted door leads into the pool garden and planting immediately crowds in about. Clumps of the large variegated hosta (*Hosta fortunei* var. *aureomarginata*) flank the door on the pool side, and there are pots of different lilies. On either side the walls are swathed with *Clematis × jouiniana* whose bold panicles of lavender flowers are a splendid ornament late in the season, continuing as late as October. In one corner there is a substantial *Hydrangea sargentiana* with magnificent leaves – rich green, oval and finely hairy and carrying corymbs of mauve flowers in late summer. This great shrub, more often seen in woodland gardens, brings a note of wildness to the artificiality of the pool garden.

The pool itself inevitably dominates the space, but the other ingredients, both planting and hard surfaces, have been planned on an appropriately bold scale. On one side a hedge of Leyland cypress (*× Cupressocyparis leylandii*) has shot up to a height of 30ft/9m. Many gardeners are snooty about this widely planted tree but in this context I find its rather shaggy surface effective, making a good foil for the expanse of water and surrounding tiles. It is an admirable wind-shield – an important consideration in the elevated, windy position occupied by this garden. Leyland cypress is popular for the very reason that makes it a tricky customer – its incredible rate of growth soon makes it an embarrassment if it is allowed to grow without constraint. It may, however, be pruned quite severely without harm. Here, scaffolding is put up every year in March, and the sides

The pavilion brings an exotic note to the swimming-pool garden but its sharp edges are eroded by lavish planting. Building materials are simple: breeze blocks are either hidden behind planting or rendered in pale natural-coloured stucco.

trimmed and the top of the hedge cut back to reduce the height.

The far side of the garden is dominated by a glamorous pavilion. It is constructed of rendered breeze-blocks, painted pale beige with white trimmings, and given simple but effective decorative touches: a central pediment and two wings are crowned by tall, pointed finials and the ogee-shaped entrance is edged with Gothic moulding. The pavilion's back wall is pierced by a window of exactly the same size and shape as the entrance, and has pretty Gothic glazing bars. Through this window can be seen a wonderful prospect, with unspoilt rural landscape falling away abruptly on its far side. The facade is shrouded with planting – on one side the Climbing Noisette rose 'Alister Stella Gray', with profuse richly scented cream double flowers, and 'Maigold' with sprightly yellow flowers; on the other, the corner is filled with the vigorous *Clematis viticella* with elegant little purple-violet flowers carried on slender stems and borne over a long season, starting in the summer.

The left-hand wall is clothed in substantial shrubs and climbers: Moroccan broom (*Cytisus battandieri*) with beautiful silver leaves and pineapple-scented yellow flowers; *Rosa* 'Sombreuil, Climbing', a magnificent old Tea rose with sumptuous double flowers, creamy pink and finely scented; the modern rose 'Golden Wings', with primrose-yellow single flowers, next to the climbing rose 'Paul's Lemon Pillar', with huge cream-yellow flowers; the great shrub *Hydrangea villosa*, with decorative felty leaves and sprays of purple flowers; the tree mallow (*Abutilon vitifolium*), with lilac flowers; and the vigorous 'Leverkusen' rose, with lemon-yellow double flowers.

Apart from cutting back the Leyland cypress hedge, the chief work in maintaining this garden is the annual pruning of the roses, which takes place in early March. All shrubs and climbers are mulched with garden-made compost

The entrance to the swimming-pool pavilion is swathed with roses. On the right are 'Maigold' and 'Alister Stella Gray', both sweetly scented and repeat flowering. Pots of agapanthus and lilies are grouped on either side and views of the countryside are glimpsed through the pavilion window.

and fish, blood and bone in the spring. All the pots are terracotta and need meticulous watering in hot weather. Weeding is done between the paving slabs surrounding the pool but if any seedlings look promising – and match the prevailing blue, white and yellow colour scheme – they are left.

The success of this swimming-pool garden comes from the happy – and intrepid – intermingling of different ingredients. The entrance is half concealed in a mass of the rose 'Cerise Bouquet' which cascades over the surrounding wall, and the doorway's arched shape echoes the shape of the facade of the pavilion. It was a brilliant idea to reveal the marvellous view through a window in the pavilion's back wall. Most of the planting is both bold and permanent, but groups of potted plants – many of them tender – form moveable ornaments which can take advantage of the protected position. The effect is of a swimming pool that happens to find itself in the middle of a floriferous garden, rather than of a garden whose abundance has to be restrained to accommodate the pool. Thus, a virtue has been made out of a feature that is hard to place in a garden.

THE SWIMMING-POOL GARDEN

1 *Clematis viticella*
2 *Rosa* 'Maigold'
3 *Rosa* 'Alister Stella Gray'
4 × *Cupressocyparis leylandii*
5 *Achillea grandifolia*
6 *Rosa* 'Leverkusen'
7 *Rosa* 'Easlea's Golden Rambler'
8 *Abutilon vitifolium*
9 *Hydrangea aspera*
10 *Rosa* 'Paul's Lemon Pillar'
11 *Rosa* 'Golden Wings'
12 *Cytisus battandieri*
13 *Rosa* 'Sombreuil, Climbing'
14 *Hydrangea sargentiana*
15 *Clematis × jouiniana*
16 Hosta sieboldiana var. *elegans*
17 Hosta fortunei var. *aureomarginata*

A SUNKEN GARDEN ENLIVENED BY A DECORATIVE RILL

A beautifully made garden of Arts and Crafts influence deftly connects different parts of a much larger garden.

In this 3 acre/1.2ha garden, enclosures of different character are linked by paths, *allées* and well-planned axes. At the centre of it, both a feature in its own right and a meeting point of paths leading to other parts, is this sunken garden with its decorative rill. In its strongly architectural feel, its careful use of stone and wood, and its excellent craftsmanship, it has strong affinities with the Arts and Crafts gardens that flourished at the beginning of the 20th century. The finest of these gardens made a happy marriage between pure architecture – putting much emphasis on local building materials and vernacular styles – and planting of complementary character. It is a formula that still has great influence, producing some of the most attractive of modern gardens. Here, the relation of this central point to the rest of the garden is a model of sensitive design.

The sunken garden is a key site in the garden. Running across it is the principle lengthways axis of the garden, aligned on the house, while the main cross axis runs along its length. It is thus in a commanding position. Linking other enclosures, it will, inevitably, be more visited than any other part of the garden, and therefore requires a variety that does not quickly stale and a character that fits harmoniously with other, very different, parts of the garden.

Although the garden *is* sunken, the difference in height between it and the surrounding areas is quite small – only 15in/35cm. This is nevertheless quite enough to mark it off as a separate area, as well as providing, from its upper perimeter, a sense of looking down on the pattern spread below. The overall dimensions are 50ft × 32ft/15m × 9.6m, which is close to the area of the average town garden. The retaining walls are made of brick: three courses laid lengthways and the uppermost course laid on edge. Broad stone steps lead up out of the centre of each side. Two steps are all that is needed and they are given interest by the lower step being made wider than the upper one. The whole of the lower part of the garden is surfaced in finely laid natural stone paving. It is, for those who worry about such things, a very low maintenance garden.

Water is the vital ingredient in this sunken garden. A narrow rill – only 12in/30cm wide – runs the whole length of the garden, emerging from a trough at its southern extremity and flowing to a point just before the steps which lead out of its northern end. In the centre the rill opens out into a rectangular pool with bulrushes and clumps of *Iris ensata* 'Rose Queen' in each corner.

Each of the openings that lead out of the sunken garden is marked by a pair of clipped shapes of box or yew, or by ornaments: stone balls or urns. Towards the house, steps flanked by tall cones of clipped yew (*Taxus baccata*) lead up towards a formal parterre which is spread out under the east-facing facade of the house – handsomely half-timbered, rearing up like the prow of a ship. Here are sweeping patterns of box (*Buxus sempervirens*) and silver box (*B. sempervirens* 'Argenteovariegata') and tall obelisks swathed in the clematis 'Royal Velours' – the only flowering plant in

The Arts and Crafts character of the sunken garden is emphasised by finely detailed hard ingredients. The lattice-work fencing is supported on uprights capped with acorn finials and the York-stone paving is beautifully laid.

this part of the garden. The entrance to this enclosure is flanked with narrow beds at the upper level, with a huge bush of the pink sweetly scented rose 'Fantin-Latour' underplanted in summer with cherry pie (*Heliotropium arborescens*), a good pale clone, 'Lord Roberts', with a particularly delicious scent.

Steps to the north, flanked by urns, lead to a pergola, on the axis of the rill, which carries the eye to a pale bench flanked by dark green urns and backed by the bold forms of delphiniums and tall irises. The shady pergola makes an abrupt change of mood from the open sunken garden. A wide gravel path runs its length, and between its uprights clumps of catmint (*Nepeta* 'Six Hills Giant') throw out their flowering stems across the path. The pergola is planted with roses such as 'Zéphirine Drouhin', 'Sanders' White Rambler' and 'Champneys' Pink Cluster'.

To the east of the garden, steps lead to an opening in a hedge of yew – with 'shoulders' cut into each side. Here a grass path runs along a simple *allée* of pleached limes (*Tilia platyphyllos* 'Rubra') underplanted with purple sage (*Salvia officinalis* Purpurascens Group) and *Viola riviniana* Purpurea Group (formerly *Viola labradorica purpurea*). This passage, of austerely simple planting, forms a link between richly decorative parts of the garden.

The south end of the rill has a different character from the rest. Here a water spout fills the scalloped stone trough from which water flows to the rill. The trough is flanked by little beds planted with thalictrums, geraniums, ferns and hostas, all benefiting from the humidity of the atmosphere. Flights of steps lead on either side to a gravel walk and sitting places on the upper level. There are no flowering plants – a tall cone of yew rises from the gravel and a passage leads through to other parts of the garden between hedges of beech (*Fagus sylvatica*). The retaining wall is embellished by a finely made lattice-work wooden fence whose upright supports are crowned by acorn-shaped finials.

The best position from which to see the whole of the sunken garden is from the sitting place by the lattice-work fence at its southern end. You will probably enter this from a long walk of maples and other shrubs, backed by a yew hedge. A narrow opening in the yew hedge – exactly aligned on the rill – leads through to the sunken garden at

WOLLERTON HALL SUNKEN GARDEN

1 *Thalictrum aquilegiifolium*
  'Thundercloud'
2 Fern, unnamed
3 *Wisteria sinensis* 'Alba'
4 *Hosta sieboldiana* var. *elegans*
5 *Geranium maculatum*

6 *Athyrium filix-femina*
7 *Polystichum setiferum*
8 *Dryopteris affinis* 'Pinderi'
9 *Epimedium × rubrum*
10 *Thalictrum delavayi* 'Album'
11 *Lamium maculatum*, silver form

12 *Iris* 'Tropic Night'
13 *Mertensia pulmonarioides*
14 *Viola* 'Foxbrook Cream'
15 *Tellima grandiflora* Rubra Group

the heart of the larger garden. The centre is clear and uncluttered in its formality, marked only by the rill and its central pool whose crisp edges are only slightly ruffled by planting. All about, above the surrounding hedges of beech and yew, there are features to catch the eye – the half-timbered facade of the house itself rising emphatically to one side, a number of good trees, and the lavishly planted pergola.

To me, the outstanding quality of the little sunken garden lies in the soothing atmosphere that results from the harmony of its proportions, the subtlety of its detail and the peaceful sound of gently falling water. It makes a calm interlude at the centre of the richly planted outer garden, linking it harmoniously to the other garden rooms.

A BEAUTIFULLY MADE SEAT AND ARBOUR IN A HIDDEN GARDEN

In the context of a much larger area this hidden garden provides a secluded sitting place where harmonious planting gives an atmosphere of repose.

It is hard to imagine a garden without somewhere to sit. All gardeners want a place where, from time to time during their labours, they can rest, admire their handiwork and reflect on their garden. But a seat of striking presence can, like this one, give decisive character to an entire area of the garden. The arbour shown here is coolly classical, based on a design by the 18th-century architect and garden-designer William Kent, but the principle that it puts into practice – of making a decorative seat the focus of attention – is one that can be applied in many different ways.

This secluded corner of a large garden is tucked away in an agreeably elevated position that gives it an airiness on hot summer days. The entire area is only 21ft × 25ft/6.5m × 7.5m, and is divided by a cruciform pattern of gravelled paths lined with bricks set on their edges. Although it commands views of the house below, and of a path that winds along the flanking hill, it is essentially inward-looking. The approach to it is by a little 'hall' of hedges of the purple plum *Prunus cerasifera* 'Nigra' (formerly *P*. 'Pissardii Nigra'). This makes an attractive hedging material, its leaves changing from ruby-red new foliage in the spring to a sombre purple-black in late summer. It is, however, very vigorous and needs frequent clipping to make a good hedge – every fortnight in the peak growing season. This is possible for a small area of low hedging but would be burdensome for anything much larger.

Frequent clipping also stimulates the repeated formation of the attractive pinker juvenile growth.

A path of pale grey granite chippings leads into the garden. The pedimented arbour, facing the entrance and forming the strong visual centrepiece of the whole arrangement, is made of white-painted wood with inserts of trellis work, and its curved bench fills its width. It occupies an open sunny position facing south-west.

The arbour's importance to the area is emphasised by the symmetrical planting that flanks it. On each side is a little standard tree of the Japanese willow *Salix* 'Onusta', and beside the entrance are groups of plants that are virtually symmetrical: clumps of pink Japanese anemones (*Anemone* × *hybrida*), the double shell-pink Portland rose 'Comte de Chambord', and the creeping cranesbill *Geranium sessiliflorum* 'Nigricans' × *traversii elegans* which strays across the gravel. Among these are the pale silver *Artemisia arborescens* and the herbaceous Roman wormwood (*Artemisia pontica*), with its handsome froth of pewter-grey aromatic foliage. Each corner of the meeting place of the two paths is marked with a rounded cushion of the deep purple *Berberis thunbergii* 'Atropurpurea', edged with ribbons of the palest silver-grey lamb's lugs (*Stachys byzantina*).

As the beds extend away from the arbour the symmetrical planting is abandoned, though the essential palette of pink and silver, with occasional notes

The white-painted arbour rises coolly at the centre of the hidden garden. It is strongly symmetrical and the planting at its base sketches in a loose but romantic symmetry which makes a good foil to the severity of the arbour.

The fine filigree grey foliage of *Artemisia arborescens* rises up behind the deep shining bronze-purple of *Berberis thunbergii* 'Atropurpurea Nana' fringed by the pink flowers of *Lamium* 'Wootton Pink'. The berberis is edged with the silver leaves of *Stachys byzantina*.

of deep purple, is maintained. To one side is *Rosa glauca* (formerly *R. rubrifolia*) whose grey-purple foliage and sharp little purple-pink flowers precisely fit the colour scheme. Near it is planted a clump of *Aster lateriflorus* 'Horizontalis', with lilac flowers and foliage that turns copper in the autumn. In front of the rose the yarrow *Achillea millefolium* 'Lilac Beauty' has flat umbels of lilac-pink flowers borne over a very long period. On the far side of the arbour the soft pink flowers of the large campanula *C. lactiflora* 'Loddon Anna' rise above the perpetual-flowering richer pink rose 'Mary Rose' – one of David Austin's English roses. Beneath it, overlapping the gravel path, are *Heuchera micrantha* 'Pewter Veil' with pale pink flowers and curious pewter-grey leaves, and *Lamium maculatum* 'Wootton Pink' with its grey foliage and silver-pink flowers.

The colour scheme of pink, purple and silver-grey is carried over into the beds facing the arbour – beds that are backed by *Prunus cerasifera* 'Nigra' making a bold horizontal containing line. There are a number of different roses here, including two groups of valuable repeat-flowering shrub roses which grow no taller than 4ft/1.2m: the Floribunda

'Mevrouw Nathalie Nypels' with deliciously scented warm pink flowers, and the old China rose 'Hermosa', with shell-pink double flowers. Both of these are beautifully displayed against the purple hedge. Structure is given by shapely mounds of silver *Santolina chamaecyparissus* and the gleaming deep purple foliage of *Pittosporum tenuifolium* 'Tom Thumb', through which the cranesbill *Geranium* 'Salome' threads itself. A happy recent experiment is the association of purple-leafed *Cotinus coggygria* 'Royal Purple' with bedded-out plants of the tender Australian *Plectranthus argentatus* with magnificent broad silver leaves. At one end of the garden is a large purple-leafed filbert, *Corylus maxima* 'Purpurea', whose bold foliage has a marvellous varnished surface which sparkles in the shade.

The planting in this garden is planned chiefly for summer. In the spring a scattering of plants are decorative against the fresh young foliage of the prunus hedge. Self-sown columbines (*Aquilegia vulgaris*) are encouraged – but only the pink forms, which intermingle attractively with the foliage of the thistle-like *Galactites tomentosa* and with a pink-flowered form

BOSVIGO PINK AND SILVER GARDEN

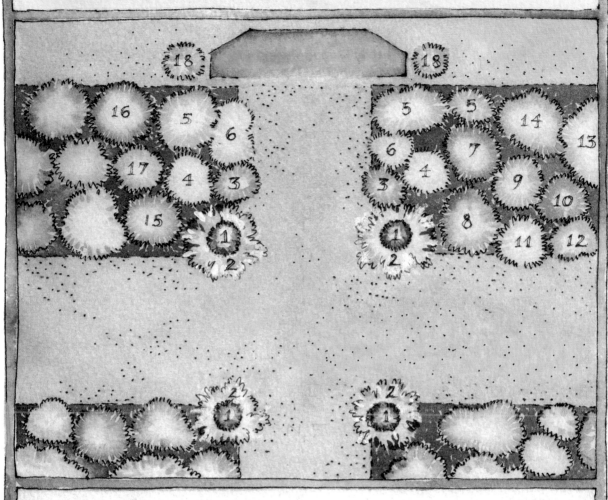

1 *Berberis thunbergii*
   'Atropurpurea Nana'
2 *Stachys byzantina*
3 *Geranium sessiliflorum*
   'Nigricans' × *traversii*
   elegans
4 *Artemisia arborescens*
5 *Anemone* × *hybrida*
6 *Artemisia pontica*
7 *Rosa* 'Comte de Chambord'
8 *Heuchera micrantha* 'Pewter Veil'
9 *Aquilegia vulgaris* (pink form)
10 *Rosa* 'Mary Rose'
11 *Lamium maculatum* 'Wootton
   Pink'
12 *Penstemon* 'Evelyn'
13 *Cosmos bipinnatus* 'Purity'
14 *Campanula lactiflora* 'Loddon
   Anna'
15 *Astrantia maxima*
16 *Rosa glauca*
17 *Achillea millefolium* 'Lilac
   Beauty'
18 *Salix* 'Onusta'

of the hairy chervil (*Chaerophyllum hirsutum* 'Roseum').

This is a garden designed for sitting in; it is a peaceful enclosure whose simple geometric layout and harmonious palette of colours encourage repose. Whereas many gardens offer places to sit that are clearly on a route to other parts of the garden, this garden goes nowhere and the obvious goal is the seat itself. The design of the arbour is gentlemanly and I like the fact that the temptation to add climbing plants has been resisted. Instead, it rises with cool, untramelled distinction from the planting at its feet. The atmosphere of the place is one conducive to peaceful meditation, not to oblivious sleep.

FORMAL HERB BORDERS LEADING TO A SHADY SUMMERHOUSE

Simple planting in a sophisticated design gives these unusual borders, and their protected sitting place, interest throughout the year.

Herb gardens have in recent years become fashionable garden features. Some are thoughtfully designed, but in too many a profusion of plants becomes a rather scruffy end in itself. In these borders the herbs are used in a restrained and considered way, to provide a muted palette of colours in keeping with the contemplative mood of the place. The borders lie at the heart of a large garden in which fastidious planting is matched everywhere by marvellously chosen paths, good garden buildings and a sense of unaffected decorative style in every detail.

The entrance to the borders is marked by a pair of square columns of yew (*Taxus baccata*) crowned by giant spheres of clipped yew. This monumental entrance draws attention to the borders and entices the visitor to explore them. A central path leading to a summerhouse at the far end is 4ft/1.2m wide and surfaced with fine grey gravel with a margin of a single course of square granite setts; the borders themselves have raised edgings of stone. Half way down, the path opens out into a circle, and at its centre an old millstone is set flush with the gravel, ringed with an outer circle of setts.

The summerhouse is open where it fronts onto the borders, allowing scents to waft in. At first it seems to mark a dead end but there is a concealed door leading from one side into the rest of the garden. The design of the summerhouse is marked by the handsome simplicity that rules the character of this garden.

Stone pillars, matching in atmosphere the yew entrance, support a roof of stone tiles, and the floor is paved in flagstones.

The borders are backed by tall hedges of yew rising 7ft/2m high. Each border has a pair of 6ft/1.8m box shapes (*Buxus sempervirens*) clipped into narrow corkscrews. Further permanent evergreen structure is given by a series of domes of golden box (*Buxus sempervirens* 'Latifolia Maculata') which are placed in pairs where the paths widens out into a circle, and mark the end of the path where it abuts onto a terrace in front of the summerhouse. The range of herbs used is not enormous but vividly shows their variety, particularly of ornamental foliage. There are three different sages – common (*Salvia officinalis*), purple-leafed (*S. officinalis* Purpurascens Group) and variegated (*S. officinalis* 'Icterina'). All these benefit from gentle shaping to form billowing mounds. Forming a background to the borders are tall bushes of rosemary (*Rosmarinus officinalis*) which, apart from their statuesque shape and delicious scent, have the attractive habit of bursting into flower in mild weather in almost any season. Bronze fennel (*Foeniculum vulgare* 'Purpureum') casts its airy veils of foliage up to 6ft/1.8m high and makes a decorative background to other plants. Of similar height, and shapely presence, is lovage (*Levisticum officinale*), whose ornamental glaucous foliage gives off an exhilarating scent of celery. Both lavender (*Lavandula angustifolia*) and

In late summer the herbs' seedheads and browning top growth add a new decorative dimension to the borders. By this time of year the herbs sprawl across the path, giving off their scent as you pass by on the way to the summerhouse.

thyme (*Thymus vulgaris*) are used at the front of the borders, spreading over the stone edges. Sweet cicely (*Myrrhis odorata*), with its delicate fern-like foliage and fragrant smell of aniseed, is especially handsome in a shaded corner where its white flowers are seen to great advantage. It is, however, a prodigious self-sower and has to be watched very carefully.

Herb gardens require hard work to keep them in order. Some herbs – mints, for example – have notoriously wandering roots and can be constrained by embedding them in pots or by boxing them in with pieces of slate. Other herbs, among them fennel and many of the alliums, self-sow with abandon. No herb is long-lived and the sages, which may be clipped into rounded shapes for a few years, eventually become so sprawling and straggly that they have to be replaced. Rosemary will also quite quickly become ungainly, but it, too, may be clipped to keep it in order. Herbs have very different cultivation needs. Many of the woody plants like rosemary, thyme, santolina and helichrysum thrive in well-drained soil in a sunny position, whereas some of the herbaceous plants need heavy, moist soil to give of their best. Herb beds do not make much decorative contribution to the garden early in the year. However, they provide excellent places in which to plant spring bulbs whose flowering will be over by the time the herbs' foliage is becoming ornamental. On the other hand, herbs do keep up their ornamental momentum very late in the year – top growth and seedheads continuing to look splendid deep into winter. They are at their most ethereally beautiful when furred with frost.

None of these plants has showy flowers and the essential atmosphere of this place comes from the subtle contrasts of foliage and habit – well displayed against the sombre green of the yew hedges – and the refinement of the details of the summerhouse and the path leading up to it. There is repetition

in the planting and gently sketched hints of symmetry. The photographs shown here were taken in August when the garden is charged with atmosphere – many of the herbs are running to seed and on a hot day the buzzing of bees fills the air. The summerhouse faces south and the enclosing yew hedges form a suntrap magnifying the fragrance of the herbs. In this season the walk to the summerhouse is a progression of scents – lovage, marjoram, thyme, fennel and sweet cicely.

From the cool shade of the summerhouse a different vista presents itself. At the far end of the path, beyond the yew entrance, a tall yucca (*Yucca gloriosa*) in a pot makes a gleaming focal point. It directs the eye upwards towards the sky, drawing attention to a distant upright conifer which rises on the skyline exactly above it. 'No plants,' wrote Gertrude Jekyll of her favourite yuccas, 'make a handsomer full-stop to any definite garden scheme.' The essential character of these borders is inward-looking and this sudden, expansive revelation of the skyline and another world outside has an exhilarating effect.

From the summerhouse the eye is drawn down the path towards a glowing *Yucca gloriosa* in an ornamental pot. It points to the sky, drawing the eye upwards to the horizon which is dominated by soaring conifers.

YORK GATE HERB GARDEN

1 *Myrrhis odorata*
2 *Melissa officinalis* 'Aureum'
3 *Allium hollandicum*
4 *Rosmarinus officinalis*
5 *Salvia officinalis* 'Icterina'
6 *Rumex acetosa*
7 *Salvia officinalis*
8 *Salvia officinalis* Purpurascens
   Group
9 *Melissa officinalis*
10 *Thymus vulgaris*
11 *Thymus × citriodorus*
12 *Levistichum officinale*
13 *Helichrysum italicum*
14 *Lavandula angustifolia*
15 *Origanum vulgare*
16 *Buxus sempervirens* 'Latifolia
   Maculata'
17 *Foeniculum vulgare*
   'Purpureum'
18 Various mints in pots
19 *Artemisia abrotanum*
20 *Teucrium scorodonia*
21 *Origanum vulgare aureum*
22 *Santolina chamaecyparissus*
23 *Origanum vulgare* 'Nanum'
24 *Satureja montana*
25 *Cotoneaster dammeri*
26 *Colchica hedera* 'Dentata
   Variegata'
27 *Taxus baccata*

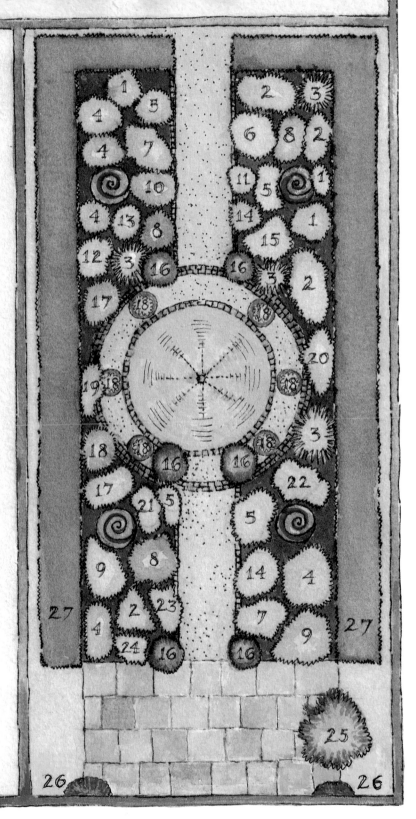

A TERRACE GARDEN IN A COUNTRY TOWN

Repeat planting and a calm colour scheme give harmony to the transition between house and garden.

A well handled transition between house and garden can enhance both, as well as providing additional interest in itself. This paved terrace runs across the back of the house in the busy centre of a small town, enjoying a protected west-facing position. In the summer it is exposed to the sun from about midday onwards, and makes a marvellous place to sit on warm summer evenings. It is overlooked by study windows on the ground floor and by bedroom windows above, while a garden door from the back hall of the house gives easy access. Being so visible from the house, and forming the main entrance point to the rest of the garden, this terrace is a key part of the layout.

The rather intransigent paved terrace was already in place when the present owners bought the house. It is 24ft/7.2m wide and 10ft/3m deep, paved in 24in/60cm square composition slabs. Beyond it a broad lawn extends at an angle deep into the garden. The owners felt that something was needed to mark the transition from the formality of the Georgian house to the informality of the garden, and to give the terrace a feeling of enclosure without obscuring light or views. They decided on a formal framework containing informal but repeat plantings that would provide ornament and interest to the terrace but would not be so dramatic or visually 'busy' as to stop the eye from wandering more deeply into the garden beyond.

A pair of 8ft/2.5m wide beds edged in box (*Buxus sempervirens*) was made, running the whole length of the garden edge of the terrace. A gap in the centre, two paving stones wide, forms an entrance to the lawn and the rest of the garden. These beds run north/south, in total a distance of 20ft/6m, and thus provide a variety of different exposures; the north-facing end, for example, lying in the shade of a very high wall of the neighbouring house, receives direct sunlight only on a late summer's evening.

The path between the two beds was given decorative emphasis by arranging the box so as to form a right-angled indent on each of the four corners. Ornaments were placed in each of these corners: a pair of handsome old stone cannonballs in two of them, and a pair of simple but finely made terracotta pots with clipped shapes of variegated box (*Buxus sempervirens* 'Argenteovariegata') in the other two. Within the beds, height and all-year-round decorative interest is given by three centrally planted standard *Salix helvetica* 6ft/1.8m high. These are always shapely, even in winter, with crowns of dense tangles of leafless branches. In late winter, glistening caramel-coloured buds are followed by pinkish catkins and in spring the leaves are a beautiful silvery grey. The foliage becomes a little dull towards the end of the summer, and falls early, but this may be enlivened by training a small climber up each standard, such as *Clematis* 'Minuet', which produces its delicate purple flowers in July and August.

Forming a base for each of the silver-leafed willows are clumps of *Artemisia arborescens* 'Faith Raven', which sprawl about the lower part of the trunks, echoing the pale silver of the foliage of the willows. The artemisias are

In the box-edged beds running along the terrace self-sown white foxgloves are encouraged. The essentially symmetrical design is strong enough to accept such intrusions harmoniously. In late afternoon the sun shines through the planting, giving it a further dimension.

The terrace seen from the window of a first-floor bedroom photographed in June. The awkward plan of the garden is clearly seen, with the wavy hedge on the left and the chief axis at an angle to the house. The formal terrace beds, with their geometric layout, create a solid visual base for the garden.

cut back quite hard in the spring, both to encourage plenty of new foliage – always much paler than old foliage – and to give them a cushion shape to echo that of the rounded crowns of the willows. They also need to be trimmed back from time to time during the growing season. Planted among the artemisias are miniature Floribunda roses, 'Orchard Pearl'. These grow no more than 24in/60cm high, and if regularly dead-headed produce throughout the season a succession of semi-double warm cream flowers that fade to white. They have something of the character of the old shrub roses and are deliciously scented.

At the shady end of the north-facing bed a group of hostas – among them, 'Krossa Regal' and 'Honeybells' – is planted at the foot of the willow. Other shade-loving plants, also with striking foliage, are planted nearby: the hart's tongue fern (*Asplenium scolopendrium*) and a form of *Helleborus foetidus* with especially beautiful claret-coloured stems, 'Wester Flisk'. Elsewhere in the beds, repeat plantings of herbaceous plants keep to a colour scheme of blue, purple and white; these include the pale violet *Viola cornuta* and its white form; *Geranium* 'Johnson's Blue' and *G.*

wallichianum 'Buxton's Variety'. This latter is especially valuable, having beautiful shapely leaves and producing its violet flowers with a pale central eye from midsummer right through to the first frosts. The silvery sea holly *Eryngium bourgatii* with its metallic blue thistle-like flowers is beautiful against the silver artemisia, while the intense blue flowers of *Platycodon grandiflora* growing through the artemisia look marvellous against the foliage in August. Clumps of *Iris tectorum* have ethereal, clear blue flowers in May, and the bold foliage rises decoratively above the box hedges. All along the terrace side of the hedges are clumps of *Cyclamen hederifolium* and *C. coum* for winter interest.

In this intensively planted area a good mulch of compost in early spring makes a lot of difference. Foliar feeding, particularly of the box hedges, later in the season is also beneficial. Ideally, the box hedges should be clipped three times a year – in spring, and again in early and late summer. The crowns of the willows can be kept shapely by pruning when they are dormant. If the artemisias are too vigorous in the summer, stifling other plants, they can be pruned back. They may need

BEAUMONT HOUSE TERRACE GARDEN

1 *Hosta* 'Honeybells'
2 *Hosta* 'Krossa Regal'
3 *Salix helvetica*
4 *Asplenium scolopendrium*
5 *Epimedium grandiflorum*
6 *Helleborus foetidus* 'Wester Flisk'
7 *Viola cornuta*
8 *Corydalis flexuosa*
9 *Iris tectorum*
10 *Platycodon grandiflora*
11 *Geranium* 'Johnson's Blue'
12 *Geranium wallichianum*
'Buxton's Variety'
13 *Eryngium bourgatii*
14 *Rosa* 'Orchard Pearl'
15 *Artemisia arborescens* 'Faith Raven'
16 *Salvia officinalis* Purpurascens
Group

spraying against black aphids two or three times in the season.

This small area is full of interest and makes a smooth transition between terrace and lawn. The planting within the beds is generous but it is given harmony by the repetition of plants and a restricted colour scheme. The pale flowers and grey foliage are beautiful against sunlight – as they are seen for much of the day by those sitting on the terrace or looking out of the groundfloor windows.

This kind of arrangement could make a perfect garden in itself, perhaps for elderly gardeners with limited space. Because access to it is across a paved terrace, it makes a good wet-weather garden; if it were only very slightly narrower, virtually all maintenance could quite easily be done without treading on the soil.

A SITTING PLACE EMBOWERED IN FLOWERS IN A WALLED GARDEN

A paved terrace makes a sitting place in the centre of a deep border against a high stone wall.

The positioning of a sitting place – even of a simple bench – is a matter of importance in a garden. It is not merely what is seen from the sitting point that is important but – particularly if it is in a dominant position – its appearance from other parts of the garden. The bench in this photograph is a striking design but it is also painted a brilliant white; it is bound to have commanding presence, however powerful the planting that surrounds it.

This walled garden, overlooked by the eastern windows of the house and adjoining it, is a slightly irregular rectangle. The garden walls are 8ft 6in/2.6m high and in one corner is the entrance to a 19th-century conservatory – a splendid architectural ornament. Borders run along the south-facing and west-facing walls, with an uninterrupted lawn in the middle of the enclosure. In the centre of the west-facing border a paved terrace has been made, 10ft/3m wide and the whole depth of the border, with a decorative Chinoiserie-style bench neatly positioned against the wall at the back. This bench gets much of the sun and from here there are views of the pretty facade of the house, the south-facing border and, to the side, of the decorative conservatory.

The planting around such a feature is of course vitally important. In this case, none of the planting is high enough to obscure the views from someone sitting on the bench but it is sufficiently lavish to give the feeling of gentle enclosure. Trained on the wall behind the bench are a group of climbing plants which form a bower over it. One of these, *Trachelospermum jasminoides* 'Variegatum', is a beautiful evergreen plant with gleaming narrow grey-green leaves with white margins and a profusion of little white flowers in summer; its heady tropical scent will carry great distances. Intertwined with it is one of the best honeysuckles, *Lonicera × italica* (syn. *L. × americana*). Flowering profusely over a long period in June and July, this has bold panicles of pink flowers, creamy yellow within, and a fortissimo scent. It may be an obvious idea to have a climbing scented plant close to a sitting area but it is quite easy to overlook the obvious. Flowering at the same time is a Viticella clematis, 'Little Nell', with pale-mauve flowers smudged with white stripes. This scrambles through a handsome grapevine, *Vitis vinifera* 'Ciotat', of the type called 'parsley' vines, with very decorative deeply cut leaves. It is one of the sweetwater grapes, and is, in a suitable site, among the earliest to fruit. The tendrils of the vine brush the back of the bench and the whole group of climbers billows outwards slightly from the wall, embowering the bench and making a loosely shaped canopy for the whole sitting area.

The planting on either side of the paved area is dominated by pinks, reds and purples, which are planned to perform most vigorously in the summer months. It is a mixed planting, although herbaceous plants are in the majority

The bench is enclosed in a profusion of planting. On the wall the honeysuckle *Lonicera × italica* intermingles with *Trachelospermum jasminoides* 'Variegatum', both marvellously perfumed and forming a delicious cocktail of scents.

A detail of the planting to the right of the bench. The trailing stems of blood red *Penstemon* 'Rich Ruby' stand out against the pale pink *Sidalcea malviflora* 'Sussex Beauty'. In the foreground is the warmer pink of *Rosa* 'The Fairy'.

and use is made of spot planting of tender annual plants. There is no precise symmetry but some plants are placed on both sides and colour associations are carefully judged. Flanking the bench are large clumps of the meadow cranesbill *Geranium pratense* 'Plenum Violaceum' which display its double flowers of sumptuous violet from June onwards. There had been a pair of standard grafted *Salix helvetica* in this position but one died so its partner had to be removed. On either side of the paved area is the Polyantha rose 'The Fairy'. This perpetual-flowering rose has a sprawling habit – rising no more than 24in/60cm – which makes it an admirable partner for low-growing herbaceous plants with which it may intermingle. It has cupped semi-double mid-pink flowers and gleaming toothed leaves. It looks very pretty against the grey Cornish slate of the paving and the same pink is echoed in the repeat-flowering rose 'Kathleen Harrop', trained on the wall behind. On each side 'The Fairy' is associated with the loosestrife *Lythrum salicaria* 'Blush' whose tall spires of flowers make an emphatic vertical contrast to the sprawling rose. This new loosestrife cultivar has none of the purple of the

type; instead it is of a warm rosy pink and flowers for several weeks from June onwards. Penstemons, always valuable for the way in which they associate with other plants, provide notes of pale purple: *Penstemon* 'Sour Grapes' and deep red *P.* 'Rich Ruby' make lively partners for the rose. An even paler pink than that of the rose is provided by *Sidalcea malviflora* 'Sussex Beauty', *Lamium maculatum* 'Wootton Pink' and a handsome bergamot, *Monarda* 'Beauty of Cobham'. In high summer these plants are packed together, creating a lavish but harmonious colour effect. But their contrasting shapes also provide interest: the upright emphasis of penstemons, loosestrife and sidalcea, whose flower colours are also an essential part of the scheme, and other plants which make their contribution almost entirely through foliage or habit. The tender *Eucomis bicolor*, for example, on the very edge of the border, has a subtle colouring of cream and green, and a fleshy flower stem crowned by a topknot resembling a miniature pineapple. In the middle of the border *Cimicifuga racemosa* has a strongly architectural character with spreading finely-shaped leaves that are a lively fresh green. Its fluffy bottle-brush flowers create a froth of

BOSVIGO WALLED GARDEN

1 *Geranium pratense* 'Plenum
   Violaceum'
2 *Lythrum salicaria* 'Blush'
3 *Penstemon* 'Sour Grapes'
4 *Rosa* 'The Fairy'
5 *Lamium maculatum* 'Wootton Pink'
6 *Eucomis bicolor*
7 *Origanum vulgare* 'Aureum'
8 *Penstemon* 'Rich Ruby'
9 *Sidalcea malviflora* 'Sussex Beauty'

10 *Monarda* 'Beauty of Cobham'
11 *Eupatorium rugosum*
12 *Phlox* unnamed
13 *Cimicifuga racemosa*
14 *Anemone hupehensis* var. *japonica*
15 *Trachelospermum jasminoides*
   'Variegatum'
16 *Lonicera* × *italica*
17 *Clematis* 'Little Nell'
18 *Vitis vinifera* 'Ciotat'

19 *Malva moschata*
20 *Geranium wallichianum*
   'Buxton's Variety'
21 *Geranium himalayense*
   'Plenum'
22 *Cleome*, unnamed, purple
23 *Hosta sieboldiana*
24 *Geranium* 'Ann Folkard'
25 *Thalictrum polygamum*

pure white in midsummer.

The maintenance of this area requires no special attention. The climbing plants need tying in and cutting back where appropriate. The bench is left out-of-doors all the year round, and washed down in early spring. There is no spring planting scheme here, which makes it easier to top-dress the borders in early spring with as much mushroom compost and well-rotted manure as possible.

On a late summer's afternoon the sun falls away from the sitting area, but it is still bathed in heat and light. From the bench there is much to engage the attention. Scattered in crevices between the paving stones are small cranesbills such as *Geranium sanguineum striatum*, the little *Alchemilla erythropoda* and miniature alpine pinks (*Dianthus* species). The wall of the house is cast into shade but the adjacent border, at right angles to it, now catches the sun in a dramatic way. The planting here is bolder than in the borders that flank the bench. At this time of day in the light of the declining sun rich purple flowers, the strong foliage shapes of irises and the spreading, toothed fronds of the stately *Melianthus major* are revealed at their most dramatic.

A PAIR OF MIXED BORDERS WITH A GAZEBO AS THEIR CENTREPIECE

Carefully planned borders, with a relaxed appearance, lead up to an ornamental gazebo.

Few things in garden design are harder to achieve than naturalness – art without artifice. With their intimacy and lack of fuss, these borders have an atmosphere that is essentially English. Yet this relaxed air needs careful planning and impeccable maintenance if it is not to become a jungle in which the thugs oust the more delicate plants and the whole becomes a shapeless jumble. At a glance, the colour scheme seems haphazard but it conforms to principles that are essential to good planting.

This large country garden, 3 acres/ 1.2ha in all, has been made almost entirely over the last ten years. Its underlying framework, perfectly clear in a plan of the garden, consists of a grid of straight lines. This is certainly one of the sources of orderliness and harmony that a visitor experiences walking in the garden, but plans can be deceptive, for the straight lines and ninety-degree junctions are blurred by rich planting, changes of level and, above all, by changes of mood.

The garden follows in the tradition of gardens of compartments: each enclosure has a distinctive atmosphere but is firmly linked to a strong pattern of paths, vistas and interconnecting features. The borders shown here link a circular area of lawn, with a sundial at its centre, to a beautifully made wooden gazebo also set in a circular area, surfaced with gravel and echoing the circular space at the other end. The borders continue beyond the gazebo and are finished by a cross axis.

The mown grass path between the borders is 3ft 4in/1m wide and edged with square paving stones which provide a useful margin over which plants can flop without damaging the grass. Roses – all perpetual-flowering varieties – are used repeatedly, and these have a constant presence from late June onwards, while the herbaceous foreworks wax and wane: the crimson-purple Damask *Rosa* 'De Rescht', a standard bush of the cream Floribunda rose 'Len Turner', the red-purple English rose 'Prospero', the pink Floribunda 'Queen Elizabeth' and the Hybrid Musk 'Sadler's Wells' whose rich red semi-double flowers are pink at the centre. Their colours, throughout the summer, are echoed by those of the herbaceous planting. The flowers of red valerian (*Centranthus ruber*) vary from a warm chalky pink to a true red, while its highly ornamental foliage, a fine glaucous grey, looks especially handsome on the white-flowered form, *C. ruber albus*. Valerian self-seeds lavishly, producing widely varying colours but always with a tendency towards the least distinguished wishy-washy pink. The richer colours and the white are excellent plants for repeat planting. In July, delphiniums produce an emphatic new range of colours, from the lilac-mauve of 'Conspicuous' and the soft lilac-pink of 'Pink Delight' to the intense ultramarine of 'Faust'. Although there are some elegant associations of colour (*Delphinium* 'Faust' intermingled with the pale lilac *Campanula lactiflora*

At the end of June the gazebo is all but hidden in plants. Behind chalk pink or white *Centranthus ruber* rise the rich blue spires of *Delphinium* 'Faust' and the gazebo is swathed in *Rosa* 'New Dawn'.

Pale yellow hollyhocks intermingle with the modern Hybrid Musk rose 'Sadler's Wells' and in the background are clouds of *Campanula lactiflora* 'Loddon Anna'.

'Loddon Anna', for example) the guiding principle has been to include almost all colours with the exception of 'hot' colours such as orange. This allows pale yellow hollyhocks (*Alcea rosea* seedlings) to intermingle with pink and red *Rosa* 'Sadler's Wells', exactly the sort of thing scorned by 'good taste' gardeners but the very essence of the uncontrived liveliness which gives cottage gardens their character. It was the sort of thing, too, approved of by Gertrude Jekyll, who planted the rich golden-yellow *Coreopsis lanceolata* among blood-red dahlias and flaming scarlet penstemons.

The gazebo rises serenely amid the exuberant profusion of the borders. It is octagonal, built of a wooden framework filled with panels of trellis. Its roof is open and wires stretched across the timbers support climbing plants. It has a Chinoiserie character, with arching tops to each of the entrances, and is stained a very handsome dark grey-blue.

This colour was carefully chosen to relate to two rather different colour schemes. The gazebo is, as I have described, at the centre of the cottage-garden scheme with whose colours it harmonises easily, but looking north, an entirely different garden is glimpsed: a hot scheme of brilliant oranges, reds and yellows.

The planting on the gazebo itself is of restrained pinks and blues. The repeat-flowering climbing rose 'New Dawn' is the chief ornament here, with its beautiful pale pink flowers, delicious scent and glossy foliage. Clematis are also trained on the gazebo, chosen to flower from very early in the year (*Clematis macropetala*) to late in the season (*C. campaniflora*). Apart from these species there are also such showy cultivars as 'The President' and 'Royalty'. All have purple or blue flowers, which look well against the colour of the woodwork.

The maintenance of these borders is determined by the climate. This is a cold area, where a temperature as low as −25°C/−13°F has been experienced in recent years. So the dead top growth of all perennials is bent over and left in position through the winter to form a protective layer for the crowns of plants underneath. It is removed in March, when it is shredded and composted, and at this stage the borders are all given a thick mulch of well-rotted manure – about three years old – to which is added any available home-made vegetative compost. The planting within the

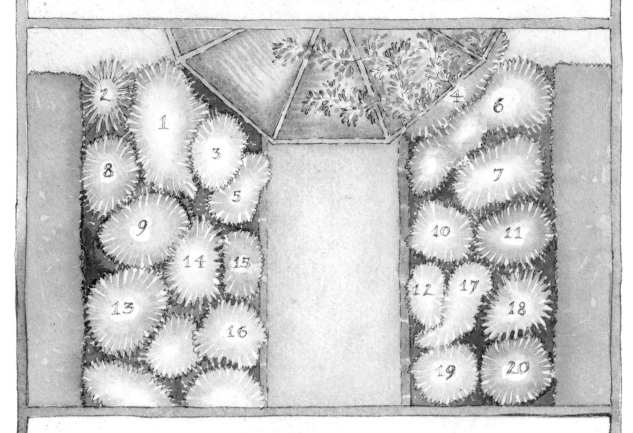

WOLLERTON GAZEBO BORDERS

1 *Thalictrum flavum* sbsp.
   glaucum
2 *Iris* 'Jane Phillips'
3 *Convallaria majalis*
4 *Rosa* 'New Dawn'
5 *Anthemis tinctoria* 'Sauce
   Hollandaise'
6 *Alcea rosea*, yellow
7 *Phlox paniculata* 'Fujiyama'

8 *Alcea rosea nigra*
9 *Rosa* 'Ballerina'
10 *Phlox*, unnamed, pink
11 *Campanula latifolia*
   'Brantwood'
12 *Artemisia pontica*
13 *Cephalaria gigantea*
14 *Delphinium* 'Faust'
15 *Centranthus ruber albus*

16 *Geranium himalayense*
   'Plenum'
17 *Lythrum salicaria* 'Robert'
18 *Dictamnus albus*
19 *Phlox*, unnamed, deep pink
20 *Rosa* 'Handel'

borders is sufficiently dense to act as a weed suppressant, and during the season the chief work is deadheading roses and perennials, and securing the scrambling new shoots of clematis to the gazebo itself.

By mid-July, when the photographs shown here were taken, the planting of the borders has assumed its maximum growth. The bushy shapes of roses and of valerian contrast with the soaring delphiniums and hollyhocks, while achillea and *Knautia macedonica* flop over the path, almost meeting in the centre. The gazebo, all but lost in a blur of planting, still provides a shapely presence at the heart of it. Approaching the gazebo from the west, the visitor is also aware of the skyline where the mounded shapes of Norway maples dominate the horizon. From the gazebo, however, the view is concentrated on the intricacies of the garden that spreads out all around.

A FLOWER GARDEN MADE WITH AN EYE FOR COLOUR AND PATTERN

A pattern of beds, each planted with a restricted colour scheme, creates a harmonious flower garden like no other.

Artists who make gardens bring to the task special skills which often produce results of great originality. The makers of this garden both trained as artists, and this has had a profound bearing on the way in which they have gone about their work. The inspiring flower garden shown here is radically different from any other in this book, and makes one look at the art of gardening with fresh eyes.

The garden is in Northumberland, in exceptionally beautiful and unspoilt rural country. The flower garden occupies half of a rectangular space enclosed by the house, an outhouse and stone walls. This is divided across the middle by a yew hedge, and the square of the flower garden is further divided into an elaborate grid of beds with a pattern of colours. The paintings of Piet Mondrian, with their grid of black lines and rectangles of a single colour, were a strong influence.

At the southernmost edge of the flower garden, overlooked by the windows of the house, the flower colours are cool, with a square bed of pinks and whites and flanking rectangular beds of yellow and white. In the centre are three square beds, with orange in the middle and blue on either side. The final section is a square within a square, with a low box hedge separating the two, and here the colours are deepest reds and purples surrounded by greys and pastel colours. Running down either side of the whole area are beds of yellow and white plants, many with gold foliage.

A schematic account of a garden's plants is no substitute for being in the garden, and here you have the impression of wading through a sea of harmonious plants. I use the word 'sea' advisedly, for most of the flowering plants in the central beds rise to nothing much more than 36in/90cm.

The planting plan on page 71 shows one of the long narrow beds (only 6ft/1.8m wide) restricted to flowers of yellow or white. At the head of the bed is a clipped hump of an unusual box – one of many in the garden. This is *Buxus microphylla* var. *insularis* (formerly *B. microphylla* var. *koreana*), a particularly tough species with leaves varying from bronze to olive green. The flowering plants are almost entirely herbaceous, interspersed with a few small shrubs such as rockroses (*Helianthemum* species). Although not all are species, the plants are all wild in character. There are several cultivars – of the owner's own eagle-eyed selection – but no hyper-hybridised garden thugs with excessively large flowers of chemical colour. An easy harmony comes from restricting the colour of the plants, though there is no fastidious handwringing about delicate associations, but harmony also comes from restricting their height. The edges of the bed are often fringed with creeping plants, many of an alpine persuasion and sometimes with golden foliage, such as *Erodium chrysanthum*, creeping golden thyme (*Thymus serpyllum* 'Aureum') and *Saxifraga* 'Bob

The flower garden is enclosed in stone walls but the rural landscape is not excluded. The harmony of the planting comes from colour grouping and a systematic, but quite unobtrusive, underlying pattern of modular beds.

In the late afternoon of a summer's day the low sun catches the heads of flowers and emphasises structural planting of low box hedges and other shapes. The rounded buttresses of clipped yew behind the hedge echo the distant crowns of trees on the horizon, linking garden and countryside.

Hawkins' forming a dense mound of fine cream-variegated foliage. Plants such as these blur the bed's edges and provide a decorative horizontal foreground for the more vertical plants behind them.

In high summer, which comes late to this place situated 700ft/210m above sea level, the whole central area of the flower garden is a mass of flowers. The outlines of beds, and even the paths which run between them, are virtually invisible. Nonetheless, while the underlying patterns may be less obvious, they are still there, making an essential contribution to the garden. Among the flowers – almost all herbaceous – topiary shapes, low box hedges and the occasional stone ornament act as firm points of reference. They are used to mark the centre, head or corners of a bed – crisply outlined shapes in the flowery profusion.

The entrance to the flower garden lies through a yard with workaday rural buildings. It is flanked by plain stone urns of strong vernacular character, and a simple plank gate in the stone wall leads into the flower garden. In classical garden design this would mark the opening of a path, with some vista leading straight ahead. Here, you make a step or two and are immediately stopped by a cross-ways bed with a thicket of *Stachys byzantina* blocking progress. You are forced to look up and consider where to go next. You are forced, in fact, to survey the whole garden, and it is a bewitching sight.

Although there is plenty to focus the attention on within the flower garden it would be wrong to think of it as inward-looking and sealed off from its surroundings. The best view of it is to be had from a little flight of stone steps which rises to first-floor level on the facade of the house. From this elevated position the pattern of beds and the blocks of colour are clearly distinguished. On either side of the central beds, along the flanks of the garden, are bold ribbons of golden planting – yellow flowers or golden foliage. As your eye moves across the beds, from cool to hot colours, the rural setting is revealed above the stone wall that forms the garden's limit – a field with grazing sheep, with the land sloping upwards, and trees and farm buildings on the horizon. This extraordinarily beautiful and intimate setting must, consciously or otherwise, have influenced the planting of magical simplicity within the garden.

HERTERTON FLOWER BORDERS

1 *Buxus microphylla* var. *insularis*
2 *Iberis saxatilis*
3 *Aquilegia chrysantha*
4 × *Solidaster* 'Lemore'
5 *Thlaspi alpinum*
6 *Aubrieta deltoidea* 'Aureovariegata'
7 *Erysimum cheirii*
8 *Potentilla recta* var. *pallida*
9 *Polemonium foliosissimum flavum*
10 *Gypsophila repens*
11 *Rudbeckia fulgida speciosa*
12 *Buphthalmum salicifolium*
13 *Senecio doronicum*
14 *Aquilegia flabellata alba*
15 *Sisyrinchium*, unnamed
16 *Thymus vulgaris aureus*
17 *Viola* 'Virginia'
18 *Astrantia major*
19 *Solidago caesia*
20 *Campanula rotundifolia* var. *albiflora*
21 *Potentilla aurea*
22 *Achillea clypeolata*
23 *Potentilla aurea* 'Plena'
24 *Alyssum murale*
25 *Ranunculus acris* 'Flore Pleno'
26 *Achillea* 'Taygetea'
27 *Achillea ptarmica* 'Perry's White'
28 *Viola*, cream form
29 *Ornithogalum pyrenaicum*
30 *Hieracium waldsteinii*
31 *Verbascum chaixii*
32 *Allium moly*
33 *Anthericum liliago*
34 *Lychnis coronaria* Oculata Group
35 *Helenium* 'Riverton Beauty'
36 *Saxifraga* 'Bob Hawkins'
37 *Erodium chrysanthum*
38 *Helianthemum*, unnamed, cream

A VILLAGE GARDEN WITH STRONG BONES

Hidden behind the house, a garden with a boldly formal layout is embellished with generous planting and lively decorative details.

One of the most dependable recipes for a satisfying garden design is a boldly symmetrical layout which establishes a firm framework within which the owner may indulge in generous planting. In the case of this garden, the space available – a former school playground – was not itself symmetrical but the simplicity of the layout – a central path flanked by two rectangular beds – imparts a satisfying air of symmetry to its irregular surroundings, and the unpretentious liveliness of the planting quickens the pulse.

The house lies on a village street and its garden is hidden at the back. French windows in three of the rooms give onto the garden, making it very much a continuation of the rooms of the house. Several upstairs bedroom windows have particularly good views of the patterned planting below. An unexpectedly generous broad central path extends from the centre of the house, establishing a strong axis about which the other ingredients are disposed. Rectangular beds on either side are the same width as the path. In a small garden it is all too easy, by scaling down the ingredients, to achieve a rather mean result, and a generous path such as this, far from seeming to occupy too much room, gives an air of spaciousness. A narrow path, unadorned, would also have led the eye – and the feet – too directly to the focal point of this vista, which is an octagonal summerhouse with a steeply pitched roof. Surfaced with pebbles, and with a strip of gravel down each side, the path has bold clumps of lavender (*Lavandula angustifolia*) and geraniums scattered along it.

The flanking beds are edged in box (*Buxus sempervirens*), 16in/40cm high and about the same width. These hedges make a strong frame for the lavish planting – mostly of white, purple and crimson – within the borders. Many of the plants are repeated on either side but any symmetry is sketched in with the lightest of hands. Each of the beds has a pair of standard *Rosa gallica* 'Versicolor' (also known as 'Rosa Mundi'). This ancient rose, with richly scented flowers striped in crimson, has a tendency to flop when grown in the usual way as a bush. It is rarely seen grown as a standard, which has the welcome effect of holding the flowering stems aloft, brandishing the flowers like exotic flags. Other roses are scattered in each bed, with several specimens of 'De Rescht', a Damask rose with very double flowers of deep crimson and exotic scent. It is an exceptionally good shrub rose for the smaller garden, growing no more than 4ft/1.2m and continuing to flower after the first flush in June. Other roses of old-fashioned character, also repeat-flowering, are the Hybrid Perpetual 'Ferdinand Pichard' with crimson-striped flowers echoing 'Rosa Mundi', and the Polyantha 'Yvonne Rabier' with semi-double white flowers. Herbaceous underplanting includes fennel (*Foeniculum vulgare* – invasive but a beautiful background plant with its feathery foliage), foxgloves (*Digitalis purpurea*), tobacco plants (*Nicotiana* species), the brilliant blue borage (*Borago officinalis*) with downy foliage, and rue (*Ruta graveolens*). Some of these

Looking north from the house terrace, the conical roof of the summerhouse provides a firm focal point for the garden's composition. But hard edges are blurred, lavish planting flows over box hedges, lavender plants and geraniums stud the path, and the summerhouse itself is draped with roses.

are self-sown from year to year and contribute to the uncontrived appearance of the planting, which makes such a satisfying contrast to the firm framework that contains it. Although there are areas where the colour scheme is fairly tightly controlled, there never seems to be any great striving for effect.

The focal point of the garden is the stone summerhouse which faces south-west. The steeply-pitched conical roof is covered in the distinctive stone tiles found in so many old houses of the area, and crowned at its pinnacle with a stone ball. In front of it is a pair of obelisks made of composition stone but now well-weathered and virtually indistinguishable from real stone. The summerhouse is garlanded in climbing plants but not so lavishly as to conceal its architectural character. A honeysuckle ramps on the roof, intertwining with the old climbing Tea rose ' Sombreuil, Climbing'. This rose – one of the hardier Tea roses – has huge double creamy-pink flowers with a good scent and is repeat-flowering. On the other side a group of clematis includes 'Lazurstern', 'General Sikorski' and the spring-flowering *C. montana* 'Superba'

which intermingles with the early-flowering rose 'Gloire de Dijon.' Because of their south-westerly orientation, the walls of the summerhouse provide a good site for all these flowering climbers. On a warm June evening its shady interior is suffused with delicious scents. To one side is a large Jerusalem sage (*Phlomis fruticosa*) with its distinguished grey foliage and cheerful – even rather strident – yellow flowers. The effect of this is to avoid the too calculating atmosphere that spoils many gardens. Although there is throughout the garden a lively decorative sense, there are no plants of great rarity.

One of the most striking things about this garden is that it has no lawn. Most gardeners succumb too easily to the tyranny of grass, with the burdensome regime of mowing, feeding and weeding that it implies. In large gardens it somehow seems worthwhile, and maintenance is easier to arrange on a larger scale; in small gardens it will take up a disproportionate amount of work.

There are plenty of sitting places in the garden: on the paved terrace at the back of the house, in the summerhouse, as well as benches tucked into odd corners – all giving views of the garden.

One of the hardest things in a small garden is to achieve variety without creating a muddle. The firm design here is balanced with exuberant planting. There are hints of symmetry but it is never absolute. The same plants are repeated here and there, which gives harmony without seeming excessively straitjacketed. All the hard materials used are in sympathy with the limestone that is the universal building material of this part of the world. Not only the stone garden walls (laid without mortar, just like the field boundaries of these parts) but the stone roof of the summerhouse and the paths are all in harmony. Yet because of the strong bones and the liveliness of the planting the effect is far from soporific.

Within the sharply defined borders an air of informality is given by self-sown plants. The blue flowers and felty leaves of common borage (*Borago officinalis*) and tall purple flowering spires of foxgloves (*Digitalis purpurea*) rise in front of the crimson *Rosa* 'De Rescht'.

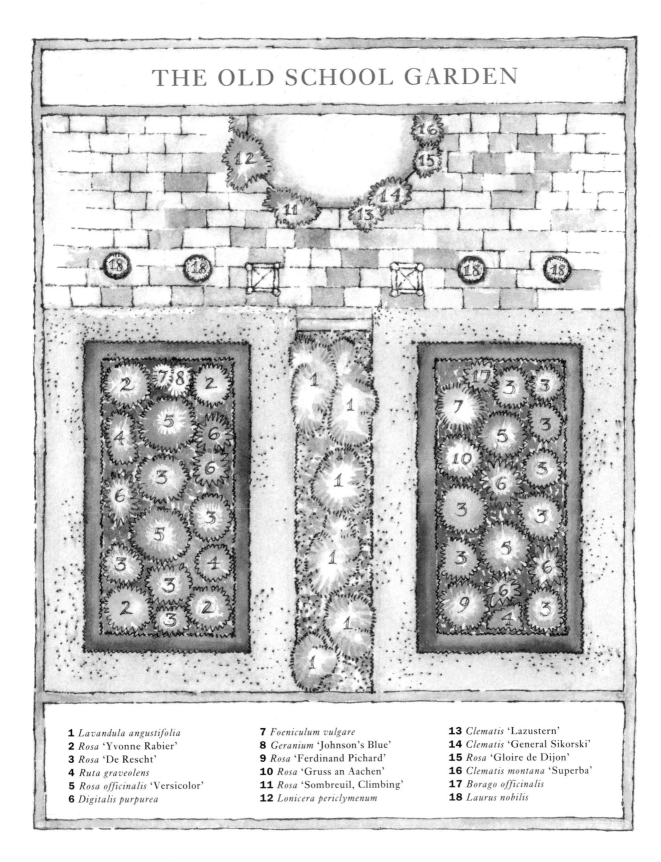

THE OLD SCHOOL GARDEN

1 *Lavandula angustifolia*
2 *Rosa* 'Yvonne Rabier'
3 *Rosa* 'De Rescht'
4 *Ruta graveolens*
5 *Rosa officinalis* 'Versicolor'
6 *Digitalis purpurea*
7 *Foeniculum vulgare*
8 *Geranium* 'Johnson's Blue'
9 *Rosa* 'Ferdinand Pichard'
10 *Rosa* 'Gruss an Aachen'
11 *Rosa* 'Sombreuil, Climbing'
12 *Lonicera periclymenum*
13 *Clematis* 'Lazustern'
14 *Clematis* 'General Sikorski'
15 *Rosa* 'Gloire de Dijon'
16 *Clematis montana* 'Superba'
17 *Borago officinalis*
18 *Laurus nobilis*

A KEY VISTA IN AN AWKWARDLY SHAPED WALLED GARDEN

Imaginative planning gives these mixed borders of shrub roses and herbaceous planting a sense of space.

The lesson of this garden is that a firm pattern of paths and features can impose logic on an irregular and illogical space. This enables borders leading off the chief axis at the heart of a walled garden to form a major ornamental interlude.

The whole area of the garden is ¾ acre/0.3 ha but the shape is very irregular, a kind of truncated triangle with no logical structure of its own. The owners of the garden solved the problem in a striking and simple way. From the entrance in one corner of the walls they made a long straight path leading to the entrance of the house, with tall hedges of yew and a narrow brick path. This forms the visual spine of the garden, linking the whole area. Openings on either side of the hedge afford glimpses of other areas and lead to two major planted features – a secret, enclosed garden on one side, and the borders, making a strong cross vista, on the other.

An archway of clipped yew forms the entrance to the borders, which are separated by a grass path and backed by hedges – a 4ft/1.2m high hedge of box (*Buxus sempervirens*) on one side and a much taller one, 7ft 6in/2.25m high, of *Prunus cerasifera* 'Pissardii' on the other. The pink-purple of the prunus hedge makes an excellent background to the pinks, purples and occasional sharp reds which dominate the borders' colour scheme. At the far end, the grass path opens out into a little lawn where a stone sundial acts as an eyecatcher.

Roses are the main woody plants used in the borders, appearing regularly along their length. Some of these are perpetual-flowering varieties such as 'White Pet' and 'The Fairy', but most are shrub roses which flower only once, producing flowers of unrivalled beauty and scent in their season but for the most part not very attractive passengers when not in flower. In a small garden the ability of roses to produce flowers throughout the season is obviously an attractive quality, but many gardeners enjoy the association of a flowering plant with a particular season – a daffodil that flowered throughout the year would quickly lose its charm.

An excellent way to use single-flowering roses is to accommodate them, as here, in a large mixed border. In this way they may, when no longer performing, be lost in a profusion of herbaceous planting that will grow up after the roses have flowered and be supported by their branches. In the middle of one of the borders, for example, is the rose 'Tuscany Superb', an old Gallica rose also known as the 'Old Velvet Rose', with – when in flower – double flowers of a marvellous deep maroon. Rising to a height of around 4ft/1.2m, it has at its feet the sea holly *Eryngium × tripartitum* which produces a froth of intense inky blue flowers carried on blue stems. On one side is the goat's rue *Galega* 'Lady Wilson' which forms a billowing mound of lavender flowers. Rising behind the rose on one side is *Campanula lactiflora* 'Loddon Anna' whose shapely long bell flowers are pale lilac-pink. In the corner where the yew and box hedges meet is the substantial daisy *Aster laevis* 'Calliope'.

Further along the border, on the same side, the rose 'Geranium' – a

An interesting skyline adds an extra dimension to borders. To the right a decorative dovecote, complete with white fantail pigeons, rises up against a background of mature trees. At the back of the border to the right, the statuesque rose 'Geranium' adds powerful structure.

The scarlet mophead flowers of *Monarda* 'Adam' stand out among trailing flower stems of the goat's rue *Galega* 'Lady Wilson' (*left*) and the rosy purple spires of *Stachys macrantha* 'Superba'.

seedling of unknown origin but with a powerful wild character – rises high at the back, throwing its arching stems of brick-red single flowers over the neighbouring plants in late June. After this single flowering the rose's decorative role is finished, except for handsome long orange-red heps, but scrambling up its feet is the herbaceous *Clematis integrifolia* with clear blue flowers and attractively backward-curving petals. Beside it is the statuesque *Kitaibela vitifolia* – as high as 6ft/1.8m – with toothed palmate leaves and mallow-like pink flowers. On the far side of the rose is another herbaceous perennial of bold character – *Strobilanthes atropurpureus*, with nettle-like leaves and violet flowers. In front are the cranesbill *Geranium psilostemon* with its magenta flowers, and the pink marsh mallow *Althaea officinalis* 'Romney Marsh'.

An unremitting narrowly restricted colour scheme can be wearisome, and the predominant pinks and purples here are seasoned with sprightly reds – the scarlet of *Monarda* 'Adam', the trailing potentilla 'Gibson's Scarlet', *Penstemon* 'Garnet' and, scrambling through the rose 'Königin von Dänemark', the cherry-red clematis 'Sir Trevor Lawrence'. These sharp notes are very telling among the generally soft colours.

Well-kept mown turf is one of the most attractive surfaces for a path between borders. In this case, being to one side of the garden's chief axis, there is not an immense amount of wear, but a regular programme of feeding, weeding and mowing is nevertheless needed to keep it looking good, and attention must be paid to plants flopping attractively over the edge of the borders, which will tend to kill the grass.

The path – 5ft 6in/1.6m wide – allows two people to walk side-by-side with unhurried ease, but does, however, lead finally and illogically towards a wall. Were this visible and unadorned it would stop you uncomfortably in your tracks. As it is, the sundial provides an apparent destination, and behind it a splendid Moroccan broom (*Cytisus battandieri*) flaunts its silver leaves and golden flowers against the wall.

The borders – twice the width of the path – give a relaxing feeling of space. The skyline, enlivened by mature trees beyond the garden wall, is clearly visible above the hedges backing the borders, and, built into the wall itself, is a splendid ornamental brick dovecote where white doves flutter and coo.

STONE HOUSE COTTAGE BORDERS

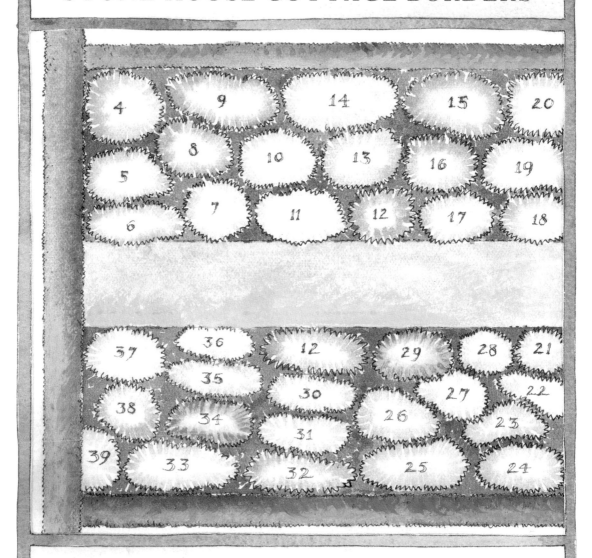

1 *Taxus baccata*
2 *Buxus sempervirens*
3 *Prunus cerasifera* 'Nigra'
4 *Aster laevis* 'Calliope'
5 *Phlox paniculata* 'White Admiral'
6 *Dendranthema* 'Clara Curtis'
7 *Eryngium* × *tripartitum*
8 *Rosa* 'Tuscany Superb'
9 *Campanula lactiflora* 'Loddon Anna'
10 *Galega* 'Lady Wilson'
11 *Nepeta* 'Souvenir d'André Chaudron'
12 *Agapanthus* Headbourne Hybrid
13 *Monarda* 'Adam'

14 *Cichorium intybus* 'Roseum'
15 *Rosa* 'Blanchefleur'
16 *Stachys macrantha* 'Superba'
17 *Phlomis bovei* sbsp. *maroccana*
18 *Knautia macedonica*
19 *Ceanothus* × *delileanus* 'Gloire de Versailles'
20 *Buddleja alternifolia* 'Argentea'
21 *Eryngium bourgatii* 'Oxford Blue'
22 *Centaurea* 'John Coutts'
23 *Campanula latiloba* 'Highcliffe Variety'
24 *Phlox paniculata*
25 *Cichorium intybus*
26 *Thalictrum rochebruneanum*
27 *Geranium psilostemon*

28 *Phlomis tuberosa*
29 *Sedum spurium* 'Atropurpureum'
30 *Phlox paniculata* 'Rosalinde'
31 *Aconitum carmichaelii* 'Barker's Variety'
32 *Eupatorium purpureum*
33 *Phlox paniculata* 'Alba'
34 *Cirsium rivulare* 'Atropurpureum'
35 *Lysimachia ephemerum*
36 *Senecio cineraria*
37 *Campanula glomerata* 'White Barn'
38 *Geranium endressii*

A WALLED GARDEN
IN A LARGER
LANDSCAPE

A formal garden, planted with a restricted colour scheme, is harmoniously related to the house and the surrounding area.

This new garden in southern California, made by the owners in 1994, introduces several valuable ideas in garden design. It is a satisfying self-contained garden in its own right but is at the same time visually integrated both with the house which it ornaments and with the beautiful landscape that surrounds it. Jutting out eastwards from one end of the house, from which it is separated by a stone-flagged path, the garden is exactly aligned with large French windows opening out from the master bedroom. So, from their bed, the owners have a commanding view of its enticing interior.

The surrounding landscape is clearly visible over the 4ft/1.2m garden walls, making it important that the design reflects something of the natural qualities of the trees and rough-hewn rocks beyond. The most striking ornaments of the landscape are old Coastal evergreen oaks (*Quercus agrifolia*) with broad crowns, sprawling branches and deeply gnarled bark. Some splendid specimens of these trees rear up behind the walls.

The walls enclosing the garden are covered in stucco, whose warm texture, slight irregularities and rounded contours have a sympathetic presence. They are precisely the same colour as the walls of the house, a subtle pale grey-brown. The area of the enclosed garden is only 21ft × 30ft/6.5m × 9m and, as the plan on page 83 shows, the planting possibilities even in this small space are considerable. There is a single entrance, a gap in the walls exactly facing the bedroom windows. Borders just under 6ft/1.8m wide run along the walls, and a rectangular central bed of the same width provides a strong central axis to the garden, emphasised by a fine old oil jar in a central position in the back bed, whose plain hand-thrown surface fits in with the natural character of the surroundings. Paths of pale stone chippings, just wide enough for one person, are neatly edged in metal strips.

The planting is mixed herbaceous and woody, and flower colour is chiefly white, with dashes of pink, blue and purple. The central bed is filled with white bedding roses, a mixture of 'White Meidiland' and 'Gourmet Popcorn'. Patches of candytuft (*Iberis saxatilis*) run along the edges, blurring the boundary between bed and path. White or gently pink roses are trained on the walls, in some cases flopping over the top, half-concealing the wall. Perpetual flowering varieties of rose are used, such as 'Iceberg, Climbing' and 'Sally Holmes', a Floribunda whose single flowers are the palest pink. There is much repetition of plants, with occasional exactly symmetrical arrangements giving emphasis. The oil jar, for example, is flanked on either side by the rose 'Iceberg, Climbing', with spreading plants of the low-growing *Pinus monticola* 'Minima' overlapping the path at the front. This is a selected variety of the western white pine – a Californian native – and the same pine is used at the entrance to the garden, below a pair of *Cistus* 'Doris Hibberson' which flop over the path on either side. All the way round, roses are trained against the walls, and have chiefly herbaceous plants

A fine old oil jar makes a simple but effective focal point in the walled garden. The walls are almost concealed in lavish planting which softens the boundary between the garden and surrounding landscape in which old evergreen oaks (*Quercus agrifolia*) make striking ornaments.

The walled garden lies at one end of the swimming pool, with a magnificent backdrop of evergreen oaks. The window at the end of the house is that of the master bedroom which faces into the interior of the walled garden.

at their feet, often lapping over the gravel path. The path is just 36in/90cm wide and its margins are frequently obscured by the plants pressing in on either side. Some of the herbaceous plants, such as delphiniums (various Pacific Coast hybrids), and valerian (*Centranthus ruber*) rise spire-like amid the profusion, forming shapely punctuation marks. Although the planting is dominated by white flowers, the occasional notes of blue from delphiniums, and pink from *Penstemon* 'Apple Blossom', *Diascia integerrima* and pinks (*Dianthus caryophylla*), greatly enliven the effect. The planting all round the beds is sufficiently dense almost to obliterate the walls and seems to merge with the natural vegetation beyond.

The position occupied by this walled enclosure in relation to the whole plot is instructive. From within, it has the charm of a secret garden. From the outside, it has a completely different role to play. Its long southern wall, with fronds of roses foaming over the top, rises above the end of a swimming pool. The pool, running parallel to the long side of the house, is built on a simple terrace with little planted ornament. The views from the terrace are magnificent:

southerly to the Pacific Ocean over wooded slopes at one end, and to the natural woodland and scrub on the hills above the walled garden to the north. The colour of the pool lining is a sombre inky blue, so much more sympathetic in a context such as this, with the wilder landscape so visible, than the shrill turquoise so often seen. Such bright and unnatural colours may be permissible only where they are not juxtaposed with the naturally softer tones of the landscape.

In this part of Southern California, in the mountains above Santa Barbara, the climate is extraordinarily benign, the elevated position and the proximity of the ocean preventing excessive heat. The planting in the walled garden takes advantage of this, giving a profusion of flowers from spring right through into winter. Because of the more or less constant growth, dead-heading of the perpetual-flowering roses goes on throughout most of the year. A general fertiliser is applied virtually every month, except in December and January when the short lull in growth gives an opportunity to prune the roses; by April they are once again in flower. Since there is virtually no rain during the summer, a concealed irrigation system

SANTA BARBARA WALLED GARDEN

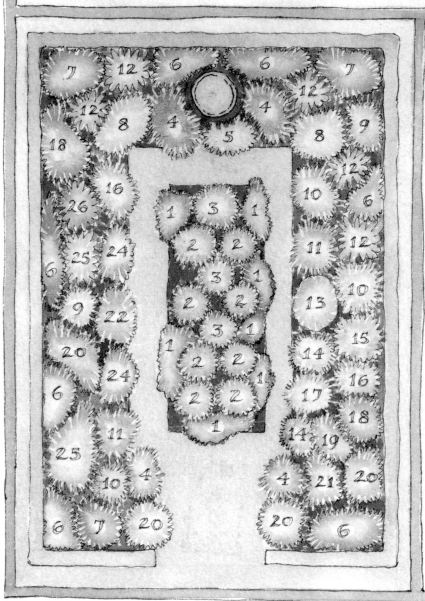

1 *Iberis saxatilis*
2 *Rosa* 'White Meidiland'
3 *Rosa* 'White Popcorn'
4 *Pinus monticola* 'Minima'
5 *Salvia chamaedryoides*
6 *Rosa* 'Iceberg, Climbing'
7 *Spiraea × vanhouttei*
8 *Fuchsia × colensoi*
9 *Penstemon* 'Apple Blossom'
10 *Nepeta racemosa*
11 *Juniperus procumbens*
12 *Delphinium* Pacific Hybrid
13 *Thymus polytrichus*
   britannicus
14 *Helianthemum nummularium*
15 *Sedum* 'Autumn Joy'
16 *Centranthus ruber albus*
17 *Dianthus caryophyllus*
18 *Rosa* 'Sally Holmes'
19 *Rosa* 'Comte de Chambord'
20 *Cistus* 'Doris Hibberson'
21 *Geranium sanguineum* var.
   striatum
22 *Diascia integerrima*
23 *Aster × frikartii*
24 *Geranium macrorrhizum*
25 *Nicotiana alata*
26 *Digitalis purpurea*

has been installed. Plants grow vigorously here and in the medium term some thinning will become essential.

Small enclosed gardens can often seem horribly claustrophobic. Here, the danger is avoided because the walls are not very high, because the planting, although profuse, has shapely structure, and above all because of the exhilarating views above the garden walls. The noble spreading branches and evergreen canopy of the Californian oaks, plainly visible beyond, provide exactly the right strong, natural shapes to contrast with the dextrous sophistication of the garden. 'Borrowed' ornaments as beautiful as these can form one of the most powerful ingredients of a garden. Gardeners lucky enough to possess such natural advantages should always find a way to give them their true worth, as this garden triumphantly has.

OVAL BEDS SOLVE THE PROBLEM OF A DIFFICULT CORNER

Three oval beds on a steep north-facing slope are linked to provide
a stepped passage connecting different parts of the garden.

The challenge of a really difficult site can sometimes produce inspired solutions. The problem here was a steeply sloping north-facing site in an old garden. Existing mature hedges meant that the space available was already determined, which added a further constricting element. In addition to that, the area was slightly irregular, narrowing towards the bottom. Steps seemed essential as a way of negotiating the slope which is too steep for a mere path – though a steep flight of steps plummeting down the slope might easily have turned the whole area into a precipitous gorge.

The solution adopted is highly original, in effect making giant steps out of three oval beds, around which brick paths loop their way in a gentle winding descent, providing plenty of opportunity to admire the plants that press in all about. A dry-stone wall surrounds each bed, retaining the ground at the sides but swooping down to ground level between each bed to allow passage from one level to the next. The wall is capped with a neat coping of dressed stone but the gaps in the dry stone are host to all sorts of plants – ferns, corydalis, spleenwort, moss and stonecrop. This is exactly the kind of naturalstic planting in a formal context that Gertrude Jekyll admired so much. The broad shape of the beds, and the walls running across the downward axis of the place, make it seem much larger, encouraging a sense of leisurely progression.

At the head of the oval beds a thatched wooden summerhouse serves several purposes. It is an eyecatcher, of course, as well as a link between two axes – that of the oval beds and that of a long narrow path running at right angles along the contour of the slope (and richly planted with flowering shrubs, particularly rhododendrons and magnolias). It also provides a sitting place from which two quite different views are offered. On one side the eye is drawn into the garden; on the other, it is drawn downwards, across the oval beds and the planting below, with distant views of old woodland and rural countryside beyond the walls of the garden. The summerhouse is wreathed in clematis and its exterior of thatch and unbarked wood gives it a strongly rustic character.

The site is not only north-facing but is shielded on either side by tall hedges of × *Cupressocyparis leylandii* and a golden thuja (*T. plicata* 'Aurea'). This limits the planting, which is dominated by the sort of plants more often found in a woodland setting: trilliums, the yellow-flowered *Uvularia grandiflora*, hellebores, astilbes, epimediums and pulmonarias. Some of the same plants are repeated in each bed, and running roughly down the centre through all the beds is a river-like stream of the brilliant blue *Corydalis flexuosa*, providing a link between the beds and giving a witty illusion of tumbling water. Many plants have bold foliage – bergenia, ferns, ligularia, trilliums and the curious *Paris quadrifolia* – with shapes strong enough not to be overwhelmed by the powerful architectural form of the boldly swooping walls.

The banks on either side of the beds

A rustic summerhouse is a focal point at the top of the oval beds. It also has an opening to one side, linking it with a cross axis. The blue of *Corydalis flexuosa* flows down the slope like a stream.

The light and airy foliage of *Cornus controversa* 'Variegata' catches the light, making it an admirable foil to colourful planting below – on the left a rich red form of *Aquilegia vulgaris* and, in the foreground, the rose-brown of *Dicentra* 'Stuart Boothman'.

are also planted. Here again there is repetition, and occasional symmetry. The silver-leafed shrub *Cornus alternifolia* 'Argentea' – a marvellous plant for any garden – is planted on each side of two of the ovals, and the central bed is flanked by *Berberis thunbergii* 'Rose Glow' whose translucent leaves do indeed glow when the light is behind them. Beside the berberis, the herbaceous potentilla *P. × hopwoodiana* throws out cream and apricot-pink flowers, while swags of *Campanula porscharskyana* cascade down the walls below. The summerhouse has little beds on either side, in which the silver-leafed cornus is planted with miniature azaleas, alpine phloxes and self-sown *Aquilegia vulgaris*. Among these are the occasional exquisite rarity such as the sinister *Arisaema ciliatum*, with deepest plum-coloured stems, and the exquisite lily-like *Nomocharis pardanthina* with downward-hanging white flowers freckled with purple.

A splendid *Cercidiphyllum japonicum* marks the foot of the oval beds, its autumn foliage a dramatic cocktail of red and yellow. The shady bed below is scattered with ferns, hostas and a distinguished peony, *Paeonia veitchii* var. *woodwardia*, with glaucous foliage

and the palest pink single flowers. Beyond the tree a circular sitting place – already in position before the oval beds were made – gives views in different directions. Looking back up the slope, the skyline is dominated by a magnificent old copper beech (*Fagus sylvatica* Atropurpureum Group). Distant ornamental trees such as this help to fix garden features in the larger landscape, giving them a context and a meaning.

The maintenance of these beds is not arduous. They are weeded and watered as necessary throughout the season, and in the autumn, when the herbaceous growth has died down, it is all cut back and removed, allowing the *Corydalis flexuosa* to develop. In early spring the beds are fed with a general fertiliser and mulched with a shredded mulch made of leafmould, well-rotted dung and bracken; this is light enough in texture to allow the erythroniums and wood anemones to come through. The *Berberis thunbergii* 'Rose Glow' is cut back hard in the winter to a 12in/30cm dome to keep it in scale. This also has the effect of making the new growth, which has the best colour, more vigorous.

The challenge of a particularly tricky garden design problem, when happily

GARDEN HOUSE OVAL BEDS

1 *Ligularia dentata* 'Desdemona' and
   Chionodoxa forbesii 'Pink Giant'
2 *Helleborus orientalis* (pink)
3 *Pulmonaria saccharata*
4 *Corydalis flexuosa* 'China Blue' and
   Viola 'Belmont Blue'
5 *Corydalis cheilanthifolia*
6 *Epimedium grandiflorum* 'Nanum'
7 *Trillium ovatum*
8 *Bergenia ciliata* f. *ligulata*
9 *Helleborus orientalis* (yellow)
10 *Trillium sessile*
11 *Primula* 'Devon Cream'

solved, often results in an unexpectedly successful new feature. The solution adopted here was a bold one that creates a highly original feature out of an awkward site, adding emphatically to the character of the garden as a whole and fitting in harmoniously with its other ingredients. From the summerhouse at the top of the hill the oval beds present a dramatic sight. Nothing is quite symmetrical and the powerful forms of the swirling walls embracing the beds create a restless, muscular energy as they descend the slope. But this restlessness is held in check by the peaceful high hedges, the thatched summerhouse at the summit, and the harmonious, repeated planting of the beds and their margins. All ingredients are held firmly in a kind of dynamic balance. In a busier part of the garden it would have created visual excess but here the tension between excitement and repose is turned to advantage.

A PATH AND A SUMMERHOUSE: KEY FEATURES IN A TOWN GARDEN

A decorative path between an avenue of conical spruce makes a bold link between the house and an extraordinary summerhouse.

The walled garden of which this is a part is ¼ acre/0.1 ha in area but seems far larger. It lies behind an old terraced house in a small town, or large village, on the borders of Belgium and the Netherlands. The site has many of the limitations that countless urban gardens have, but in this case they have been triumphantly overcome to create a marvellous garden that overflows with lessons for gardeners. The most important single principle is – be bold. Too many small gardens are mean in ambition and fiddly in execution. A boldly conceived design may have far more telling impact in a small garden than it can in a larger landscape, and is much easier to achieve.

Here, a path linking the house to an extraordinary summerhouse and thence to other parts of the garden is an object lesson in bold and simple planning. At a slightly lower level than the paved terrace that runs along the south side of the house is a rectangular lawn. Running straight across the lawn and away from the house is a 7ft/2m wide, beautifully made path of square paving stones arranged in strips alternating with strips of bricks. The path is a central decorative device, a dominating axis treated in a highly ornamental way. But the point of a path is that it must go somewhere, and this one leads, as straight as an arrow – admittedly with distractingly pretty planting on either side – to the summerhouse and the heart of the garden. The summerhouse was the single distinguishing feature of the garden when the present owner came thirty-five years ago. Fashioned of the dogwood *Cornus mas*, which has been trained to form a roof and walls, this hundred-year-old structure has three arched openings facing the house. It is 25ft/7.5m wide and its interior, with an elegant cast-iron bench, not only forms a cool summer's retreat but also gives framed views of garden and house. A metal superstructure still exists inside, on which the plants – about a dozen of them – were originally trained, but the growth of a century has been such that it now immensely exceeds the size of this armature. The attractions of *Cornus mas* for such an ornamental summerhouse are many. The pointed leaves are quite small so that the 'walls' have a regular texture, and their attractively sombre green colour makes an excellent background. It flowers as early as February or March, producing a profusion of little yellow flowers on bare wood that is one of the most dazzling sights of early spring. The fruit borne in the summer is a bright shining red, like a cherry; indeed, its English common name is cornelian cherry. The foliage has good autumn colour – a fine pale yellow – and after the leaves have fallen in late autumn the intricate twiggy framework of branches is laid bare, making a fascinating winter ornament. It needs to be gently trimmed two or three times a year to maintain its outline, with individual branches being removed rather than comprehensively shorn. It is given a single major clipping in mid-June – no later, as flowers are

A view from the sitting terrace to the summerhouse of clipped *Cornus mas*. The path is lined with rows of erigeron and lavender, behind which rises an avenue of spruce, *Picea glauca* var. *albertiana* 'Conica'. The detail is simple and all parts relate to each other.

The powerful shapes of the conical spruces make a fine contrast to the flowery planting on either side of the avenue – the border seen beyond is full of old roses. The velvety texture and rich green colour of the conifers provide permanent ornament in the garden.

produced on the previous year's growth so it is important not to clip too late in the year when growth has almost ceased.

The path to the summerhouse is edged with a rounded hedge of lavender (*Lavandula angustifolia*) and scatterings of *Erigeron*. Beyond the lavender hedges are, on either side, stately rows of the spruce *Picea glauca* var. *albertiana* 'Conica'. These so-called dwarf conifers grow naturally into broadly-based trees of striking conical shape, and after thirty-five years have grown to a height of 8ft/2.5m, with bases over 6ft/1.8m in diameter. The individual trees vary slightly in height and show gentle billowing variations in outline. It is not an unusual tree but is more often seen in collections of conifers and rarely used to such dramatic effect as it is here where its character is displayed to exceptional advantage. It was a daring stroke to use it in this confined garden and the trees have now assumed a monumental character. In high summer, they make a bold contrast with the lavishly flowery planting behind them. The owner is worried that the cones have now become out of scale and, as they are still growing, that the problem will become worse. This is a dilemma which afflicts all those who garden in restricted space

– almost any tree or shrub will, one day, become far too big. But the prospect of a plant growing too big should never dissuade a gardener from planting it and relishing its well-behaved youth.

From the terrace by the house the upright shapes of the spruces are seen to be a recurrent theme in the garden. In a neighbouring enclosure and rising far above surrounding planting is a pair of swamp cypresses (*Taxodium distichum*) which, though looser and narrower, repeat the conical shape. One day they too may prove an embarassment but, for the moment, they provide emphatic structure. Nearby, the tip of a fastigiate golden elm (*Ulmus minor* 'Dampieri Aurea') can be seen from the house terrace – one of three of this unusual tree in the garden. Lastly, beyond the garden's boundaries are the soaring shapes of Lombardy poplars (*Populus nigra* var. *italica*) making a link between the rural landscape and the patterned garden within the walls. The skyline of a garden is always important; the gardener can do little about its defects, but handsome features may always be 'borrowed' or referred to within the garden to marvellous effect. This borrowing makes a happy connection between artifice and nature.

AN AVENUE AND A SUMMERHOUSE

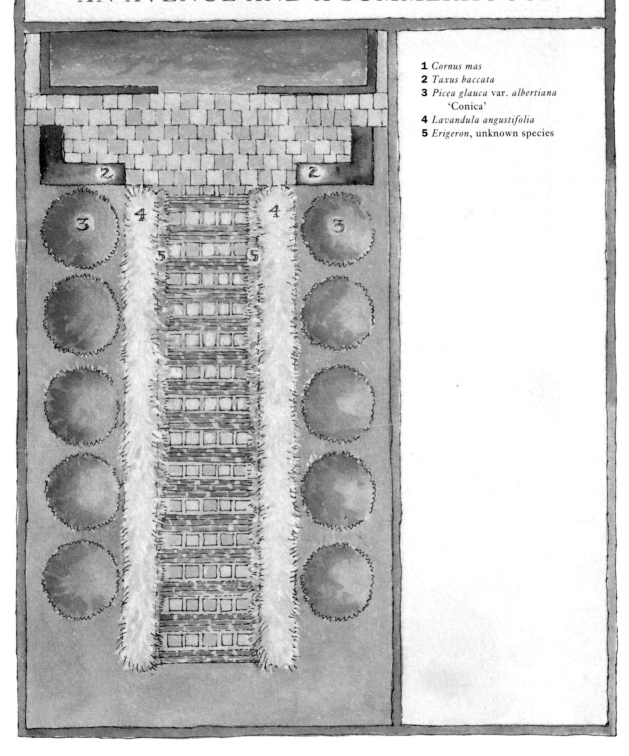

1 *Cornus mas*
2 *Taxus baccata*
3 *Picea glauca* var. *albertiana*
   'Conica'
4 *Lavandula angustifolia*
5 *Erigeron*, unknown species

MAKING A VIRTUE OUT OF LIMITED URBAN SPACE

A small town garden combines interesting plants and lively design to make a varied and exciting urban oasis.

What is the best way to deal with severely limited space? Many gardeners adopt the principle of reducing plants and features to a bare minimum. In this town plot, however, in an area of 40ft × 17ft/11.4m × 5.2m, the garden designer Anthony Noel has fashioned for his own garden an intricate and richly planted space which ignores the potential limitations of its small size. The garden, which faces south-east, is walled in brick and lies behind a terraced house. It is crammed with features yet manages to achieve, by meticulous upkeep, an atmosphere of calm and repose.

At the centre of the garden a lawn of intense green and impeccable surface has the air of a precious rug in the middle of a room. It is surrounded by flagstones of varied sizes, which nibble in to the edge of the lawn, giving it a discreetly ragged margin. (In a situation like this it makes all the difference to use real stone, with its attractive varied surface and irregularities of texture, rather than the flat and repetitive surface of many composition slabs.)

On either side of the lawn are two built features, used like miniature stages. Facing south-west is a little recessed sitting area with an elaborate cast-iron seat painted a dazzling turquoise. It is flanked with box (*Buxus sempervirens*) clipped into spirals, and a pair of Versailles boxes with standard fuchsias underplanted with trailing *Helichrysum petiolare*. The boxes are painted in stripes of white and turquoise, matching the colour of the seat. Throughout the garden there are many painted surfaces (including striped flower pots) with colours chosen (and changed at intervals) for specific local effect. Pots stand round about the seat: two large pots of marguerites (*Argyranthemum foeniculaceum*) and smaller ones of lilies (the flamboyant, sweetly scented 'Stargazer') and cacti. Plants grow between the cracks of the paving stones: decorative alpine strawberries and white thrift (*Armeria maritima* 'Alba'). Much of the ornament here and elsewhere in the garden consists of moveable décor, allowing different arrangements at different times in different parts of the garden.

Facing the sitting area on the other side of the lawn is a little pool with water-jets. A bronze mask let into the brick wall spouts water into a rectangular raised pool below, and jets of water play onto the surface of the mask. More pots of 'Stargazer' lilies, as well as pots of clipped box, decorate the edge of the pool. On either side of the pool, grown in containers, are magnificent climbers from tropical Africa: *Gloriosa rothschildiana*. These would not survive a hard winter out-of-doors but, supported on bamboos, make marvellous pot plants, flaunting their brilliant scarlet and gold flowers against waxy foliage. On one side the plant intermingles with the striped Bourbon rose 'Variegata di Bologna'.

The walls, especially their tops, have been drawn into the decorative scheme of the garden, with climbing plants boldly used. Relishing the contrast, found in many old country gardens, of vigorous plants growing against a background of stonework, crumbling

A cast-iron seat, painted a brilliant turquoise, is flanked by pots of 'Stargazer' lilies which are both dramatically decorative and richly scented. White thrift (*Armeria maritima*) and wild strawberries are scattered in cracks between the paving stones.

mortar and bricks, the owner has successfully imported something of this atmosphere into his own town garden. The dramatically variegated ivy *Hedera colchica* 'Sulphur Heart' (formerly *H. colchica* 'Paddy's Pride') hangs in heavy swags at the entrance to the garden. The scented rose 'Madame Alfred Carrière' clothes a west-facing wall. On the south-facing wall is the variegated summer jasmine (*Jasminum officinale* 'Argenteovariegatum'). In a small garden it is relatively easy to fill the air with scent and here, in high summer, the perfumes of roses, jasmine and lilies are an emphatic ingredient.

A town garden often has the valuable attribute of combining different microclimates in a small area, and well-designed gardens will capitalise on the possibilities. In a south-facing bed, underneath the variegated jasmine, several plants make the most of this privileged position: the long-flowering Mexican daisy (*Erigeron karvinskianus*), the South African *Melianthus major* with magnificent leaves, the French lavender *Lavandula stoechas* sbsp. *pedunculata* and the Mediterranean *Santolina chamaecyparissus*. The far north-facing end of the garden has by contrast several shade-loving plants: hostas (including

the beautiful and deliciously scented *H. plantaginea*), *Arum italicum* sbsp. *italicum* 'Marmoratum' with glistening, patterned foliage, and the Japanese painted fern (*Athyrium niponicum* var. *pictum*), accompanied by London pride (*Saxifraga × urbium*) – a nice mixture of the grand and the humble.

An intensively planted small garden like this needs high standards of upkeep – languishing or unhappy plants are all too obvious in a small space. This garden has light, sandy soil, so the owner feeds it well with manure and other fertilisers, and it is watered lavishly in dry weather. Dead-heading is carried out regularly, and dead leaves are removed. The lawn is mowed at least every week in summer and kept meticulously free of debris. Because the only way into the garden is through the house, all garden rubbish has laboriously to be bagged and removed the same way.

Small gardens tend towards reticence and meanness. Here, many of the effects are similar to those found in large gardens, without being absurdly out of scale. The design of a small garden can provide a challenge which, if met with suitable panache, may make a splendid virtue out of the potential handicap of limited space.

A LONDON TOWN GARDEN

1 *Cordyline australis*
2 *Rosa glauca*
3 *Lonicera japonica* 'Halliana'
4 *Hedera canariensis* 'Gloire de Marengo'
5 *Hosta sieboldiana* var. *elegans*
6 *Arum italicum* sbsp. *italicum* 'Marmoratum'
7 *Paeonia suffruticosa* sbsp. *rockii*
8 *Saxifraga umbrosa*
9 *Anemone hupehensis*
10 *Alchemilla mollis*
11 *Paeonia mlokosewitschii*
12 *Rosa* 'Variegata di Bologna'
13 *Rosa* 'Madame Alfred Carrière'
14 *Armeria maritima* 'Alba'
15 *Lathyrus latifolius* 'White Pearl'
16 *Ophiopogon planiscapus* 'Nigrescens'
17 *Anemone × hybrida* 'Honorine Jobert'
18 *Hosta plantaginea*
19 *Iris* 'Superstition'
20 *Eucomis bicolor*
21 *Acanthus spinosus* Spinossisimus Group
22 *Jasminum officinalis* 'Argenteovariegatum'
23 *Melianthus major*
24 *Lavandula stoechas* sbsp. *pedunculata*
25 *Agave americana* 'Mediopicta'
26 *Wisteria sinensis* 'Alba'
27 *Helichrysum petiolare*
28 *Rosa × odorata* 'Viridiflora'

A WALLED GARDEN WITH A PARTERRE AND LIVELY NEW BORDERS

Features from the past have been skilfully preserved and embellished with exuberant new plantings in an enclosed garden attached to a historic house.

The idea of a garden enclosed by old stone walls has irresistible allure. This one, lying within a larger garden, has a particularly beautiful setting at the foot of a marvellously romantic 14th-century fortified manor house. In addition to the incomparable setting, the chief attraction of the walled garden lies in its decorative formal layout with largely replanted borders surrounding it.

There are probably only two ways of dividing up an enclosed, regular space such as this one. The most usual is to make a four-square cruciform pattern of paths, so that the shape of the enclosure dominates the arrangement within. The other is to take advantage of the strong framework of walls to weave a freer, contrasting pattern in which symmetry has its place but where the arrangement of beds and planting is less constrained. The first is solid, calm and logical; the second allows the imagination free rein.

The walled area forms a rectangle, 100ft × 70ft/30m × 20m. Almost filling the centre is a 19th-century parterre of beds edged with box (*Buxus sempervirens*), where four beds shaped like *fleurs de lys* are disposed about three circular beds, with gravel paths winding between. The central bed of the three has a stone edging and a Victorian cast-iron basket planted with *Rosa* 'De Rescht' and tender bedding plants that change from year to year. The *fleur de lys* beds are planted in pairs, both with roses: one pair has 'Gruss an Aachen', a Polyantha rose with creamy pink flowers, and the other has 'Heritage',

one of David Austin's English roses, with pale pink double flowers. Both are well scented and perpetual-flowering – valuable qualities in so prominent a position. All the beds have an underplanting, in mixed colours, of the annuals *Echium vulgare* and *Salvia horminum*, which often also self-seed. In the centre of each bed is a standard mop-headed hawthorn (*Crataegus oxyacantha* 'Paul's Scarlet') with double scarlet flowers. They are clipped once a year to form well-defined balls.

Densely planted mixed borders, their margins blurred by abundant planting and by graceful curves, line the garden walls. The planting is a mixture of woody plants – particularly shrub roses – and herbaceous, but the latter dominate. A south-facing border lying at the foot of the castle walls gives an idea of the flavour of these borders. This one is backed by an informal hedge of the Hybrid Musk rose 'Felicia' which has elegantly formed shell-pink double flowers, a delicious scent, and is recurrent-flowering; it makes a good, hardworking background to the decorative planting below. Other roses include the exquisite Damask rose 'Madame Hardy', with double white flowers with creamy-pink undertones and a sweet musky scent; the repeat-flowering Bourbon rose 'Madame Pierre Oger', with silver-pink cupped flowers; and the valuable Hybrid Musk rose 'Ballerina' which has single pink flowers with a pale eye. These are underplanted with herbaceous perennials

Clumps of santolina flank an entrance to the walled garden. The box-edged beds are filled with the roses 'Gruss an Aachen' or 'Heritage', and a hawthorn (*Crataegus laevigata* 'Paul's Scarlet') trained as a lollipop marks the centre of each bed.

in pink, purple, blue or white. The planting has the appearance of relaxed artlessness which successfully conceals much thought and hard work. There is harmony both in the controlled colour scheme and in the relative size of the plants. Accidental harmony comes, too, from many self-sown seedlings of plants such as *Aquilegia vulgaris*, foxgloves (*Digitalis purpurea*) and opium poppies (*Papaver somniferum*). In this profusion other plants give structure by virtue of their strongly shaped foliage or striking habit. Here are the spherical flower-heads of *Allium christophii* and *A. hollandicum*, the statuesque thistle *Onopordon acanthium*, the flowering spires of *Verbascum chaixii* 'Mont Blanc' and the powerful toothed and veined leaves of *Salvia sclarea* var. *turkestanica*. These last will also self-seed but they have, in fact, been raised and carefully placed for best effect. Smaller plants weave their way through others, scattering harmonious splashes of colour. The purple of *Penstemon* 'Sour Grapes', the scarlet of *Potentilla nepalensis* 'Miss Willmott', the trailing lavender flower-stems of catmint (*Nepeta* × *faassenii*) and the pink and

white of *Lychnis coronaria* Oculata Group. The very edge of the border is laced with smaller plants like pinks (*Dianthus* cultivars), violas and *Lamium maculatum* 'Beacon Silver'. There are no great rarities and, taken together, they show the lively effect that can be achieved from a largely traditional selection of plants.

A similar range of plants, with the occasional exotic interloper, is found in the other beds. And although this is not a large area, a few substantial shrubs or small trees add character. *Buddleja* 'Lochinch' throws out arching panicles of well-scented lavender flowers, in harmony with the prevailing colour scheme. The evergreen *Photinia davidiana* 'Palette' has lustrous leaves variegated in pink and white. Overhanging an entrance is the beautiful American snake-bark maple *Acer pensylvanicum*.

Generous planting needs generous feeding and for many years immense quantities of spent mushroom compost were added to the beds. Feeling that a change was needed, the gardener now gives an annual top-dressing of rotted farmyard manure and a little bonemeal here and there. There is a regular programme of rose spraying to keep black spot and greenfly at bay, with weekly sprays starting in March and continuing through the summer.

A walled garden such as this one can be treated in isolation from the rest of the garden, which allows greater freedom of planting and design. Outside the walls here, there are links with the planting within but the effects are on a grander scale, appropriate to the splendid setting of a medieval moat and distant views of ancient parkland. Inside, the atmosphere is much more intimate. The enclosing stone walls provide a solid frame for the garden's different ingredients, and the planting has a festive, exuberant air, making a happy contrast to the stern ramparts of the castle.

Seen from the roof of the castle the walled garden reveals the lively pattern of its beds. The edges of the beds running along the walls are allowed to encroach on the gravel path. Beyond the walls are the moat and ancient parkland.

A CASTLE WALLED GARDEN

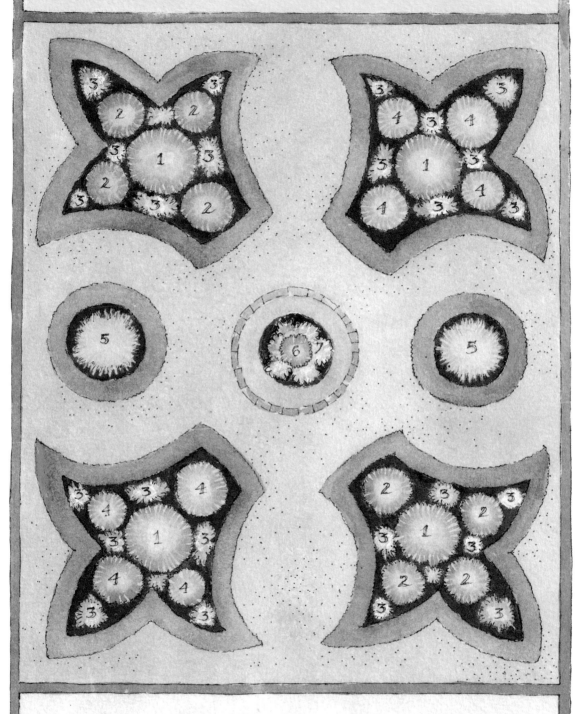

1 *Crataegus laevigata* 'Paul's Scarlet'
2 *Rosa* 'Gruss an Aachen'
3 *Echium vulgare* and *Salvia horminum*
4 *Rosa* 'Heritage'
5 *Lavandula spica*
6 *Rosa* 'De Rescht'
7 *Pelargonium* 'Blue Beard'

A FORMAL ROSE GARDEN CHANGED INTO A 'TROPICAL' GARDEN

The framework of a historic garden is used to make a thrilling new garden.

In recent times it has been fashionable in British gardens to use a limited range of polite colours: pinks, blues, whites, pale yellows and silvers, for example. Such schemes slip inconspicuously into almost any setting, but often lack character. A new attitude towards colour – and form – has been making an impact in the last few years, and a garden like this one could inspire you to revamp an outmoded corner of your own.

One of the pioneers in this field is the English gardener and writer Christopher Lloyd. The garden he looks after had belonged to his parents and is a shrine to the Arts and Crafts movement of the early years of the 20th century. Unlike many shrines, however, it is a living place and, like all the best modern gardens, subject to constant experiment.

The formal rose garden was made for Mr Lloyd's parents to the designs of Sir Edwin Lutyens, who had restored the house and made other contributions to the gardens. It is a secluded spot, protected on one side by an outhouse and on the other three sides by 6ft/1.8m high hedges of yew (*Taxus baccata*). The beds were originally laid out in a pattern, and each contained one or two species of roses. Mr Lloyd changed the roses from time to time, although some remained from his parents' time. In summer it is a hot, dry part of the garden and, as a rose garden, was, after the end of July, devoid of interest.

Mr Lloyd eventually decided to remove almost all the roses. Keeping the existing pattern of beds separated by narrow stone paths, he introduced a mixed scheme, with many tender plants, which capitalises on the benign microclimate and provides a garden which continues to be dramatically decorative right up until the first frosts. The idea was to create 'a jungle of luxuriance' in which exotic leaf forms, rich colours and density of planting would be the ruling principles.

Most of the plants are herbaceous, and many are too tender to withstand a winter in the south-east of England. Some woody plants are 'stooled' (cut down to the ground) in early spring, with the result that they throw out vigorous new shoots with foliage of startling size – an idea of particular interest to gardeners with limited space. As a tree, *Paulownia tomentosa* will in appropriate conditions grow as high as 50ft/15m; if stooled, it produces fleshy shoots rising to 10ft/3m in a good season, with magnificent five-sided downy leaves, 36in/90cm across. The tree of heaven (*Ailanthus altissima*) will make an even larger tree than the paulownia and it, too, lends itself particularly well to stooling. Its distinguished pinnate leaves will be up to 36in/90cm long, twice the size of the normal adult foliage, making a marvellous ingredient for a lively border. The shrub *Rhus* × *pulvinata* Autumn Lace Group (syn. *R. glabra* 'Laciniata') if cut back will also produce leaves 36in/90cm long, which are feathery, pinnate and borne on striking plum-coloured stems. They also have the virtue of rich red autumn colouring.

Throughout the garden use is made

On the right the stiff blade-like leaves of *Phormium* 'Sundowner' thrust through the grey foliage of *Artemisia* 'Powis Castle'. In the background tall purple *Verbena bonariensis* mixes with white *Nicotiana sylvestris*.

Luxuriant planting and rich colours are the rule in this garden. Orange-red *Dahlia* 'Ellen Houston' with dark foliage rises in the foreground with the filigree foliage of *Rhus* × *pulvinata* Autumn Lace Group growing through. At the back are the fleshy leaves and pale pink flowers of *Canna* 'Louis Cayeux'.

of tender exotic foliage. The Japanese banana (*Musa basjoo*), one of the hardier bananas, will in favourable conditions unfurl its immense leaves to a height of 10ft/3m, giving a splendid sense of tropical exuberance. The castor oil plant (*Ricinus communis*) from North Africa is seen here in the cultivar *R. communis* 'Carmencita', with gleaming mahogany palmate leaves and scarlet prickly seedheads. *R. communis* 'Impala', similar but more vigorous, is also used. *Canna* 'Striata' has sharp green leaves striated in fine gold lines, with apricot flowers borne on downy pink stems.

The planting plan opposite shows one of the sections of the garden and gives a good idea of the characteristic style of the whole. The paths that separate the beds are quite narrow, the planting within them dense, and many of the plants are tall; some actually brush your face as you pass – self-sown *Verbena bonariensis* at the edge of some of the beds rises easily to 6ft/1.8m. You have the impression of being submerged in a jungle.

The contrast of leaf forms and the sprightly colours of flowers give a fortissimo effect – like the juxtaposition of *Canna* 'Louis Cayeux', with stately glaucous foliage and rich pink flowers,

and the New Zealand flax *Phormium* 'Sundowner', with sword-like variegated leaves suffused with pale gold and pink. Immediately behind the canna is the little trailing Mexican *Ipomoea lobata* (syn. *Mina lobata*) which scatters its startling scarlet and yellow flowers hither and yon at the tips of its tendrils. Dahlias are used to great effect throughout the garden. In this section are the rich orange-yellow 'Chiltern Amber', the blood-red 'Ellen Houston' (with handsome dark leaves) and 'Alva's Doris', a rich red cactus type.

Other exotic foliage in this part of the garden is provided by *Eucalyptus gunnii* which is raised from seed every year and whose juvenile foliage, a glowing glaucous-grey, is a lovely ornament. The ginger (*Hedychium flavescens*), from Bengal, has bold broad leaves and elegant spires of yellow flowers. The Egyptian *Cyperus papyrus* (whose fibre was used for paper-making) throws out exciting mop-heads of leaves at the tips of tall reed-like stems. The rice-paper plant from Taiwan (*Tetrapanax papyrifer*) has magnificent fan-like leaves. In cooler climates this shrub behaves like a herbaceous plant, being cut to the ground each winter.

This *is* a labour-intensive style of

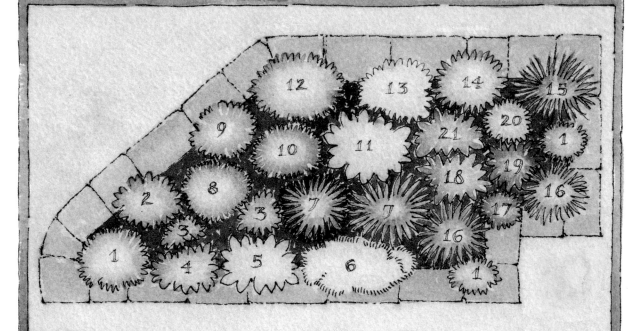

GREAT DIXTER TROPICAL GARDEN

1 *Verbena bonarienis*
2 *Nicotiana sylvestris*
3 *Ipomoea lobata*
4 *Dahlia* 'Alva's Doris'
5 *Canna* 'Louis Cayeux'
6 *Artemisia* 'Powis Castle'
7 *Phormium* 'Sundowner'
8 *Rosa* 'Chanel'

9 *Begonia* 'Cleopatra'
10 *Rhus × pulvinata* Autumn Lace
   Group
11 *Canna* 'Erebus'
12 *Dahlia* 'Ellen Houston'
13 *Hedychium flavescens*
14 *Dahlia* 'Chiltern Amber'
15 *Cordyline australis*

   'Atrosanguineus'
16 *Cyperus papyrus*
17 *Oxalis vulcanicola*
18 *Tetrapanax papyrifera*
19 *Canna indica* 'Purpurea'
20 *Eucalyptus gunnii*
21 *Ricinus communis* 'Impala'

gardening. The verbenas, for example, are used as flexible ornaments. Some are removed to open a vista; others are cut back to change their period of flowering or to rejuvenate them. Most of the plants are too tender to survive reliably many winters in south-east England – though it is surprising what *does* survive: both the banana, protected with fern fronds, and *Canna indica* 'Purpurea' have survived recent winters. Furthermore, the best performance of many plants is only achieved by lavish feeding and watering. Because so much of the planting is in effect annual, there is always scope for experiment and fine tuning – luxuries which few gardeners have the opportunity to indulge in on any scale.

This exotic garden is a separate world, tucked away from the rest of the garden and visually cut off from it. Here are no conventional borders, viewed like paintings from a distance and with plants graded in size from front to back. The exuberant planting is visible through a veil of purple flowers of *Verbena bonariensis* in front of some of the borders. In this garden you are physically engulfed by a profusion of plants; your senses are assailed by the jungle-like depth of planting and the intensity of colours that embrace you as you pass.

A PAIR OF TRUE HERBACEOUS BORDERS FORM A HIDDEN GARDEN

The strength and character of herbaceous planting are vividly displayed in these subtle borders.

Few gardeners today would contemplate planting a true herbaceous border, believing that the burden of maintenance would be more than they could face. Furthermore, such borders have little ornament out of season. Instead, most favour the mixed border, in which herbaceous and woody plants intermingle, often with the addition of evergreens for winter interest and structure. Herbaceous borders *are* hard work but the rewards are many and they can be adapted to gardens of whatever scale. Even a small garden can provide space for some herbaceous planting, and the season can always be extended by an underplanting of spring bulbs.

As these borders powerfully show, there is a marvellous freshness in the foliage of herbaceous plants, and a softness in the contrasting shapes of habit and foliage. The woody framework of so many shrubs imparts an unyielding stiffness, whereas the fleshy stems and soft foliage of most herbaceous plants give a character of inherent gracefulness that no other planting can provide. The borders shown here do in fact contain one or two species of woody plants, but are dominated by herbaceous perennials.

These borders, tucked away and concealed behind a thick hedge of *Thuja plicata* (this, the western red cedar, makes a fast-growing hedge that grows best in heavy moist soil), form part of a very large and complex garden where the owner can afford the luxury of features that do not need to perform in every season. The borders are nevertheless fully integrated into the overall garden layout. They are arranged in two pairs with a gravel path between, and at their centre, marking the cross axis of paths, is an airy octagonal gazebo built of white-painted wood and trellis work and swathed with the pale pink Climbing rose 'New Dawn'.

The borders are entered at one end through an opening in a hedge from a shady path, and at the other end lead to a door into a yard for greenhouses. At either end a simple white-painted wooden gate set in brick piers has vertical slats with spaces between, allowing tantalising glimpses of what lies beyond. The tops of these gates are arched, echoing the dome of the central gazebo. All this – apart from being logical – gives the layout a sense of purpose. Few things in garden design are more irritating than arbitrary routes and awkward relationships. As Russell Page wrote in his masterly *Education of a Gardener* – 'if the main lines of a composition are right, the detail may look after itself.'

The borders are 8ft/2.5m wide and 50ft/15m long. They are just wide enough to accommodate three ranks of plants, which are sufficiently closely planted to intermingle but have enough space around them to reveal their characteristic shapes. This is important, for one of the great charms of herbaceous borders is the undulating pattern of mounds and contrasting foliage. The path between the borders is only 4ft/1.2m, and in high summer,

By June the edges of the path have become hidden by plants and the framework of the gazebo is almost concealed by *Rosa* 'New Dawn'. To the right, the bold upright form of *Campanula lactiflora* White has statuesque presence.

The hooded flowers of *Stachys macrantha* 'Superba' are a rich rosy purple, seen here attractively associated with the thistle-like flowers of *Eryngium bourgatii.*

when the foliage of hostas, penstemons, cranesbills and sedums flops over the gravel, it is narrower still.

The beds are backed by 8ft/2.5m hedges of beech (*Fagus sylvatica*) – one of the best hedging materials, with soft young foliage that flutters in the breeze and magnificent autumn and winter colouring. Each bed has two columns of evenly spaced clipped silver pear (*Pyrus salicifolia*) quite close to the hedge, and these loosely formal shapes give subtle structure. Further structure is given by the repetition of herbaceous plants. *Hosta sieboldiana* var. *elegans*, which has boldly veined rather upright glaucous leaves, is repeated at irregular intervals at the front of the borders. Also repeated is the statuesque *Campanula lactiflora* White, rising a good 5ft/1.5m, with superb spires of white tubular flowers whose petals curve back elegantly at the tips. Planted in each of the four beds is a form of betony (*Stachys macrantha* 'Superba'). It has dark toothed leaves and flowers of a sharp rosy purple.

One problem with herbaceous plants is that many of them need support. Individual staking is laborious and requires skill if it is to look good. By far the most effective and least obtrusive stakes are the old-fashioned 'pea-sticks',

traditionally cut from coppiced hazel wood (*Corylus avellana*). However, in these borders the problem is solved by stretching a net across those areas of planting that need support. Fishing net with 6in × 6in/15cm × 15cm mesh is supported on stakes driven into the ground at 8ft/2.5m intervals to hold the netting at a height of 24in/60cm. The netting is put into place in March and removed when the top growth is cut down in November. Entirely concealed when the plants are in full growth, this is an excellent way of providing support, and the netting can also be sloped up towards the back to accommodate taller plants.

These borders were designed for his own garden by the garden designer and writer Martin Lane Fox. I always find it especially interesting to see the kinds of gardens that garden designers contrive for themselves, for in their professional work they will so often have to yield to the demands of their clients. Hidden behind their high hedge, on the periphery of the larger garden, these borders give the impression of a place where the owner had indulged his own pleasure in plants that he loves. Here, harmony reigns, and there is no need to astound the visitors.

HAZELBY BORDERS

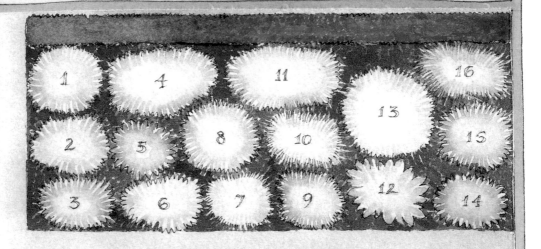

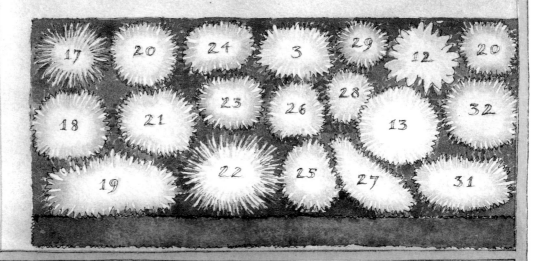

1 *Campanula lactiflora*
2 *Achillea* 'Salmon Beauty'
3 *Eryngium bourgatii*
4 *Cephalaria gigantea*
5 *Paeonia,* unnamed, red
6 *Stachys macrantha* 'Superba'
7 *Artemisia* 'Powis Castle'
8 *Lychnis chalcedonica* 'Alba'
9 *Penstemon,* pink, unnamed
10 *Perovskia* 'Blue Spire'
11 *Phlox,* unnamed, pink
12 *Hosta fortunei*
13 *Pyrus salicifolia* 'Pendula'

14 *Centaurea dealbata* 'John Coutts'
15 *Aster × frikartii*
16 *Foeniculum vulgare* 'Purpureum'
17 *Agapanthus,* unnamed, white
18 *Calamintha nepeta nepeta*
19 *Polygonum amplexicaule*
20 *Penstemon* 'Middleton Gem'
21 *Lysimachia ephemerum*
22 *Miscanthus sinensis* 'Variegata'
23 *Astrantia major rubra*
24 *Geranium wallichianum*

'Buxton's Variety'
25 *Thalictrum aquilegiifolium* var. *album*
26 *Thermopsis lanceolata*
27 *Campanula lactiflora*
28 *Nepeta* 'Souvenir d'André Chaudron'
29 *Penstemon* 'Sour Grapes'
30 *Hosta sieboldiana elegans*
31 *Sidalcea* 'Loveliness'
32 *Achillea* 'Apple Blossom'

A COLOUR BORDER FOR LATE SEASON DISPLAY

In this long border, in a key position in a large garden, plant form is as important as the modulation of colours from 'hot' to 'cool'.

Owners of small gardens may be unwilling to devote space to a feature that, however striking, starts to perform only after midsummer. However, by incorporating spring bulbs and early-flowering herbaceous plants, a border like this could easily be extended to provide ornament in the first half of the season as well.

The position of this great single border is an important one in the garden. It faces one side of the house and runs along a lawn which links different parts of the garden. From the side of the house it presents itself, at a distance, in full panorama, but it is also visible from other approaches.

Borders are often arranged in pairs on either side of a relatively narrow passage, so that they are seen obliquely – or head-on only from relatively close to. A bold painterly scheme such as this one is seen at its best head-on but from quite far away, without the distractions of deforming perspective or the sense of urgency engendered by a narrow path.

The border is planned on a generous scale: it is 16ft/4.8m wide and just under 100ft/30m long. It is backed by a hedge of yew (*Taxus baccata*) 6ft/1.8m high, and a narrow grass path runs between it and the plants at the back of the border, to allow both the clipping of the hedge and the maintenance of tall plants at the back. A border of this size needs the setting of a large garden but the principles of planting are applicable to one of any size, and an exactly equivalent effect may be achieved with a scaled-down planting plan.

Although colour is deployed in this border with particular skill – ranging from the vibrant and dramatic to the cool and peaceful – it would be wrong to think of it merely as a 'colour border', for contrasts of foliage and habit are also essential ingredients. Running from north-east to south-west, the planting starts at the northern end with cool whites, pinks and silvers which modulate to yellow and gold. In the centre section the scheme moves into its most exciting mood of reds, purples and oranges, with splashes of rich yellow. Finally, at the southern end, the colours soften to blues, violets and white. To explain how this works in detail I shall describe the planting in the central part.

Rising high at the back of the border in the 'hot' section is *Rosa* 'Geranium' (syn. *R. moyesii* 'Geranium'). This great species rose is a valuable border plant of statuesque presence, throwing out long thorny stems which cast sprays of flowers over other plantings. Its lightly scented flowers are scarlet and – a marvellous bonus for a late-flowering border with this colour scheme – its hips are strikingly ornamental, flask-shaped and a lively orange-red in colour. To one side, trained on a pole, is the clematis 'Kermesina', a viticella type with crimson flowers in late summer. In front of these is a group of the ornamental red orach (*Atriplex hortensis* var. *rubra*), an admirable example of a hardy annual plant that can have real presence in a border. It will grown to 6ft/1.8m and flaunts its bold, triangular toothed leaves over a long season. Pinching out the tip will make it bushier; in very dry weather it tends to grow rather leggy. It will

On a late summer's evening the light strikes the plants from behind, emphasising shapes and causing colours to glow. Scarlet pelargoniums lie among the foliage of ruby chard and red dahlias rise from the shapely leaves of *Ricinus communis*.

self-seed gently from year to year and is an admirable foliage plant for any scheme of reds and pinks. Two substantial clumps of red-hot pokers provide fine architectural form and long-lived colour – the more frequently seen *Kniphofia uvaria* 'Nobilis', rising up to 5ft/1.5m, with rich orange-red flowers lasting well into the autumn – and *K.* 'Erecta', similar but a little smaller. Alongside it is one of the best of the really vibrant blood-red dahlias, 'Blaisdon Red', which is still in flower when *Rosa* 'Geranium' behind it is splendidly festooned with orange hips.

Annuals, varying from year to year, also make a decorative contribution. Some of these, like the orach, self-seed. Love-lies-bleeding (*Amaranthus caudatus*), with exotic flowers like dangling red tassels, is another prolific self-seeder. The castor oil plant (*Ricinus communis*), which has beautiful palm-shaped leaves, will grow as tall as 5ft/1.5m. One of the handsomest cultivars, used here, is *R. communis* 'Carmencita', with red-brown foliage and vivid red seed-pods. It is planted in association with the cerise pelargonium 'Arley Red', love-lies-bleeding, red orach and the russet-orange flowers of *Helenium* 'Moerheim Beauty.' Two sorts of beet (*Beta vulgaris*) also contribute ornamental foliage: *B. vulgaris* 'Bull's Blood' and 'Ruby Chard', both of which have upright, fleshy leaves with striking red stems. Although the colours are chiefly red and purple the scheme is spiked with splashes of yellow. There is the cool pale amber of the rose 'Sunset Song' and the much sharper yellow of *Helenium* 'Sunshine' at the front of the border. It was Gertrude Jekyll who wisely advised designers of single colour borders to add dashes of appropriate contrasting colours – 'a blue garden, for beauty's sake, may be hungering for a group of white lilies, or something of palest lemon-yellow.'

Much maintenance is required to make borders such as this a success. In late autumn herbaceous top growth is

In late summer the border takes on a golden hazy character, with seedheads and browning top growth giving a soft background colour to the brightness of yellow heleniums, orange crocosmias, blood-red dahlias and crimson amaranthus.

cut down and the ground is weeded and forked over. The following April a top-dressing of fish blood and bone is lightly dug in. In alternate years, a good mulch of mushroom compost is given, but this brings too much nitrogen to the soil if used excessively, so garden-made compost is used every second year. Dahlias are planted out early in June, with stakes put in at the same time. After a diluted disinfectant in January to ward off black spot, the roses are – when possible – given a fortnightly spraying with an all-purpose 'cocktail' throughout the summer. The yew hedge is clipped in August.

In August and September the colours of the 'hot' section of this border seem to shimmer in the sun. In overcast weather they are scarely less attractive, smouldering with an intense glow. And the liveliness of the colour is matched by the striking effect of the variety of plant forms: the upright blade-like foliage of crocosmias, the arching stems of the rose 'Geranium', the exotic palmate leaves of the castor-oil plant, the drooping flowers of *Amaranthus caudatus* alongside the firmly upright red-hot pokers.

KEMERTON COLOUR BORDER

1 *Helenium* Sunshine hybrid
2 *Crocosmia* 'Star of the East'
3 *Solidago* 'Crown of Rays'
4 *Rosa* 'Sunset Song'
5 *Euphorbia dulcis* 'Chameleon'
6 *Antirrhinum* 'Black Prince'
7 *Centaurea* 'Black Ball'
8 *Helenium* 'Moerheim Beauty'
9 *Atriplex hortensis* var. *rubra*
10 *Ricinus communis*
   'Carmencita'
11 *Dahlia* 'Blaisdon Red'
12 *Kniphofia uvaria* 'Nobilis'
13 *Kniphofia* 'Erecta'
14 *Amaranthus caudatus*
15 *Pelargonium* 'Ashley Red'
16 *Beta vulgaris* 'Bull's Blood'
17 *Crocosmia* 'Lucifer'
18 *Clematis* 'Kermesina'
19 *Rosa* 'Geranium'
20 *Knautia macedonica*

A GRAVEL GARDEN AND ITS DROUGHT-RESISTANT PLANTS

A former car park is transformed into a brilliant display of flowering plants which flourish without irrigation.

The interest in the natural habitats of garden plants is of fairly recent origin. It began in the 19th century when huge numbers of exotics were brought back to Europe, and gardeners looked for places where they would grow successfully at home. In some cases they were spectacularly successful: the magnificent tender rhododendrons from the western Himalayas, for example, that flourish in the wet, mild climate of the south-west Cornish coast. William Robinson's book *The Wild Garden* (1870) laid great emphasis on growing hardy plants in habitats as close as possible to those enjoyed in the wild, and in the 20th century this idea has been extended to encourage the idea of gardening in harmony with nature. The possibility of dramatic changes in climate caused by the 'greenhouse effect', as well as regular bans on watering, have given this impetus a particular urgency.

The garden shown here is in one of the driest parts of England, the county of Essex on the east coast, which enjoys – if that is the word – no more than 20in/50cm of rain a year. The bulk of this rainfall comes in the winter months, leaving the gardening season particularly exposed to the problems of drought. The cost of watering is high, and many gardeners find such artificial conditions uncongenial. Beth Chatto, who made this garden, is a gardener and nurserywoman who has always emphasised the importance of a plant's habitat. She became known for her exhibits at the Chelsea Flower Show, in which plants, grouped by habitat, were disposed in a convincingly natural way.

As an experiment, Beth Chatto decided to cultivate a new area of her garden in which there would be no watering at all. Plants chosen for their resistance to drought would have to depend on what was naturally available – conserved, to some extent, by a mulch of gravel that helps prevent surface evaporation. The deeper the mulch, the more effective it is, though most loss of water from the soil is in fact caused by the plants themselves, transpiring moisture through their foliage. Plants from dry habitats have naturally evolved over time to conserve moisture, but a substantial broad-leafed tree from a wetter environment will disperse into the atmosphere two or three hundred gallons of water a day, and no amount of mulching will have much impact on conserving water in the soil. It is therefore only by using plants that have minimal moisture needs that mulching will make any practical difference.

The design of this gravel garden is naturalistic, with sweeping borders and island beds of irregular outline. It is protected from bitter north-east winds by a tall hedge of × *Cupressocyparis leylandii*, and gravel is used over the whole area, dissolving boundaries between path and bed. Furthermore, the edges of the beds are blurred by many self-sown creeping plants, such as thymes, which threaten to reclaim the paths from under your feet. Although the garden is in a sense a horticultural

Plants are packed closely together, as in nature, and by late July form a seamless tapestry of colours. Here are the shapely yellow bracts of *Euphorbia characias* sbsp. *wulfenii* (*top*), trailing stems of *Nepeta* 'Six Hills Giant', and the vivid pink flowers of *Cistus* 'Silver Pink' showing well through the fine silver foliage of *Artemisia* 'Powis Castle'.

test-bed – designed to find out which plants will work in these conditions – it is laid out with a sharp eye for associations of colour and of form. There is another, and important, source of harmony: plants from similar habitats always go well together. Anyone who has walked in the hills of, say, southern Spain, will have noticed the astonishingly harmonious spread of cistus, artemisia, lavender, euphorbia – plants which appear to have been arranged by the hand of a skilled gardener.

In one respect, however, the gravel garden is quite unlike anything you would ever see in the wild. Nature, for example, tends to distribute large communities of a few plants in a single area. Here, in a relatively small space, is a huge variety of species which, although they may have similar habitats, come from many different parts of the world.

An informal layout such as this one puts particular emphasis on the planting, which becomes the chief source of harmony and interest. The winding paths and margins of the beds, while creating sympathetic naturalistic shapes, are too fluid to make any firm pattern or design.

The repetition of plants over a large area is always a source of harmony. It is the way that nature herself generally arranges things. The onion *Nectaroscordum siculum* sbsp. *bulgaricum* seeds itself about profusely and is ornamental over a very long period – from its pink-brown hanging bell-like flowers in the spring to its upward-pointing umbels of rocket-like seedheads in summer and autumn. The self-seeding biennial Scotch thistle (*Onopordum acanthium*) is of spectacular presence, with statuesque silver-grey leaves and mauve shaving-brush flowers. While, scattered liberally in exactly the way in which it might be found in its native Greece, the beautiful Madonna lily (*Lilium candidum*) adds to its magnificent heads of white flowers the further beauty of delicious scent.

Grasses, which make such attractive companion plants, are widely used. *Stipa tenuissima* forms graceful clumps, crowned in summer by seedheads, pale gold flecked with purple, which catch the slightest breeze. *Stipa gigantea* throws out arching stems, up to 8ft/2.5m high, bristling with dangling golden anthers. Different species and cultivars of a single genus are also frequently used – geraniums, cistus, thymes, bergenias, alliums, lilies and sea hollies.

Throughout the garden there are brilliant associations of plants. A pale pink toadflax (*Linaria purpurea* 'Canon Went') threads its way between the silver leaves of the sea holly (*Eryngium giganteum*). The deep red penstemon 'Andenken an Friedrich Hahn' is planted next to giant seedheads of *Allium christophii* whose stems take on a plum-coloured bloom as they age. Fruity pink *Alstroemeria* Ligtu Hybrid flops among the silver-grey leaves of the shrub *Atriplex halimus*. The sumptuous blue of the flax *Linum narbonense* glows among the stems of pale mauve- flowered *Verbena bonariensis* and smaller, deeper mauve *Verbena rigida*.

The tall stems and decorative seedheads of *Nectaroscordum siculum* rise among the plump silver flowers of the knapweed *Leuzea centauroides*, with a sheaf of rich yellow wild Spanish broom, *Spartium junceum*, in the background.

BETH CHATTO'S GRAVEL GARDEN

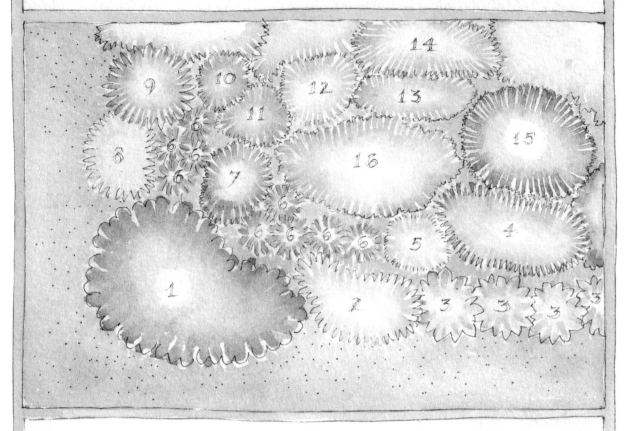

1 *Bergenia* 'Beethoven'
2 *Stachys byzantina* 'Big Ears'
3 *Verbascum bombyciferum*
4 *Alstroemeria* Ligtu Hybrid
5 *Lavandula angustifolia* 'Hidcote'
6 *Allium hollandicum* 'Purple

Sensation'
7 *Erysimum* 'Bowles' Mauve'
8 *Stachys byzantina* 'Primrose Heron'
9 *Euphorbia stricta*
10 *Anthemis punctata* sbsp.*cupaniana*
11 *Origanum laevigatum* 'Hopleys'

12 *Artemisia ludoviciana* var.
incompta
13 *Ceanothus thyrsiflorus* var. *repens*
14 *Elaeagnus* 'Quicksilver'
15 *Berberis* × *stenophylla*
16 *Atriplex halimus*

Many of the drought-resistant plants come from climates, such as that of the Mediterranean, very much balmier than that of Essex. However, the hardiness of a plant is determined by other factors than that of temperature. Most of these plants, even in the warmest of climates, would be killed if their roots were buried in sodden heavy soil, but the soil in this part of the garden, chiefly sand and gravel, provides excellent drainage. Furthermore, in those parts of the country, like Essex, where there are high levels of sunshine, the wood of shrubs will ripen so that they are more able to withstand hard frost than the soft and sappy growth of wetter, milder places.

A naturalistic style of planting such as this could be taken to ludicrous lengths, so that a garden is scarcely a garden at all. The success here depends on many of the traditional principles of garden design: colour associations, harmony of plant groupings and lively contrasts of leaf and form. But underlying all this is the deeper, more unexpected, harmony that comes from the fact that all the plants have in common the ability to survive conditions of drought.

OLD-FASHIONED HERBACEOUS BORDERS IN A CASTLE GARDEN

At the heart of an ancient walled garden an axial path is flanked
with borders of flowers.

Kellie Castle in Scotland occupies an enviable site: a wooded position on slopes that lead down to the banks of the Firth of Forth at Pittenweem. The castle is of a characteristic Scottish kind, welcoming rather than forbidding, rising high with crow-stepped gables, dating from the late 14th century with many later additions. A walled garden, no more than 1 acre/0.4ha in extent, nestles against the north side of the castle. It is irregular in shape – rectangular, with one sloping corner – but internal harmony is given to it by the grid of paths and vistas that divide its space. Kellie is not only on a domestic scale but it uses a style of planting, and a mixture of the ornamental and the productive, which makes it a valuable model for other small gardens.

The castle was the childhood home of the architect Robert Lorimer who in 1880 as a sixteen-year-old schoolboy laid out the garden, following traces of a garden which may go back to the 17th century. In a lecture given in 1899, he described the ideal of those times: 'Great intersecting walks of shaven grass, on either side borders of brightest flowers backed up by low espaliers hanging with shining apples.'

The decorative heart of the garden consists of the pair of herbaceous borders that you see as you first enter the garden. The entrance is through an opening in the stone wall, from where a narrow path of fine sea-pebbles cuts straight across to the far wall, dividing the garden in two unequal parts. The far end of the path is marked by a wooden bench of Arts and Crafts character, designed by Robert Lorimer's son, the sculptor Hew Lorimer. Beyond the garden wall is a backdrop of fine old trees. At each end of the path is a wide metal arch covered with the rose 'Dorothy Perkins' which, with its clear pink flowers and light scent, became one of the most popular of climbing roses after its introduction in 1902.

The axial path runs north-west/south-east and is edged on either side with hedges of box (*Buxus sempervirens*). Behind them, herbaceous borders are backed with espaliered pear trees trained on wires to a height of 7ft/2m. The outlines of the box hedges are not too sharply defined and plants flop over from time to time. Half way along the path's length it is intersected at right angles by a grass path, giving enticing views of other parts of the garden.

The borders are entirely herbaceous and in spite of a certain amount of repeated planting and some excellent colour associations, the wide range of colours give it an uncontrived air. There is no spring planting; the borders are planned entirely for summer effect, only starting to perform in June and remaining richly decorative deep into the autumn. There is much yellow in the colour scheme – with heleniums, golden rod (*Solidago* species), achillea and *Thalictrum flavum glaucum* – which intermingle happily with the violet-blue of *Echinops ritro*, the pale lavender of goat's rue (*Galega officinalis*) or much

In the late afternoon in early July the low sunlight shows the borders at their best. The rose 'Dorothy Perkins' garlands the arch. On the right the rich orange-red of *Helenium* 'Moerheim Beauty' glows in the part shade. The trees on the skyline add to the sense of enclosure.

Drifts of plants in the style of Gertrude Jekyll add to the old-fashioned character of the borders. At the back the pale violet of goat's rue (*Galega officinalis*) rises above the feathery flowers of golden rod (*Solidago*) with golden helenium and yellow achillea at the front.

stronger colours such as the orange-red of *Helenium* 'Moerheim Beauty'.

In the past, regular mulches of manure or mushroom compost were applied. But experiments are being made with reducing organic enrichment so that, although plants may not grow so large, they will flower even more vigorously. Flowering is also improved by increasing the vigour of plants by regular division – the plants here are divided every four years in staggered rotation, giving the opportunity to improve the soil at the same time.

Plants are supported by netting stretched over the whole width of the borders. This is put in place in March before the foliage has grown too high, and attached to wooden posts 18in/45cm high at the front and around 36in/90cm at the back, to which are also fixed the wires that hold the espaliered pears. By mid-summer the plants have grown through and the netting is entirely concealed by foliage. At the end of the season the netting must be removed to be cleaned and stored for the winter, which necessarily means removing the dead herbaceous top growth. In gardens that do not use this netting system it makes sound organic sense to leave the top growth in place as a source of winter food for wild birds, in the form of seeds and bugs, and as a home for various valuable hibernating insects such as ladybirds and lacewings. In colder climates many gardeners leave the top growth in position, perhaps bent over, to make a protective eiderdown which will keep the worst of the frost off the crowns of the plants below.

Few gardens allow much choice in the positioning of borders, but because of the way the sun strikes them, borders running north and south always have a special atmosphere. In the morning or evening, when the sun is at its lowest and most flattering, it casts shadows across the planting and throws the shapes of foliage and spires of flowers into dramatic relief.

Herbaceous borders are often thought to be much harder work than mixed borders, yet because all the plants are of the same type, they are in some ways easier to cultivate and maintain than a mixed border. Furthermore, if there are woody plants in a border it is impossible to use the system of netting to support the plants. From the purely aesthetic point of view, herbaceous borders always have a particular charm, with the soft outlines of the plants moving freely in the breeze.

KELLIE CASTLE BORDERS

1 *Rosa* 'Dorothy Perkins'
2 *Pulmonaria saccharata*
   Argentea Group
3 *Galega officinalis*
4 *Leucanthemum × superbum*
5 *Rosa × alba* 'Semi Plena'
6 *Centaurea montana alba*
7 *Echinops ritro*
8 *Phlox paniculata*
9 *Knautia macedonica*

10 *Potentilla* 'Monsieur
    Robillard'
11 *Lilium pyrenaicum*
12 *Sidalcea malviflora*
13 *Campanula latifolia*
14 *Catananche caerulea*
15 *Campanula lactiflora*
16 *Oenothera missouriensis*
17 *Morinia longifolia*
18 *Phlox paniculata*

19 *Solidago canadensis*
20 *Thalictrum flavum glaucum*
21 *Tradescantia* 'Osprey'
22 *Achillea*, unnamed, yellow
23 *Salvia × superba*
24 *Helenium* 'Wyndley'

HOT COLOURS FOR LATE SUMMER – AND AN ELEMENT OF SURPRISE

Beside a path leading into woodland, the planting in these borders
has vibrant colours and a wild jungle-like exuberance.

In great gardens of the past it was always possible to have an area devoted to a single type of plant (roses or irises, for example), or to a seasonal scheme. The owner would simply not visit when it was out of season. Few gardeners have the space or the labour for such grand exercises today, and will try, as far as possible, to have year-round ornamental planting of one kind or another in every bed. It is, however, virtually impossible to have planting schemes that will perform with equal splendour in spring, summer and autumn, and since most gardens will reach their peak of floriferousness in the month of June, a compromise is usually reached which puts the greatest emphasis on mid-summer. This invariably means that the later months of the season will be increasingly deprived of plant interest.

The borders shown here perform for only a single season, although in this case the season is a long one. They flank a path which leads into an area of woodland whose naturalistic spring planting is a major attraction but which for the rest of the year, when much of the area is cast into deep, dry shade, has little going on.

Trees and substantial shrubs form a background, but the borders themselves receive much sunlight throughout the day. The planting starts to get into its stride in June but continues deep into autumn, with different ingredients making their appearance – 'like a series of fireworks going off, bang, bang, bang', as the owner puts it.

The colours that dominate these borders are 'hot' – rich golds and reds making a striking contrast to the cool shade of the woodland beyond. The bulk of the planting is herbaceous, with much use of bulbous plants, and a scattering of tender bedding plants to fill gaps or give notes of emphasis. The colour associations are often startling: for example, a spreading clump of the rich golden *Alstroemeria aurea* rearing up behind the blood-red dahlia 'Arabian Night'. Behind this group are bold clumps of *Lilium lancifolium* which bears its orange Turk's cap flowers on stems rising as high as 7ft/2m. Alongside the alstroemeria is a group of the perpetual-flowering Floribunda rose 'Dusky Maiden', with deep scarlet flowers of a rich velvet texture and, in front of it, the orange-scarlet of *Crocosmia masoniorum* mediating between the alstroemeria and the rose.

Running along the front of this part of the border are herbaceous plants, some of them trailing over onto the gravel path, which pick up the colour scheme of the larger plants behind. Orange-red *Potentilla* 'Gloire de Nancy' sprawls among the little viola 'Jackanapes' which produces a profusion of lemon-yellow flowers with rich deep purple markings to the tops of the upper petals. The old cottage garden plant *Geum* 'Mrs J. Bradshaw' throws its sprays of flaming red double flowers through the sheaves of shining slender red-brown leaves of the distinguished, decorative and tender New Zealand grass

Explosive colour associations dominate the borders. Golden-yellow *Alstroemeria aurea* with deep red *Dahlia* 'Arabian Night' at its feet. To the left at the back, the orange flowers of *Lilium lancifolium* rise up above red *Rosa* 'Dusky Maiden' and orange *Crocosmia masoniorum*.

A sitting place let into one of the borders is flanked by clumps of *Hypericum × inodorum* 'Summergold' and purple-leafed *Plantago major* 'Rubrifolia'. A scarlet double-flowered nasturtium, *Tropaeolum majus* 'Hermine Grasshof', trails across the path on each corner.

Uncinia rubra. This in turn intermingles with a flowing wave of the nasturtium *Tropaeolum majus* 'Hermine Grashoff' whose elegant rich scarlet double flowers mark the entrance to a recess with a bench.

The facing border continues the colour scheme with the occasional repetition of plants. Another group of the rose 'Dusky Maiden' is set off by the dahlia 'Bishop of Llandaff', with intense scarlet flowers and purple foliage. In front of the rose the bedding sage *Salvia splendens* 'Blaze of Fire' gives a burst of brilliant scarlet. To one side of it the fleshy purple leaves of ruby chard (*Beta vulgaris* 'Bull's Blood') makes a distinguished partner. Other plants of ornamental foliage play their part, such as the rhubarb *Rheum palmatum* 'Atropurpureum' which rears up behind a screen of red orach (*Atriplex hortensis* 'Rubra'). This border, which faces south-west, is much hotter than the other, and quite tender things are grown here: the dahlia-like Mexican *Cosmos atrosanguineus* with almost black flowers and a whiff of bitter chocolate; a spreading mat of the South African daisy *Arctotis × hybrida* 'Flame' with its decorative upright grey-green leaves and flame-orange flowers held well above –

decidedly tender but easy to raise from cuttings; and, above it, *Crocosmia* 'Star of the East' with large and graceful flowers of a rich apricot-orange.

Borders so full of fast-growing herbaceous plants need plenty of preparation and maintenance. In January a lavish top-dressing of mushroom compost is put down. From February onwards an unremitting battle against slugs commences: small quantities of slug pellets are used very frequently in key places, sometimes two or three times a week. In March, rose spraying starts, to control black spot and aphids. In April, as plants start to grow vigorously, staking is begun. Throughout the summer months this continues, along with weeding and the spot planting of bedding plants. In October, cutting back begins, and the removal of supports.

As you climb the steps from the house the borders are hidden from view. When you reach the top they burst suddenly into sight, an exhilarating explosion of colour. There is no distant prospect of them, and much of their drama comes from the fact that they are hidden and unexpectedly revealed. Such an element of surprise always gives excitement in a garden.

BOSVIGO HOT BORDERS

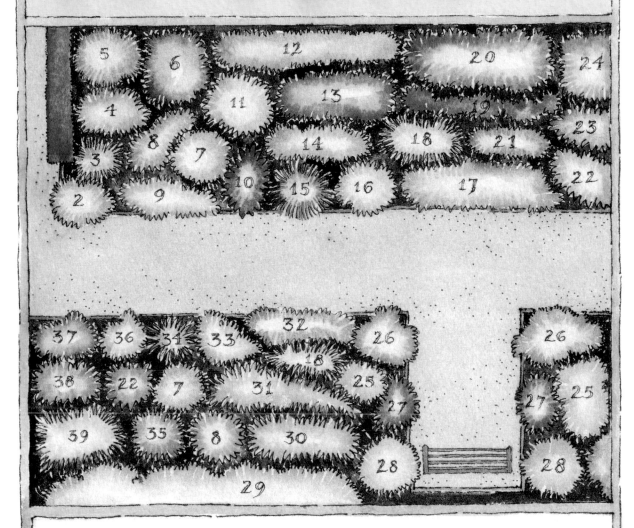

1 *Taxus baccata*
2 *Cosmos atrosanguineus*
3 *Crocosmia citronella*
4 *Lychnis chalcedonica*
5 *Foeniculum vulgare* 'Purpureum'
6 *Dahlia* 'Bishop of Llandaff'
7 *Rosa* 'Dusky Maiden'
8 *Trollius × cultorum* 'Orange Princess'
9 *Salvia splendens* 'Blaze of Fire'
10 *Beta vulgaris*
11 *Lobelia* 'Hadspen Royal Purple'
12 *Inula hookeri*
13 *Ligularia dentata* 'Desdemona'

14 *Geum* 'Princess Julia'
15 *Carex comans* bronze
16 *Rumex flexuosus*
17 *Arctotis × hybrida* 'Flame'
18 *Crocosmia* 'Star of the East'
19 *Atriplex hortensis* var. *rubra*
20 *Rheum palmatum* 'Atropurpureum'
21 *Lobelia* 'Dark Crusader'
22 *Dahlia* 'Bednall Beauty'
23 *Tithonia rotundifolia* 'Torch'
24 *Helenium* 'Wyndley'
25 *Cuphea ignea*
26 *Tropaeolum majus* 'Hermine Grasshof'

27 *Plantago major* 'Rubrifolia'
28 *Hypericum × inodorum* 'Summergold'
29 *Bidens ferulifolia*
30 *Lilium lancifolium*
31 *Rudbeckia sullivanti* 'Goldsturm'
32 *Uncinia rubra*
33 *Geum* 'Mrs Bradshaw'
34 *Crocosmia masoniorum*
35 *Lychnis chalcedonica* 'Flore Pleno'
36 *Viola* 'Jackanapes'
37 *Potentilla* 'Gloire de Nancy'
38 *Dahlia* 'Arabian Night'
39 *Alstroemeria aurea*

A HISTORIC SUNKEN GARDEN WITH A BRILLIANT DISPLAY OF BEDDING

Changing displays of bedding plants animate an ancient formal garden whose framework makes a rare foil for these lively arrangements.

The art of seasonal bedding went out of fashion in most private gardens earlier this century, partly for reasons of cost and partly because of a reaction against its regimented formality. Today, with the discovery that there need be nothing excessively formal about it, there is a renaissance of interest in the use of bedding. It can be used to fill in awkward gaps after mid-summer or, as here, to achieve brilliant colour early in the season. This method of gardening *is* labour-intensive but it produces results impossible by any other means, and may well be worth following in a smaller area than the one described here.

This sunken garden belongs to a historic Tudor manor house. The garden itself is also of Tudor origins but its layout, and the way the owner uses bedding schemes, follow principles that could easily be translated into more modest circumstances. The whole area of the sunken garden forms a rectangle 58ft × 25ft/17.4m × 7.5m in size. It extends west of the house across a lawn and is slightly shielded from it by a trellis-work screen against which ivy (*Hedera helix*) is trained and tightly clipped. Four standard yews (*Taxus baccata*), clipped into slender mushroom shapes, run along the inner side of the screen. Stone flagged paths divide the area into four lawns with, at the centre, an oval pool. Topiary of box (*Buxus sempervirens*) emphasises the plan – pairs of spreading domes at the beginning and end of the long central walk, and four giant drums of box, crowned with hemispheres and

now well over 5ft/1.5m across, beside the pool.

The only beds consist of narrow strips under the 18in/45cm-high supporting walls. These beds are 3½ft/1m wide on the long sides and 32in/80cm on the short sides. Although the ornamental planting is chiefly of bedding plants there are also permanent plants, some of them self-sown, like the violet *Viola labradorica*, honesty (*Lunaria annua*), foxgloves (*Digitalis purpureus*), lady's mantle (*Alchemilla mollis*) and the stinking hellebore (*Helleborus foetidus*). These are of a cottage-garden simplicity and make an attractive foil to the grand formality of the setting. More substantial shrubs of *Cotoneaster horizontalis* make striking sprawling shapes on the edge of retaining walls.

The spring bedding scheme shown here is dominated by tulips. Fresh supplies are brought in every year, and experiments are often made with new cultivars. Although tulip bulbs produce a new bulb each year, bulbs kept over from the previous season will vary in size, whereas graded bulbs bought from a specialist nursery will produce a uniformity of flower-size. The tulips are planted out in blocks in the last week of November, according to carefully worked out colour arrangements. Every bulb is dipped in fungicide before being planted in the narrow strip beds along with background planting of herbaceous plants which are propagated for the purpose: different cultivars of

In spring the formality of topiary and the symmetrical layout of the sunken garden is enlivened by brilliant blocks and strips of bedding. The setting is an ancient one – but the planting entirely modern.

Tulips for the spring are bedded out with carefully chosen associated seasonal plants. Here, deep purple *Tulipa* 'Arabian Mystery' is underplanted with rich blue pansies and white forget-me-nots.

forget-me-not (*Myositis scorpioides*) with blue, white or pink flowers, and various pansies. In addition, many of the permanent herbaceous plantings, such as variegated hostas, make admirable companions for the tulips.

After the middle of May, when flowering is over, the bulbs and all the debris, including petals and skin, are removed. The earth between the remaining herbaceous plants is dug over and fed with fish, blood and bone, and tender bedding plants are then put in – argyranthemums, dahlias and other annuals which change from year to year. In all, about 1,000 plants are bedded out in this part of the garden. At first the colour scheme is largely yellow and gold – from argyranthemums, Wisley primroses, yellow helianthemum, golden variegated hostas and golden origanum. Later in the summer the colours are much brighter.

In the autumn all the permanent herbaceous plants are divided, or new ones added. A careful look-out is kept for tulip fire, and if the slightest trace is found, the soil is dug out and fresh loam put in its place. The beds are all then mulched with garden-made compost (manure is never used as it is bad for tulips), and spring bedding is put into

place – three colours of the daisy *Bellis perennis*, wallflowers, pansies, forget-me-nots and sweet Williams.

A garden such as this is clearly hard work, but has the advantage of producing an early display of rich colours in spring, long before hardy perennials or most flowering shrubs will be making much of a contribution. Spring colour is dominated by yellow, and the explosion of colour from tulips and associated plants provides a brilliant spectacle.

The beds which contain the dazzling schemes described here *are* very narrow – if they were more substantial they would overpower the delightful detail of the sunken garden. As it is, they provide ribbons of colour, a lively counterpoint to the topiary, stone paths and lawns.

The paths, pool and topiary of this garden provide a permanent decorative framework in which many different planting schemes could be successfully incorporated. It is a formula which, on a smaller scale, could be adopted in any garden. Apart from the essential once-yearly clipping of topiary, and the regular mowing of the lawns, it could be made as labour-intensive – or as maintenance-free – as you wished.

CHENIES MANOR SUNKEN GARDEN

1 *Buxus sempervirens*
2 *Bergenia cordifolia*
3 *Cotoneaster horizontalis*
4 *Sedum spectabile*
5 *Hosta* 'Thomas Hogg'
6 *Hosta undulata*
7 *Teucrium chamaedrys*
8 *Astrantia major*
9 *Geranium endressii*
10 *Helleborus foetidus*
11 *Alchemilla mollis*
12 *Origanum vulgare*
   'Aureum'

NEW COLOUR BORDERS IN AN OLD WALLED GARDEN

Fastidiously chosen plants, selected for harmony and contrast of colour
and form, animate this old walled garden.

This 2½ acre/1 ha walled former kitchen garden, in the depths of the west country and at some distance from the house for which it originally provided produce, is built on a gently south- and east-facing slope. The present gardeners use the garden partly as a commercial nursery and partly as a kind of horticultural test-bed where they experiment with new plants. A special interest, however, is the use of colour, and the walled garden is now dominated by borders displaying a range of associating colours and forms. The use of colour is a fascinating subject – involving far more than just flowers that 'go together' – and the borders in this garden display subtle juxtapositions that lead to exciting and harmonious effects. In the garden, visitors can see the plants in action, displayed with great artistry and grown not in the usual regimented display beds but in the atmosphere of a private garden.

The shape of the encircling walls is unusual – roughly like a horseshoe with the south-facing wall curving round to trap the sun. Built of fine 18th-century red-brown brick, and 8ft/2.4m high, their patina and soft colour make a marvellous background for planting. Beyond the walls, to the north and the east, dense old woodland gives protection from cold and violent winds. In this benign microclimate the soil is fertile clay, just on the alkaline side of neutral, allowing the use of a very wide range of plants.

When the present gardeners came, parts of the kitchen garden had already been turned over to decorative uses and some valuable structural planting completed – including fine hedges of beech (*Fagus sylvatica*) lining the broad central path. At the lower end of this path the tops of the beech curve over, forming a shady tunnel to provide perfect conditions for the many kinds of hostas that now lap decoratively at the edges of the path.

Borders 12ft/3.6m deep, edged with gravel paths, girdle the garden walls, and the whole area is divided into four, in classical fashion, by a cruciform arrangement of paths.

The importance of colour is proclaimed, fortissimo, as soon as you enter. The main door of the walled garden is aligned with the central west-east axial path, where deep mixed borders on either side are planted in a variety of yellows, creams, whites and lime-green. In arrangements of this sort the contrast of shape is at least as important as that of colour – indeed, a limited range of colour, however harmonious, can be insipid if it lacks firm contrasts of form. Strong vertical emphases are provided by the bold jagged leaves of *Eryngium giganteum*, the softer veils of feathery *Foeniculum vulgare*, spires of 'Chandelier' lupins, the bold mop-head corymbs of *Achillea chrysocoma* 'Grandiflora' and the tall flowering stems of hollyhocks (*Alcea rugosa*). Contrasts of colour are important, too, even in a limited colour arrangement. Some golden foliage, for example, can seem merely bilious unless redeemed by the clearer, sharper yellows of such plants as *Phlomis longifolia* or *Anthemis tinctoria* 'E.C. Buxton'.

Even on a dull day the orange and yellow of the French marigolds (*Tagetes patula*) lights up, and the scarlet flowers of *Dahlia* 'Bishop of Llandaff' glow intensely in the background. The finely-cut leaves of the marigold contrast with the gleaming bronze of the dahlia foliage and that of the much coarser *Leonotis nepetifolia* at the back.

The orange Turk's cap flowers of *Lilium lancifolium* stand out against the fresh green foliage of *Colutea × media* whose decorative bladder-like seedpods are an ornament of late summer.

The borders against the south-facing wall at the top of the garden are planted in exhilarating schemes of red and orange. The plan opposite shows a section of this planting. At the back, against the wall, are substantial hardworking shrubs which perform over long periods. The vigorous evergreen privet *Ligustrum lucidum* 'Tricolor' has gleaming leaves marked with gold and white with occasional speckles of pink, making a lively background to other planting. Two modern roses pull their decorative weight: 'Parkdirektor Riggers' has striking lustrous foliage and rich red semi-double flowers produced continuously throughout the summer; nearby another perpetual-flowering rose, 'Dusky Maiden', has velvety red single flowers; while the shrub *Colutea × media* provides a subdued but decorative contrast, its fresh blue-green leaves ornamented in late summer by curious bladder-shaped pods flushed with bronze. These appear at the same season as the orange Turk's cap lily (*Lilium lancifolium*) and the piercing scarlet flowers of *Crocosmia* 'Lucifer'. The fast-growing annual *Leonotis nepetifolia* displays bold, toothed heart-shaped foliage crowned with curious sprays of tubular scarlet flowers. In front of it, flowering at the same time, is *Helenium* 'Moerheim Beauty' with golden-orange flowers. Towards the front of the border the sombre purple foliage and scarlet flowers of the dahlia 'Bishop of Llandaff' are fringed with French marigold (*Tagetes patula*) with its sprightly flowers of gold and orange. Intermingling with these are the pale apricot flowers of *Arctotis* 'Flame'. This part of the border is planted to hit its floriferous stride in June and continue, crescendo, through late summer. By the autumn, with dahlias and roses continuing to flower, and an autumnal glow suffusing the foliage, the atmosphere changes but is no less striking and decorative.

The colours in the borders modulate as they extend along the walls. Plants are arranged to form a series of harmonious pictures so that, walking along the path, you may admire them with all the attention you might pay to paintings in a gallery. However, despite the firm pattern of walls and paths, these are pictures without frames, that merge with each other as they progress along the garden's perimeter. Warm oranges, yellows and reds dissolve into purples, pinks and reds, and these in turn into

HADSPEN COLOUR BORDER

1 *Ligustrum lucidum* 'Tricolor'
2 *Leonotis nepetifolia*
3 *Crocosmia* 'Lucifer'
4 *Helenium* 'Moerheim Beauty'
5 *Foeniculum vulgare* 'Purpureum'
6 *Tagetes patula*
7 *Potentilla* 'Gibson's Scarlet'
8 *Arctotis* 'Flame'
9 *Dahlia* 'Bishop of Llandaff'
10 *Dahlia* 'Ellen Houston'
11 *Rosa* 'Dusky Maiden'
12 *Rosa* 'Parkdirektor Riggers'
13 *Rosa* 'Altissimo'
14 *Lilium lancifolium*
15 *Papaver* 'Beauty of Livermore'
16 *Euphorbia griffithii*
17 *Colutea* × *media*

creams, peaches and apricots.

The garden has a private and secret air; access to it is through doors in the high walls, and only the wooded slopes beyond link it to the outside world. Although most of the garden has been turned over to ornamental uses its original purpose as a kitchen garden is not forgotten, with a section given over to the orderly – and decorative – production of fruit and vegetables. This more mundane planting is, like the soaring bed of graded yellow to bronze sunflowers underplanted with brilliant nasturtiums, an effective and conscious contrast to the high art of the colour arrangements that run along the walls. The ornamental and the productive, judiciously placed side by side, sharpen the effect of both.

A MODERN GARDEN FOR A MODERN HOUSE

A Californian garden which makes the best use of site, climate and appropriate plants to create a striking landscape at ease with its surroundings.

It is very rare that a modern house is embellished with a suitably contemporary garden. The house shown here, in an uncompromisingly modern idiom, has a garden that is entirely in harmony with the house at its centre and with the climate of southern California where it is situated. The house, built in 1983, has an enviable position, facing south over wooded slopes that run down to the Pacific Ocean. The rainfall is low here – no more than 18in/45cm, which is concentrated in the winter months. The climate is wonderfully benign, with rare slight frosts and the greatest temperatures of summer always tempered by the effect of the maritime position. The landscape architect Isabelle Greene, who created the garden, has respected all these elements to make a strikingly 20th-century landscape that, nonetheless, shows the ancient virtues. The 18th-century poet and garden designer Alexander Pope spelled out the essential principle of garden design – 'consult the genius of the place in all.' The genius of the place includes, of course, the general character of the surroundings but it also includes the more specific matter of the microclimate.

The house is built on a slope and the garden makes a virtue of that position. A shady entrance courtyard on the north side has a decidedly oriental character. A naturalistic little pool is surrounded by randomly shaped slabs of stone, as though scattered by nature's hand, and edged with a bold clump of the Egyptian paper reed (*Cyperus papyrus*). The planting here has an entirely natural air.

A clump of sweetly scented *Trachelospermum jasminoides* nudges an outcrop of rock. An old coastal live oak (*Quercus agrifolia*), with its sprawling, gnarled limbs, has a dramatic presence in one corner – outside the garden it is one of the commonest trees of the wild landscape. From the pool a rivulet of stone slabs meanders across gravel down one side of the house where there is an arrangement of stark simplicity: hand-thrown pots are disposed on a low deck-like table. Behind, pleached against the wall, is a blood-red bougainvillea (*B. glabra* 'San Diego Red') – a particularly good colour, very much more decorative than the banal purple too frequently seen. From the edge of a terrace – from which there are marvellous views of the ocean beyond the wooded slopes – the rivulet of stone is repeated in the terraced garden that spreads out below the southern walls. This not only emphasises the importance of water in this climate but also provides a common visual theme linking the chief parts of the garden. A visitor to the garden may not notice the specific symbolism of this stony stream but its harmonious effect will certainly be an important part, however unconscious, of the visitor's experience.

The gently terraced garden to the south of the house, of which the plan on page 135 shows a part, is built up of a series of irregular beds retained by low walls resembling the traditional adobe. The pattern of slabs of natural stone seen in the garden to the front of the house is continued here, as though the rivulet had flowed under the house. It

Below the south-facing walls of the house the garden is terraced in gently descending steps. A 'river' of stone flows across a bed of 'pork and beans' (*Sedum × rubrotinctum*) and the rough surface of adobe walls contrasts with the crisp lines of the modern house. A striking harmony is achieved, using very different ingredients.

seems to flow, too, through large areas of plants – the grey-leafed *Cerastium tomentosum* (the common snow-in-summer of European gardens), the 'pork and beans' stonecrop (*Sedum* × *rubrotinctum*), and the creeping grey-blue *Senecio serpens*. These plants, all well able to withstand heat and drought, form self-sustaining carpets which make a good background for more substantial plants.

Many are also drylands plants of a powerfully sculpturesque presence: *Yucca whipplei*, a Californian native, forms an almost spherical sheaf, up to 7ft/2m across on fully mature specimens, of very narrow spiny leaves; *Agave americana* makes a compact giant rosette with blade-like glaucous-grey leaves up to 36in/90cm in length; *Agave vilmoriniana* forms a dramatically sprawling plant with long curving leaves, concave on the upper surface.

In too many collections of succulents the plants are so packed together, and of such heterogeneous character, that their true identity is hard to discern. Here, they are often planted as single splendid specimens and given all the presence, in this context, of precious sculptures in a garden of a different type. Smaller agaves, such as the artichoke-like *Agave*

parryi, a native of southern Californian drylands, are planted in little groups. A small Australian shrub, *Calocephalus brownii*, with almost white woolly foliage grows among the pale grey stone below the *Agave americana*, looking exactly as it does in the wild. Seen from the terrace above, this part of the garden has an almost abstract pattern, as though created by nature rather than a gardener. The designer was indeed inspired by the sight of crops seen from the air.

Other parts of the garden are more formally decorative. A group of figs is espaliered against the wall of the house. There is a finely designed L-shaped pergola which supports a beautifully trained Burmese honeysuckle (*Lonicera hildebrandtiana*) with creamy yellow flowers and distinguished glossy foliage, in whose shade are little beds of strawberries. The evergreen honeysuckle is extremely vigorous and needs regular clipping to keep it in order. Blocks of a single plant – *Tulbaghia* 'Silver Queen' or *Teucrium chamaedrys* – are planted with geometric simplicity. Grapevines (*Vitis vinifera*) are trained into umbrella shapes and there is a row of weeping white mulberries (*Morus alba* 'Pendula'). These more artfully organized features have the effect of emphasising the

MRS VALENTINE'S GARDEN

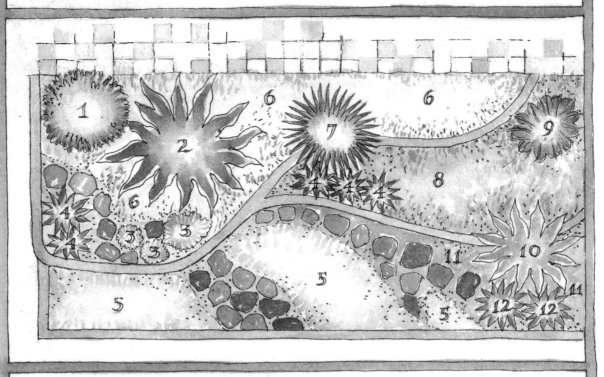

1 *Rosa* 'Iceberg'
2 *Agave americana*
3 *Leucophyta brownii*
4 *Agave parryi*
5 *Sedum × rubrotinctum*
6 *Cerastium tomentosum*
7 *Yucca whipplei*
8 *Senecio serpens*
9 *Anigozanthos flavidus* 'Yellow Gem'
10 *Agave vilmoriniana*
11 *Muehlenbeckia axillaris*
12 *Aloe vera*

powerful naturalistic planting that lies to one side.

High levels of maintenance are particularly important to this garden. The owner has no full-time gardener; instead, one or two part-timers are employed three mornings a week. The western side of the garden, containing non-drylands ornamental plants, depends on frequent watering which is provided by a computer-controlled irrigation system. The whole garden is one that requires meticulous manicuring. It is one of the paradoxes of horticulture that the natural look is not always provided by nature.

The climate is the dominant underlying factor in this garden. However, the decision to use plants that are native to the area, or come from similar climates, is one that can be applied to any garden. If plants, transplanted to an uncongenial climate or position, have to struggle merely to survive they will never form the ingredients of a successful garden. Moreover, plants that share similar habitats, even though they may come from very different parts of the world, have much in common and will, when planted together, fall naturally into an easy harmony. Many of the plants shown here are used sparsely, making sculptural contrasts against the simple architecture and displayed so that their intrinsic beauty is given full value. This is a garden of striking originality which contains many lessons for more mundane gardens.

AN ENCLOSED FLOWER GARDEN PLANNED FOR LATE SUMMER

At the heart of a large garden, this hidden enclosure is filled with plants of dramatic colours, which explode into life in late July and flower for weeks.

The border has been the traditional way of arranging flowers in a garden for well over a hundred years. Originally it had the function of a kind of frame, to display the flowers to best effect and focus attention on them. It was at first very much part of the pattern of the whole garden design, forming a block in a grid of paths and hedges or walls. Conventions sprang up about the correct ways of arranging the border, with plants disposed in a smooth gradation of size from the largest at the back to the smallest at the front. Some of these principles were merely restrictive and led to a dogged devotion to received ideas rather than a true understanding of the possibilities of gardening in borders. Gertrude Jekyll's writings on colour, and her technique of planting in bold long 'drifts' (a word first used by her in this context), had a powerfully liberating effect and her ideas have an insistent presence in gardening today. Much garden practice, acknowledged or not, is derived from her writings.

The flower garden shown here is based on the unit of the border but the effect is quite different from a Jekyll border. Instead of being an object of contemplation, like a picture, the borders in this garden are a way of immersing the viewer in a jungle of colour and form. But the calculating use of colour, particularly of adjacent complementary colours, is exactly what Gertrude Jekyll advocated.

The whole space is a rectangle, 40ft × 53ft/11.5m × 16m, enclosed on all four sides by hedges or walls. A cruciform pattern of paths, not exactly centred, divides the area into four chief spaces. The intersection of paths is marked by bold plants – an erupting sheaf of the golden variegated grass *Cortaderia selloana* 'Aureolineata', *Acanthus spinosus* – in both leaf and flower one of the finest of architectural plants – and *Ligularia dentata* 'Desdemona' with large rounded leaves which have dark purple undersides. The openings at the head of each path offer no unencumbered invitation to explore other parts of the garden. To the west a narrow slot in a hedge of beech (*Fagus sylvatica*) gives only the slightest glimpse of the garden on the other side. The brick wall to the north has an opening garlanded with attractive planting but the wooden door does not encourage exploration. On the eastern side a pair of Irish yews (*Taxus baccata* 'Fastigiata') flank an opening which gives a view which seems to be cut short by a path and border running at right angles to it. To the south a path leads to a pretty gazebo, but plants sprawl across, almost blocking the way. All this gives an inward-looking character, focusing all attention on its contents.

Two square beds dominate the space, and at the centre of each bed a purple cordyline (*C. australis* Purpureus Group) rises high in a strapwork pot on a pedestal. These form powerful shapes at the heart of the lavishly planted borders.

Borders also run along the northern and southern boundaries but they are

Yellow, scarlet and purple are the keynotes of this section of the garden. At the back are the tall flowers of *Ligularia* 'The Rocket'; in the centre, yellow loosestrife (*Lysimachia punctata*) and the flat corymbs of *Achillea* 'Coronation Gold' with a scattering of *Potentilla* 'Gibson's Scarlet' among the sombre purple foliage of *Heuchera micrantha* var. *diversifolia* 'Palace Purple'.

much narrower. Walking along the dividing paths, you have the impression of being surrounded by plants. The colour scheme is dominated by 'hot' colours – purples and reds – with touches of cool yellow. Substantial purple-leafed plants give structural emphasis – *Cotinus coggygria* 'Royal Purple', a weeping copper beech with lacquered leaves (*Fagus sylvatica* 'Purpurea Pendula'), the statuesque *Rheum palmatum* 'Atropurpureum' and *Berberis thunbergii* 'Rose Glow'. These make a fine sombre background to the fireworks of more colourful planting.

In mid July the drama starts to unfold. The black-red flowers of a sweet William (*Dianthus barbatus albus* Nigrescens Group) intermingle with the plum-coloured leaves of *Heuchera micrantha* var. *diversifolia* 'Palace Purple', with the brilliant trailing *Potentilla* 'Gibson's Scarlet' weaving through. *Dahlia* 'Bishop of Llandaff' has dark bronze leaves and clear scarlet flowers. Here it is planted with a foreground of the sage *Salvia fulgens*, with its small scarlet flowers, and a background of *Ligularia* 'The Rocket' which has dark jagged leaves and flower

stems which are almost exactly the same colour as the dahlia's leaves. The perennial *Lobelia* 'Queen Victoria' has glistening upright red-purple leaves with scarlet flowers borne from August onwards on 36in/90cm stems. It soars above the little scarlet-flowered *Salvia grahamii* with a background of Maltese Cross (*Lychnis chalcedonica*) whose flat corymbs of flowers, carried on 4ft/1.2m tall stems, a dazzling vermilion, echo in richer tone the colour of the sage. These reds and purples continue well into August, when they are joined by other plants of similar colours – crocosmias (the large scarlet-flowered 'Lucifer'), many dahlias and perennial lobelias.

Yellow flowers, like shafts of light, leaven this heady mixture of red and purple. The yellow *Achillea* 'Moonshine' is repeated, mixing well with many different plants. It is planted with a mound of golden grass (*Cortaderia selloana* 'Aureolineata') through which an orange-yellow potentilla (*P.* 'William Rollison') threads its way, and to one side there is an sprawling unnamed alstroemeria with red-brown flowers. It appears again with the long-flowering pale yellow *Kniphofia* 'Sunningdale Yellow', its neatly shaped upright flowers a good foil to the achillea's horizontal flower heads, and *Lobelia* 'Cardinalis' whose scarlet flowers will appear at the beginning of August. The dominating colour scheme of yellow, red and purple is carried over into climbing plants on the brick wall which forms the northern boundary. Here, flanking a door, are the *Clematis* 'Bill Mackenzie', with sharp lemon-yellow flowers, a deep purple-red clematis (*C.* 'Madame Julia Correvon') and a grapevine (*Vitis vinifera* 'Purpurea') with purple leaves.

The drama of this garden accelerates through the remainder of the summer into autumn, with yellow rudbeckias and heleniums now playing a part. Although there is plenty to see on the skyline, visible above the hedges and walls, the garden has a secret air. Despite the entrances and exits it gives the

The arching fronds of the ornamental grass (*Miscanthus sinensis* 'Gracillimus') sprawl gracefully over orange marigolds and lemon-yellow potentillas. In the background the scarlet flowers of *Lobelia cardinalis* rise behind the blade-like leaves of crocosmias.

WOLLERTON LATE SUMMER GARDEN

1 *Lonicera nitida*
2 *Viola riviniana* Purple Group
3 *Salvia microphylla*
4 *Lychnis chalcedonica*
5 Rose, unnamed, double yellow
6 *Elaeagnus pungens* 'Maculata'
7 *Fagus sylvatica*

8 *Sinacalia tangutica*
9 *Miscanthus sinensis* 'Gracillimus'
10 Marigold, unnamed, double yellow
11 *Lobelia* 'Queen Victoria'
12 *Crocosmia* 'Jackanapes'
13 *Lobelia cardinalis*
14 *Salvia elegans*

15 *Heuchera micrantha* var.
   diversifolia 'Palace
   Purple' and *Dianthus barbatus
   albus* Nigrescens Group
16 *Achillea* 'Coronation Gold'
17 *Ligularia* 'The Rocket'

impression of being a detour from the main thoroughfares that link different 'rooms' of the layout. There are no clear vistas drawing the eye to some other part of the garden. Although there is a strong underlying pattern of paths, the planting is so profuse as to make the edges often invisible. The paths are narrow and eroded by plants that encroach and, in one case, actually blocked with a mound of clipped box in the middle. This is not a place to be hurried through. The layout slows the step and encourages visitors to stay and immerse themselves, with sensual delight, in the excitement of the brilliant colours.

BORDERS MAKE A STRONG AXIS IN A WALLED GARDEN

A long passage of flowers makes a brilliant transition from kitchen garden to wild woodland garden, linking many other features on the way.

Major garden features are always most effective when given a powerful sense of purpose. The double borders shown here, part of a large Scottish garden, are an object lesson which could be applied in many other circumstances. Visually they span the whole width of a large walled garden, covering a distance of 150ft/45m, and linking areas of very different character.

Most visitors approach the borders from a walled kitchen garden in which the productive and ornamental are attractively intermingled. A path leading down one side of this garden culminates in a pair of white-painted iron gates, beyond which an arch of clipped silver pear (*Pyrus salicifolia* 'Pendula') frames the borders stretching away in the distance to a splendidly ornamental gate in the wall on the far side of this second walled garden. The gate and frame of silver pear are aligned on the borders, focusing the eye on the chief glory.

The two borders are unusually narrow, just over 8ft/2.5m, and separated by a grass path 3ft 4in/1m wide. They are backed by 8ft/2.5m high hedges of *Prunus cerasifera* 'Pissardii', which make an excellent background to the planting. These are cut back every year at the end of the summer to a height of 24in/60cm, and in the spring, before new growth has started, they form a lovely hedge of pink flowers – the only flowering ornament so early in the season in these borders. Both foliage and stems of the vigorous new growth are a decorative and attractive rosy colour, and the texture is softer than that of other hedging material, giving much

movement in the tall new shoots.

The planting within the borders derives its harmony from simple principles. The photographs for this book were taken in mid July when the borders were nearing their peak, so the planting I describe refers to that season. The front is dominated by plants with white, magenta and pink flowers, and there is much silver foliage. Essential plants here include the double form of the pink-flowered wild campion (*Silene dioica* 'Flore Pleno'), the silver-leafed southernwood (*Artemisia abrotanum*), white-flowered sweet rocket (*Hesperis matronalis*) and strands of the intense magenta *Geranium psilostemon* falling forwards from the large bushes that punctuate the beds. The back of the borders is dominated by yellow. The giant scabious (*Cephalaria gigantea*) produces a mound of rather coarse, toothed foliage from which rise slender waving stems, as high as 8ft/2.5m, carrying pincushion-like flowers of the palest yellow. A thalictrum (*T. flavum* sbsp. *glaucum*), with finely divided glaucous foliage has frothy umbels of pale yellow flowers. Planting is repeated in both borders, without exact symmetry but giving an air of balance. Although there is generally no excessively studious arrangement of colours there are, from time to time, brilliant combinations. The rich orange of *Alstroemeria aurea* is combined with silvery-blue delphiniums – there are many delphiniums of ancient but unknown origin in this garden. A sea holly (*Eryngium alpinum*), with intricately cut flowers of a metallic blue, is planted in front of a cascade of

The approach to the borders leads from a walled kitchen garden. An opening with a pair of white wrought-iron gates forms a strong frame, concentrating attention on the borders. At the far end of the path leading between the borders another white-painted gate closes the garden vista.

magenta *Geranium psilostemon*. The double violet flowers of *G. pratense* 'Plenum Violaceum' intermingle with the pale yellow of *Thalictrum flavum* sbsp. *glaucum*. With its pale yellow flowers, *Cephalaria gigantea* makes an admirable partner for many other plants, especially the pale orange-brown of the daylily *Hemerocallis fulva*.

Because the beds in these borders are comparatively narrow, the gradient of plants, from the lowest to the highest, is precipitous, giving you the impresssion of walking through a flowery chasm. Good support is essential for a pure herbaceous planting of this kind, and here netting is stretched over most of the border, sloping upwards at the back to support the taller plants. Given such support, many of the plants not only grow to an unusual height but also make far more shapely bushes than is usually the case. The larger geraniums, for example, if unsupported will quickly flop in the wind and rain and form a sprawling and tangled mass; here, plants such as *Geranium psilostemon* will rise to a height of 4ft/1.2m and form splendid rounded shapes.

As you explore along the length of the borders, you discover that they are not continuous. The sundial half way

down marks a major cross-axis which links other parts of the garden that lie concealed behind the prunus hedge. To either side there is a central feature of similar size and shape: to the east a circular raised bed planted with a dazzling collection of different cultivars of the shrubby *Potentilla fruticosa*; to the west, a circular pool of the same size, with a statue and a jet of water. This near symmetry has a powerful linking effect on the two halves of the garden.

The stone gate piers, capped with dashing urns of lead, have swags of the climbing rose 'Goldfinch' on either side, and hostas planted all along a narrow bed at the foot of this north-facing wall flourish in the shade. The gate, the culminating focal point of the borders, is also the start of something new. Beyond it, stone steps lead down to a wilder part of the garden, with woodland walks along the banks of a river, and handsome specimen trees.

The single axis which threads these borders runs through a complex sequence of views: from the regimented order of the kitchen garden, through narrow borders bursting with flowers, past alluring cross-axes leading to other parts of the flower garden, and finally to the informality of the wild garden.

PITMUIES BORDERS

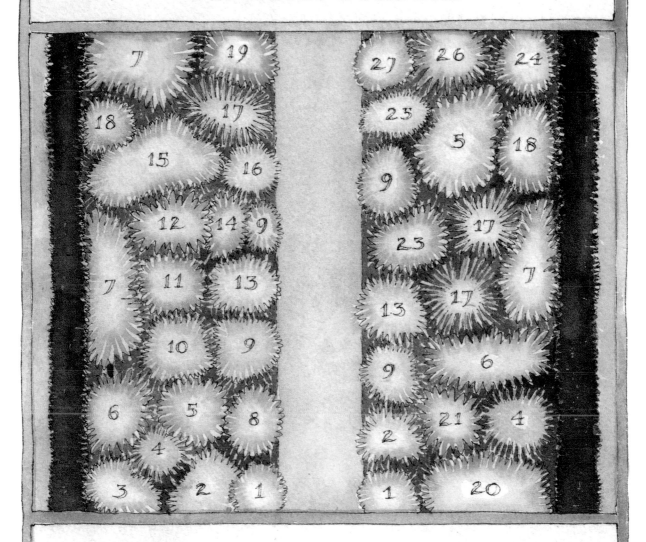

1 *Viola cornuta* Alba Group
2 *Stachys macrantha*
3 *Thalictrum minus*
4 *Foeniculum vulgare* 'Purpureum'
5 *Geranium psilostemon*
6 *Echinops ritro*
7 *Cephalaria gigantea*
8 *Lunaria annua*
9 *Silene dioica* 'Flore Pleno'
10 *Hesperis matronalis* var. *albiflora*

11 *Geranium pratense* 'Plenum Violaceum'
12 *Paeonia lactiflora* 'Lord Kitchener'
13 *Stachys byzantina*
14 *Astrantia maxima*
15 *Thalictrum flavum* sbsp. *glaucum*
16 *Artemisia abrotanum*
17 *Hemerocallis fulva*
18 *Thalictrum lucidum*

19 *Aconitum* × *cammarum* 'Bicolor'
20 *Saponaria officinalis* 'Rubra Plena'
21 *Paeonia officinalis* 'Alba'
22 *Phalaris arundinacea* var. *picta*
23 *Astrantia major*
24 *Sidalcea* 'Sussex Beauty'
25 *Veronica gentianoides*
26 *Papaver somniferum* 'Perry's White'
27 *Armeria maritima*

A HERBACEOUS BORDER CONTAINED WITHIN THE SCHEME OF THINGS

A lavishly planted deep herbaceous border inspired by the colour theory of Gertrude Jekyll.

The border is a surprisingly recent development in gardening. It first appeared in something like its modern form in the 19th century, when gardeners, inspired by the flood of new plants coming to Europe and in reaction to the 18th-century landscape style, were in search of something new. A further influence was that of painting. Both the Pre-Raphaelites and the Impressionists took a scholarly interest in colour theory, and in particular the curious effects of juxtaposing certain colours. These ideas were taken up by gardeners on both sides of the Atlantic. In the USA Louise Beebe Wilder – in particular in her book *Color in my Garden* – and in England Gertrude Jekyll, showed gardeners how they could put into practice the principles of colour theory. These sometimes rather abstract ideas caused gardeners to think about the use of colour in a new way, and to experiment with harmony and dissonance in their planting. Some gardeners understand these things by instinct – others must learn by studying the work of master gardeners.

The border shown here is almost entirely restricted to herbaceous perennials, but there are a few shrubs and climbing woody plants. It occupies a key place in a large garden, running from east to west beside a path that is an important axis, and providing a dramatic view from an open lawn.

Where this border differs from others is both in its planting and as a tightly conceived element in the overall garden scheme. The planting, as in many other herbaceous borders, is at its peak in July. Its colour scheme changes from creams and yellows at its eastern end, modulating to pinks and lilacs towards the middle, and to richer purples at the western end. This scheme is not adhered to rigidly but is the broad underlying rule.

The border is 100ft × 16ft/30m × 5m in size, backed along its whole length by a brick wall 8ft/2.5m high, with old yews and other trees rising up behind. The gravel path running along its whole length is edged on either side with strips of grass 18in/45cm wide, and is part of much larger axis linking different enclosures of the garden. At the easterly extremity of the border it passes through a gate whose brick piers are festooned with clematis, both *Clematis orientalis* and *C. tangutica* whose yellow flowers set the colour theme for this cooler end of the border. It is this end of the border that is shown in the planting plan on page 147, showing the chief colours modulating from yellows, buffs and creams to pink and red.

Trained on the wall at this end of the border are the roses 'Buff Beauty', which repeat-flowers throughout the summer, and 'Lady Hillingdon, Climbing', which produces intermittent flowers after its first flush in late June or early July. Both these have exquisite scent, and 'Buff Beauty', planted by the gate, provides a delicious whiff for the passer-by. Several herbaceous plants show their powerful structural value in the densely packed

The border is crisply edged with a strip of impeccable turf between path and plants. Trees behind the border wall make a powerful background but the exuberant herbaceous planting more than holds its own.

border. *Delphinium* 'Sungleam' holds aloft its spikes of flowers of the palest cream, and towards the back of the border *Ligularia* 'The Rocket' gives a similar vertical emphasis but with flowers of sharp yellow. To one side of it *Cephalaria gigantea*, rising equally high, holds its creamy-yellow powder-puff flowers at the tips of long wiry twisting stems that wave in the slightest air. In the central part of the border the white flower-spikes of *Lysimachia clethroides* also make firm shapes among the profuse foliage. *Verbascum chaixii*, with pretty purple spots at the centre of the flowers, has a similar effect.

Emphatically upright foliage also has a valuable role to play in giving structure to herbaceous plantings. Daylilies (*Hemerocallis*) have very handsome leaves, appearing early in the year, an attractive fresh green with a gleaming surface, and carried in bold upright sheaves. The leaves of crocosmias, narrow and blade-like, always have an air of distinction. Here, in the yellow and cream part of the border, *Crocosmia* 'Custard Cream' is very effective. *Sisyrinchium striatum* is one of the best plants, with upright leaves which have the added attraction of being pale grey-green striped with cream, and a profusion of flowers of the palest yellow.

The classic pattern for the herbaceous border is to have plants rising in a smooth progression from lowest at the front to the tallest at the back. This, apart from being hard to achieve, can give a very contrived air. Here there are several quite tall plants at the front – *Achillea* 'Lilac Beauty', *Salvia* × *sylvestris* 'Blauhügel' and *Delphinium* 'Sungleam', while in high summer the brick wall at the back of the border is all but invisible, submerged in planting. The effect here is more of a burgeoning bank of colour, erupting from the ground, and the crisp turf edges and pale grey gravel of the path at the edge of the border make a sharp contrast with the sudden profusion; even the trees beyond the wall now seem to be

A stone ornament is almost submerged in the planting at the centre of the border. Behind it is the pink rose 'Heritage' and clouds of *Astrantia major.* On the left is *Achillea* 'Forncett Beauty' and, right foreground, *Penstemon* 'Pink Profusion'.

part of a continuous scheme of planting, with the subtle colours and lively shapes of the border changing, with no sudden break, to the natural, wilder world beyond the garden.

The positioning of this border well illustrates some principles of garden design. First, it is harmoniously connected to the whole pattern of the garden. The path that runs along one side of it is one of the chief thoroughfares, leading purposefully from one part of the garden to another. Different views of the border are presented – either obliquely from the path or more or less head-on from a distance across the lawn on its south side. This creates great visual variety, because the border will present very different views according to the position of the sun. Secondly, I do not like borders that peter out weakly – it is not hard to have, at the very least, some striking plant to mark the ends. But here the effect is achieved in a different way. At one end the gateway, whose piers are crowned with bold stone spheres, makes an emphatic ornament. At the other end, where the path sweeps out into a circular area, there is a bench flanked by

WOLLERTON BORDER

1 *Rosa* 'Lady Hillingdon, Climbing'
2 *Achillea filipendulina* 'Gold Plate'
3 *Echinops ritro*
4 *Jasminum humile* 'Revolutum'
5 *Verbascum olympicum*
6 *Rosa* 'Buff Beauty'
7 *Argyranthemum* 'Jamaica Primrose'
8 *Bupleurum falcatum*
9 *Hemerocallis* 'Little Men'
10 *Nicotiana* 'Lime Green'
11 *Clematis orientalis*
12 *Aster divaricatus*
13 *Delphinium* 'Sungleam'

14 *Cephalaria gigantea*
15 *Ligularia* 'The Rocket'
16 *Clematis* 'Vyvyan Pennell'
17 *Actinidia deliciosa*
18 *Helianthus* 'Lemon Queen'
19 *Lysimachia punctata*
20 *Lysimachia ciliata* 'Firecracker'
21 *Anthemis tinctoria* 'Sauce Hollandaise'
22 *Crocosmia* 'Custard Cream'
23 *Nicotiana langsdorfii*
24 *Physostegia virginiana* 'Summer Snow'

25 *Lysimachia clethroides*
26 *Hydrangea anomala petiolaris*
27 *Eupatorium purpureum* 'Atropurpureum'
28 *Agastache cana* 'Cinnabar Rose'
29 *Papaver orientale* 'Patty's Plum'
30 *Lupinus* 'Chandelier'
31 *Verbascum chaixii*
32 *Coreopsis verticillata* 'Moonbeam'
33 *Penstemon* 'Snow Storm'
34 *Arctotis × hybrida* 'Wine'
35 *Phlox paniculata* 'Norah Leigh'

cast-iron urns planted with clipped spheres of box. This signals both the end of the border and a change of direction, for the path now does a right-angled turn into a different part of the garden. Thirdly, the lawn lying to the south of the border presents a clear, open space – in contrast to the border's intense visual activity.

Arbitrariness and surprise can create exciting effects in a garden. But, in the end, harmony comes only from an underlying pattern of colour and shapes and a sense of purpose.

AN ORNAMENTAL KITCHEN GARDEN DESIGNED TO PLEASE

Fruit, vegetables and ornamental plants in a strongly designed formal framework.

The garden shown here is part of a much larger garden but it constitutes, in a small area, a complete garden in itself. Under ½ acre/0.2ha in area, it includes many decorative features as well as practical – and useful – planting ideas. The key to its success lies undoubtedly in the straightforward, logical and subtly ornamental layout in which fruit, vegetables and 'cottage-garden' plants are grown.

The area is divided into four. At its centre is a rectangular lily pond surrounded by eight giant domes of clipped box (*Buxus sempervirens*) rising to a height of over 5ft/1.5m and almost 7ft/2m across. Three paths run through generously proportioned arched tunnels of espaliered fruit trees. The tunnels are a good 12ft/3.6m wide and curve gently up to 8ft/2.5m. The supports are quite light, for the framework is now substantially provided by the espaliered fruit trees themselves. The fruit trees are planted in opposite pairs at interval of 14ft/4m, and the main stems are trained upwards, bending over until they reach the top, their lateral branches trained at right-angles to form the framework. Most are apples, both dessert and cookers, and are chiefly old varieties long established in English orchards, such as 'James Grieve', 'Newton Wonder', and 'Laxton's Fortune'. There are also pears: 'Doyenné du Comice' and 'Conference'.

Espalier fruit trees are usually grafted on dwarf stock but all these are grown on their own roots. They have grown to a great size since they were planted in 1965, and have assumed a venerable character – their branches deeply gnarled and encrusted with moss and lichen. They do, however, need regular pruning to keep the tunnels in shape – with new growth cut back at least two or three times during the growing season. This regular pruning encourages the formation of fruit which ripens particularly well on the 'walls' of the tunnel. And the result is ornamental all the year round. In winter the leafless skeleton shows the pattern of neatly trained branches; in spring the prolific blossom – pear followed by apple – is an exhilarating sight; in the heat of summer the tunnels provide a deliciously shady walking place; finally, in autumn, the fruit is marvellously displayed among yellowing and russet foliage. The same effect could be achieved in a far more modest area. Dwarf stock, planted closer together, would be economical of space and would allow the cultivation of several varieties. It is essential to choose those that will pollinate each other, or varieties such as the 'Conference' pear, that set fruit without pollination.

The paths under the fruit tunnels are of mown turf flanked by beds running between the trunks of the fruit trees. The planting here is of the unaffectedly cottage-gardening style that is so appropriate in such a position. Self-sown foxgloves (*Digitalis purpureus*), *Alchemilla mollis*, columbines (*Aquilegia vulgaris*) and pink and lilac opium poppies (*Papaver somniferum*) are all allowed to find a home. Other plants are repeated along the length of the tunnel, including *Sisyrinchium striatum*, lamb's ears (*Stachys byzantina*), sweet Williams (*Dianthus barbatus*), wild primroses (*Primula vulgaris*) and several cranesbills

A tunnel of fruit-trees forms the backbone of the kitchen garden. It is unusually wide, and narrow beds running down either side are filled with flowers, many of them self-sown. The broad mounds of clipped box echo the shape of the tunnel's arch.

Sections of the pergola frame views of the kitchen garden. Wigwams of bamboo canes provide shapely support for different varieties of climbing beans. Beyond the rows of vegetables many varieties of sweet peas are cordon-trained on an upright framework.

(*Geranium* species).

The four beds marked off by the cruciform pattern of paths are used for different purposes. One is largely given over to a fruit cage and two are planted chiefly with vegetables. The last has a gazebo fashioned of pear trees pleached around a cylindrical metal framework in the middle of a simple lawn. The roof is supported by a rustic column, and a seat surrounds its base. The pear trees are tightly clipped to form smooth 'walls' which in early spring are smothered in white blossom.

Orderliness is the essence of the attraction of a kitchen garden, and here the rows of vegetables and fruit form a marvellously decorative pattern. Wigwams of bamboos have cultivars of runner beans (*Phaseolus coccineus*) trained up them, with white or white and red flowers instead of the usual scarlet. Gooseberries (*Ribes grossularia*) are trained as little standard trees, displaying to good effect their ornamental lobed leaves and fruit. Sweet peas (*Lathyrus odoratus*) are grown in quantity and trained on a vertical frame.

Along the southern edge of the garden, a pergola on a low wall forms a kind of screen through which there are attractive views of the garden within,

and through which you pass to enter. A grass path runs along it and there are box hedges on either side. Climbing roses festoon it, among them the flamboyant 'Easlea's Golden Rambler' with large double pale yellow flowers, the white-flowered 'White Cockade' which flowers continuously, and 'Maigold' whose yellow flowers have a hint of apricot. These intermingle with the purple-leafed grapevine *Vitis vinifera* 'Purpurea' and clematis.

Where the fruit tunnels meet at the centre of the garden the domes of box echo the gentle curve of their roof. In high summer the dappled shade within the tunnels offers a cool passage across the garden; gaps between the branches of the espaliers allow views of the full and orderly beds of fruit and vegetables; the breeze brings the piercing scent of sweet peas; and the borders lining the walls are full of flowers. At the eastern end of the garden is a dipping pool against the garden wall, with neatly enclosing hedges of *Lonicera nitida* rising to its rim, the whole embowered in honeysuckle and *Clematis* 'Perle d'Azur' trained over an arched metal frame. Here the decorative and practical are perfectly intertwined, encapsulating the essential character of the garden.

HEALE HOUSE KITCHEN GARDEN

1 *Stachys byzantina*
2 *Pulmonaria officinalis* 'Sissinghurst White'
3 *Vinca major* 'Variegata'
4 *Sisyrinchium striatum*
5 *Pulmonaria rubra*
6 *Tulipa* 'Spring Green'
7 Hyacinth, unnamed
8 *Lamium maculatum*
9 Peony, unnamed
10 *Sedum* 'Herbstfreude'
11 *Santolina chamaecyparissus*
12 *Melissa officinalis*
13 *Digitalis purpurea*
14 *Primula vulgaris*
15 *Aubrieta*, unnamed, purple
16 *Fuchsia magellanica*
17 *Alchemilla alpina*
18 *Primula auricula*
19 *Heuchera micrantha* var. *diversifolia* 'Palace Purple'
20 *Dicentra eximia* 'Stuart Boothman'
21 *Viola cornuta*
22 *Geranium clarkei* 'Kashmir White'

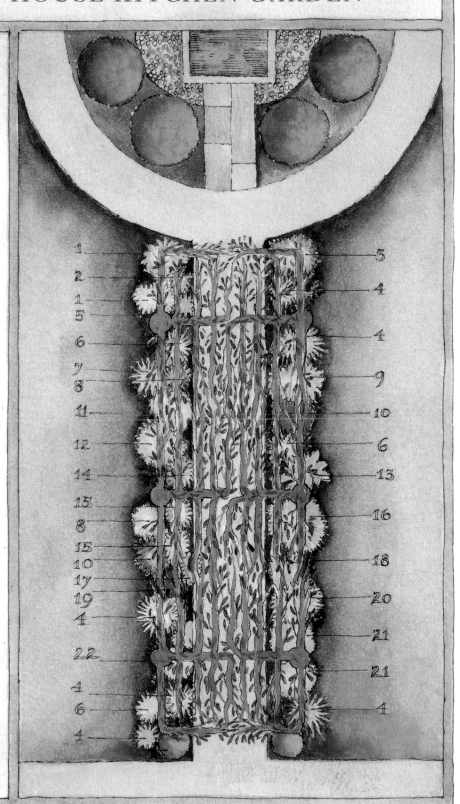

AN ORNAMENTAL AND PRODUCTIVE *POTAGER*

A decorative parterre of raised beds in which vegetables are grown in a decorative pattern of rows, with ornamental planting at the centre.

The French word *potager* simply means 'kitchen garden', with no particular suggestion of ornamental character. It has been purloined by the English to mean a particular kind of kitchen garden in which the pattern of edible plants, disposed in an arrangement of symmetrical beds, becomes an ornamental feature. French working kitchen gardens are nevertheless usually a delight to behold and have always been gardened with skill, and the finest of all ornamental *potagers* is at the Chateau of Villandry on the Loire, where the kitchen garden is raised to the status of high art. Yet this style of vegetable gardening is equally appropriate for small gardens, with the productive and the decorative attractively combined in a limited space.

The *potager* shown here is just a part of a large and productive walled kitchen garden on the east coast of Scotland. It occupies quite a small space (35ft × 26ft/10.5m × 7.8m) and is an admirable model for a self-contained kitchen garden in its own right. The beds are long and narrow – just over 4½ft/1.3m wide – retained by baulks of timber which rise 6in/15cm above the surface of the soil. Beds of this sort are familiar from medieval miniatures. In the Middle Ages the simplest way of improving poor and stony ground was to import humus-rich soil and pile it on the surface, keeping it in position with a frame of wattle, stone or wood. These beds were traditionally never more than twice the span of a man's reach – that is to say, no more than 5ft/1.5m across – so that they could be cultivated from paths on either side.

The decorative potential of raised beds such as these soon became apparent. The linear emphasis of the timber edging strongly defines the pattern of the beds (which, in a *potager*, is a large part of its charm), and the timber makes a firm boundary between bed and path, particularly important when the paths are surfaced in gravel which so easily mixes with the soil. Perhaps most important of all, it is an admirable way of raising plants, for the beds may be cultivated without digging and without harming the structure of the soil by perpetually walking on its surface. By adding compost or other organic matter to the surface and forking it lightly in, the 'lazy' beds may be kept perpetually in good heart. A last advantage is that a bed may be specially prepared, for example with alkaline soil, to suit a particular crop.

The beds shown here follow the classical pattern of a four-part division, allowing a simple rotation of crops. They are arranged in pairs, each separated by a narrow path surfaced with river gravel. At the centre of the arrangement an octagonal raised bed has a medlar (*Mespilus germanicus*) planted in the middle. A medlar is not only productive, bearing its curiously shaped fruit late in the season, but is also particularly ornamental. The bed is edged with lavender (*Lavandula angustifolia* 'Hidcote') and a mixture of ornamental and vegetable planting surrounds the medlar's trunk. The intensely blue balloon flower (*Platycodon grandiflorus*) intermingles with the

The *potager* lies at the heart of a traditional working vegetable garden in which the productive and ornamental are intermingled. The Victorian-style glasshouse contains a collection of pelargoniums and other tender plants.

On one side the *potager* is edged with a trellis-work fence and ornamental planting with a row of old apple trees behind. The opening in the fence is flanked by the rose 'Blairi Number 2' and the honeysuckle, *Lonicera periclymenum*, both of which are deliciously scented.

fern-like foliage of carrots, while tender *Cedronella canariensis*, with cedar-scented foliage and lilac-coloured flowers, rises above *Gypsophila elegans* and a scattering of *Viola tricolor*.

The sight of orderly rows of vegetables is, to my eye, irresistibly attractive, and here the vegetables are arranged in single rows running the length of the beds. The parallel rows of onions, parsnips, carrots and shallots present strong contrasts of foliage: upright fleshy stems of onions and shallots, bold leaves of parsnips, and delicate finely cut foliage of carrots. These subtle contrasts are one of the essential beauties of vegetable gardening, although more brilliant contrasts are also available. Lettuces grown here, for example, include not only the butterhead 'Tom Thumb' but also the red and plain varieties of oak leaf lettuce and the dark purple 'Lollo Rosso'. This last, if left to run to seed, will make a dramatic upright plant whose glistening leaves become even darker as they age.

It is always a problem with *potagers* that the lovely symmetry will be upset when you start to gather your crop. A further advantage of these narrow beds with their sharply defined edges is that the overall pattern is barely affected by the removal of a lettuce or two.

The setting of this charming *potager* epitomises the decorative and productive possibilities of the kitchen garden. The encircling stone walls all have flower beds at their feet, giving flashes of colour or glimpses of statuesque ornamental foliage wherever one walks. On one side of the *potager* sweet peas (*Lathyrus odoratus* cultivars) are trained, in the traditional way, in vertical cordons, with, among them, the fast-growing hyacinth bean (*Lablab purpureus*) which produces decorative white or purple flowers and, later in the season, deep purple pods.

The view from the middle of the central path which divides the garden in two reveals the essence of the kitchen garden. At this point fruit and vegetable beds press in on either side, but at one end of the path is an entrance festooned with roses and honeysuckle, while at the other end, in a sunny west-facing position, a little cast-iron bench is flanked by domes of box and buttresses of golden *Lonicera nitida*, with thyme and marjoram scattered between gaps in the stone paving. You may sit on the bench engulfed by scent and admire the intermingling of ornament and produce.

PITMUIES POTAGER

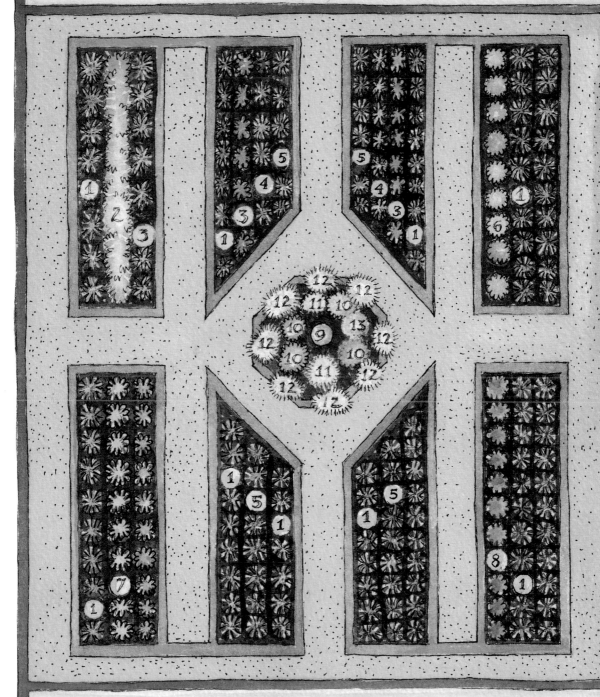

1 Onions	**6** Lettuces	**10** *Platycodon grandiflorus*
2 French beans	**7** Radishes	**11** *Cedronella canariensis*
3 Parsnips	**8** Lettuces (Lollo Rosso and Oak	**12** *Lavandula angustifolia* 'Hidcote'
4 Carrots	Leaf)	**13** *Origanum* 'Purple Cloud'
5 Shallots	**9** *Mespilus germanicus*	

A HERB GARDEN IN TOUCH WITH THE PAST

Period plants are used in a geometric pattern of beds in a secret garden.

Tucked away in a corner near the house, this little garden was created to provide a hidden retreat with an authentic period flavour. The house had been at the centre of a famous 16th-century garden, long disappeared, and the owners decided to redesign and replant this site to honour the historic character of the place. It lies to one side of the house, overlooked by its windows.

Formal gardens of the 16th century – knots or parterres – were almost always placed so that their patterns of clipped hedges and plants could be admired from above. Self-contained behind its high hedges, though here part of a larger garden, an area like this could easily be transposed to form the flexible basis for the layout of an entire garden on a more modest scale, and plants of a different period could also be used.

The site is bounded by a path linking a courtyard with the garden proper, and it has two discreet entrances – unobtrusive openings in a solemn yew hedge, which are invisible until you are upon them, giving the garden an air of surprise and mystery.

Yew hedges and a formal pattern of beds already existed when the garden designer Rosemary Verey was asked in 1980 to devise appropriate new planting, using plants available in English gardens in 1580. The use of period plants always gives a distinctive flavour to any garden scheme. Many of the bright colours (especially orange) and large flowers that are familiar to us today – the result of modern hybridisation – produce an effect quite unknown in the 16th century. The use of period plants is therefore not just an exercise in historic accuracy; it makes a striking difference to the atmosphere of a garden.

This, however, is not a purist recreation of period planting for in some cases, in the absence of surviving historic cultivars, modern varieties have been included. Variegated holly, for example, existed in the 16th century but no known cultivar of that period survives. *Ilex × altaclerensis* 'Golden King', a 19th-century variety, has been chosen as an appropriate substitute, and with its wide golden-yellow margins and prolific berries provides exactly the cheerful atmosphere that is needed. A wallflower used for spring bedding, *Erysimum* 'Cloth of Gold', with flowers of sumptuous golden yellow, is quite modern but it is known that wallflowers of this colour were used in Elizabethan gardens.

The garden measures 70ft × 90ft/21m × 27m and is divided by a cruciform pattern of mown grass paths. Their meeting point at the centre is marked by a circular bed with a stone sundial making a punctuation mark in the middle. Its base is surrounded by different species and cultivars of thyme, which have formed cushions that flow together. Here is the very dwarf wild thyme (*Thymus serpyllum*); the deliciously lemon-scented *T. × citriodorus* and its decorative cultivar 'Silver Queen' with leaves finely edged in cream; and the common culinary thyme (*T. vulgaris*) in its gold-leafed cultivar *T. vulgaris* 'Aureus'.

The sundial bed is surrounded by a circular grass path and four beds whose

At the centre of the herb garden a pale stone sundial stands in a circular bed planted with different varieties of thyme. Openings of paths are marked by mounds of silver-grey *Santolina chamaecyparissus*. The whole is overlooked by a shady summerhouse of clipped yew.

inner edge is curved to run parallel with
the paths. Each of these beds has
repeated structural planting: a clipped
lollipop of variegated holly and lollipops
and cubes of clipped box (*Buxus
sempervirens*). In addition, each bed has
low bushes of old English lavender
(*Lavandula × intermedia* 'Alba' Old
English Group), southernwood
(*Artemisia abrotanum*), cotton lavender
(*Santolina chamaecyparissus*) and rue
(*Ruta graveolens*). In the centre of the
beds a spring display of the wallflower
Erysimum 'Cloth of Gold' is followed by
annuals, a different one in each bed:
love-in-a-mist (*Nigella damascena*),
viper's bugloss (*Echium vulgare*), clary
(*Salvia sclarea*) and cornflower
(*Centaurea cyanus*). The repeated
planting of small shrubs and the
repetition of clipped shapes with the
lively colouring of annuals creates an
effect that is both restful and lively.

Each corner of the garden has a large
L-shaped bed, at the back of which more
substantial shrubs are planted. Among
these, sometimes repeated from bed to
bed, are the eglantine rose (*Rosa
eglanteria*), Spanish broom (*Spartium
junceum*) and laurustinus (*Viburnum

tinus*). Substantial herbaceous plants
such as acanthus, valerian (*Centranthus
rubra*) and foxgloves (*Digitalis purpurea*)
are planted in the centre of the beds,
with smaller plants at the front spilling
over on to the paths. Here again,
repeated planting is freely used to give
both repose and formality. Swathes of
common or purple sage (*Salvia
officinalis* and *S. officinalis* Pupurascens
Group), the apothecary's rose (*Rosa
gallica* 'Versicolor') in groups of three,
and boldly shaped stinking hellebores
(*Helleborus foetidus*) are used in this way.
The intersection of paths is marked by
planting in pairs on either side –
lavender, rosemary (*Rosmarinus
officinalis*), bay (*Laurus nobilis*) or cotton
lavender.

Owners of small gardens, anxious to
include as many different plants as
possible, may easily forget the value of
repeated plantings. Yet it is small areas
that most benefit from the harmony
created by the repetition that is the key
to the atmosphere of this Elizabethan
garden. In a restricted area it is also
important that the planting is of a
harmonious scale throughout – the only
plant that could become an
embarrassment in the long run is a
vigorously growing *Magnolia grandiflora*
in the western corner.

The soil here is very heavy, and to
make it workable much organic material
is added – both mushroom compost and
leaf mould. The beds surrounding the
sundial are dug every year in the autumn
when the spring display of wallflowers is
planted. In spring a general fertiliser is
applied, and the beds are forked over
again when the summer annuals are
planted. The yew hedges, box shapes
and lollipops of holly are all clipped
annually in August.

At the back of the garden is a shady
arbour fashioned of clipped yew, with a
wooden seat. The arbour is boldly
shaped but unobtrusive because the
surrounding hedges are also of yew. The
path leading up to it is flanked with
ramparts of rosemary, *Rosa gallica*

HOLDENBY HERB GARDEN

1 *Ilex × altaclerensis* 'Golden King'
2 *Ruta graveolens*
3 Pink, unnamed
4 *Santolina chamaecyparissus*
5 *Artemisia camphorata*
6 *Lavandula × intermedia* 'Alba' Old English Group
7 *Buxus sempervirens* 'Suffruticosa'
8 *Buxus sempervirens* 'Suffruticosa Variegata'
9 *Thymus serpyllum*
10 *Thymus vulgaris* 'Silver Posie'
11 *Thymus vulgaris*
12 *Thymus vulgaris aureus*
13 *Thymus × citriodorus*
14 *Fragaria vesca* 'Semperflorens'

'Versicolor' and *Artemisia alba* – all scented. They make a sweet-smelling approach to the arbour and on a hot summer's day will perfume its interior.

The mixture of colour and evergreen formality forms a balance of excitement and restraint in the garden. The overall design permits great versatility, for these borders could be planted in countless different ways. The paths that thread through the area allow different parts of the garden to be viewed from different angles, helping to banish the monotony that one or two restricted viewpoints can so easily enforce. The surrounding hedges and wall make the garden into a suntrap and many of the plants have marvellous scents of flower or foliage – roses, bay, thyme, rosemary, lavender. So in a single limited space all the essential ingredients of a garden have been brought happily together: harmony, a sense of repose, variety of foliage and flower, and scent.

A DECORATIVE
MINIATURE ORCHARD

In a small village garden, old varieties of apples and pears are trained to form an elegant miniature orchard adorned with flowers.

Formal kitchen gardens that are both decorative and productive have become fashionable garden features. But whereas vegetable growing is labour-intensive and impermanent (the majority of vegetables are annuals, and every time a lettuce is removed from some impeccably symmetrical arrangement the balance will be upset), the orchard described here has all the charm of a formal, productive garden together with the additional virtue that the framework of trained, shaped and pleached trees is permanently ornamental. It is also an inspiring model that may be adapted in many different ways; it can be made as elaborate or as simple as you wish. This garden is restricted to apples and pears – although there are over fifty varieties – but many other kinds of fruit could be treated in the same way. There are rich possibilities for seasonal underplanting and the fruit trees may also be used to support smaller climbing plants such as clematis, or annuals like morning glory (*Ipomoea* species and cultivars).

The little orchard forms part of an elaborate village garden in Belgium, and is divided into a series of skilfully interconnected enclosures of different character. The site, formerly a decorative herb garden, occupies a very small area – a rectangle 22ft × 43ft/7m × 13m. It is west-facing and is protected by a fine old brick wall and a hedge of yew (*Taxus baccata*). Its owner, a skilled ornamental gardener, had made the acquaintance of a fanatical collector of different varieties of apple and pear. From this neighbour she obtained a collection of apples and pears, and laid out a formal orchard to accommodate them. This part of Belgium, the

province of Limburg in the south-west, has an ancient tradition of growing fruit trees, and local nurseries, and those over the border in the Netherlands, still propagate old varieties.

A paved garden path runs down one long side of the rectangular site, and along this a screen of apples is pleached in intertwined lover's knots to a height of 7ft/2m and trained on lateral wires. There are two entrances, each with a metal framework of Gothic arches on which pears are trained. Large mounds of clipped box flank the opening, and along the path are pots of aromatic or culinary plants: purple sage (*Salvia officinalis* Purpurascens Group), lemon verbena (*Aloysia triphylla*) and strawberries. A narrow bed at the foot of the apple screen has chives (*Allium schoenoprasum*), *Campanula persicifolia*, rue (*Ruta graveolens*), cranesbills (*Geranium* species) and several varieties of sage.

The garden is laid out in geometric fashion with long thin maze-like beds edged in dwarf box (*Buxus sempervirens* 'Suffruticosa'). Narrow paths are paved with old bricks which are also used underneath some of the trained fruit trees within the beds. A rectangular bed in the centre, shown in the plan on page 163, has a tall pear, clipped into a slender cone shape and now rising to 10ft/3m in height. It is flanked by 7ft/2m-high apples and underplanted with loose hedges of lavender. There are two cultivars of *Lavandula angustifolia* here: *L. angustifolia* 'Hidcote', one of the best lavenders for hedging, forming a compact bush with narrow leaves and deliciously aromatic deep violet flowers, and *L. angustifolia* 'Rosea' which has

The decorative framework of the miniature orchard is provided by narrow brick paths, hedges and topiary of dwarf box (*Buxus sempervirens* 'Suffruticosa') and the fruit trees themselves. Two varieties of lavender decorate the centre – *Lavandula angustifolia* 'Hidcote' and *L. angustifolia* 'Rosea'.

pretty pink flowers. Pairs of topiary beehives of clipped dwarf box punctuate the lavender hedges. Surrounding the central bed are very narrow beds with a pear at each corner, and between them, pears trained into low T-shaped espaliers. In the centre of each long side is a flamboyant topiary box ornament of four spheres of descending size rising on a single stem. At either end of the rectangular central bed are smaller box-edged beds, each with a large pear trained into an obelisk and flanked by a pair of Caucasian pears (*Pyrus syriaca*) clipped into lollipop shapes.

At each end of the long west-facing wall, aligned with the openings through the apple screen, are wooden Gothic seats, painted pale beige and framed by iron arches with pears and clematis trained over them. Along the crest of the wall is the white Rambler rose 'Albéric Barbier', and more white roses and clematis are glimpsed on the top of a pergola rising above the yew hedge in an adjoining part of the garden.

A formal orchard of this kind preserves its decorative attractions throughout the year, changing with the seasons. In winter the leafless skeletons of the fruit trees and the pattern of box-edged beds makes a scene of orderly formality. The pink and white spring blossom of apples and pears is one of the most beautiful sights of the season. By the month of June the fruit, in particular that of pears and crab apples, is making a contribution to the decorative scheme. In autumn, with the branches laden with fruit, and leaf-colour starting to change, few parts of the garden are lovelier.

The making of a garden along these lines is not complicated. The fruit trees should be grafted onto dwarf stock or their vigour will be uncontrollable. It is possible to buy plants that have already been trained into standard shapes, but these are expensive and it is better to buy one-year-old plants and train them yourself in exactly the way you want. Do, when tying in new growth, use old-fashioned gardeners' twine. Nothing

in this traditional context looks nastier than the green plastic-covered wire ties that may so easily cut into the wood of the branches and deform it. Once the plants are established, they must be pruned at least three times a year – to maintain the shape, to concentrate growth in the fruit and to remove foliage obscuring light from the fruit. Most fruit trees carry fruit on lateral spurs but some are tip-bearing – make sure you know which is which, otherwise you may find yourself removing precious fruiting wood. In an intensively gardened area feeding is important, either with mulches of compost or manure or, perhaps more conveniently in a small garden, with a foliar feed which may be sprayed on.

From this Belgian fruit garden there are glimpses of the house, built of the typical slender bricks of those parts. The atmosphere of enclosed, orderly intimacy brings to mind both the productive little gardens of late medieval Flemish miniatures and the neat alleyways and courtyards of Dutch paintings of the 17th century. The formal fruit garden celebrates, in the most decorative way, a living tradition.

A Gothic seat is flanked by clumps of *Alchemilla mollis* and overhung with the deliciously scented rambler rose 'Albéric Barbier'. Behind the seat a decorative plaque commemorates a much-loved dog.

A MINIATURE ORCHARD

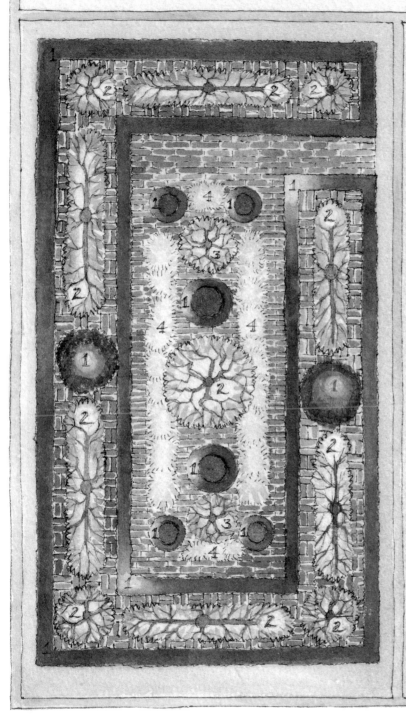

1 *Buxus sempervirens*
   'Suffruticosa'
2 Pears, unnamed varieties
3 Apples, unnamed varieties
4 *Lavandula angustifolia*
   'Hidcote' intermingled with
   L. angustifolia 'Rosea'

A PRODUCTIVE PARTERRE FOR A COUNTRY HOUSE HOTEL

A formal pattern of box-edged compartments produces fresh herbs, youthful salads and vegetables – and provides an attractive pleasure garden for visitors.

The ornamental kitchen garden is one of the most attractive forms of modern gardening. In the past, herbs, fruit and vegetables were normally banished to a kitchen garden of strictly utilitarian appearance. Such gardens, often ornamented with rows of flowers for cutting, had their attractions, but that was not their chief aim. Modern gardeners, recognising the intrinsic beauty of kitchen garden plants attractively regimented in orderly rows, are beginning to realise the decorative potential of this style of gardening.

The garden I show here is part of the old kitchen garden of a large country house which was taken over a few years ago and developed into a luxurious country house hotel with a superb restaurant attached. The herb and vegetable garden provides fresh herbs, salads and vegetables for the chef, but the owners thought it would also make an attraction for the delight of visitors coming to the restaurant and hotel.

The site, 205ft/61.5m long by 40ft/12m wide, slopes gently downwards towards the south, and the whole area is divided into geometric-shaped beds edged in hedges of common box (*Buxus sempervirens*). A central grass path forms the principal axis and is terminated by a white-painted Chinese Chippendale seat flanked by standard bay trees in pots. The pattern of beds on either side is symmetrical, with triangular or rectangular beds separated by grass paths, and a circular bed at the centre.

Restaurants often find that the actual cost of producing their own vegetables is very high – but the freshness and guaranteed quality are impossible to put a price on, and it is also possible to grow ingredients that are hard to find elsewhere. The beds at the top end of the garden, given extra protection by a tall hedge of yew (*Taxus baccata*), are reserved for the growing of early salads and vegetables – what are called in France *primeurs*: the very first, and tastiest, of the crop. A west-facing bed, running the whole length of the garden and again backed by a yew hedge, provides main crops of vegetables such as peas, broad beans, artichokes, asparagus and courgettes.

The herb beds are filled with substantial blocks of plants, with similar planting in corresponding beds on either side of the main path. One pair of beds has tall bushes of billowing rosemary (*Rosmarinus officinalis*) underplanted with waves of lavender (*Lavandula angustifolia*). Another has purple sage (*Salvia officinalis* Purpurascens Group) set off by the lively lime-green of creeping marjoram (*Origanum vulgare*). Common sage (*Salvia officinalis*) is underplanted with the glaucous foliage of rue (*Ruta graveolens*). The round central bed, of which there is a plan on page 167, has cushions of several different thymes which include lemon thyme (*Thymus citriodora*), creeping thyme (*T. serpyllum*) and its cultivar with particularly pretty pink flowers, *T. serpyllum* 'Pink Chintz'. The whole bed is edged with crescents of chives (*Allium*

A view of the parterre and adjacent herbaceous border from an upper window of the hotel. In winter, although stripped of flowers, the parterre's evergreen bones, and the framework of fruit trees, present a very decorative appearance.

In the central circular
bed different varieties
of thyme form plump,
floriferous cushions
edged with the paler
purple of the flowers
of chives, with a
lollipop of bay in the
middle. The
Chinoiserie bench is
also flanked with
miniature bay trees.

schoenoprasum), with a lollipop of
standard bay (*Laurus nobilis*) at the
centre. The round bed is flanked with
beds containing similar but not identical
planting, in each of which lovage
(*Levistichum officinale*) has a striking
presence, growing 6ft/1.8m tall and
flaunting its decorative spatulate foliage.
On one side it rises above a sea of mint,
both pineapple mint (*Mentha suaveolens*
'Variegata') and peppermint (*M.* ×
piperita), and on the other, above bay
and lemon balm (*Melissa officinalis*) – all
giving off their delicious scents.

The box hedges which edge the beds
are 12in/30cm high and wide and give
exactly the crisp outline needed to mark
out the geometric shapes. They are
clipped in June, when growth is at its
most vigorous, and again in the autumn
before there is any danger of frost. A
hard frost can damage the new growth of
box severely. Although the emphasis of
the pattern of beds is primarily
horizontal, with the occasional
punctuation mark of a standard bay tree
and some old apple trees, many herbs if
allowed to run to seed assume statuesque
shapes and produce spectacular
seedpods. By the end of June, for
example, when I photographed this
garden, sorrel (*Rumex acetosa*) had

formed billowing clouds of flowers
4ft/1.2m high, in striking colours of
pink and lime-green. Lovage, too, was
displaying its immense upward-pointing
seedheads borne on stems 7ft/2m high.
In its second year the biennial giant
angelica (*Angelica archangelica*) produces
magnificent branching stems with huge
umbels of creamy green flowers. Fennel
(*Foeniculum vulgare*) and its
bronze-leafed form (*F. v.* 'Purpureum')
also add substantial vertical emphasis.

To one side of the herb garden,
running its whole length and separated
from it by a grass path, is a pair of
herbaceous borders. The planting here is
of the old-fashioned, uncontrived sort
that seems appropriate in mood to a
kitchen garden. In high summer it is
filled with self-sown foxgloves (*Digitalis
purpurea*), tall pale-yellow scabious
(*Cephalaria gigantea*) and *Thalictrum
aquilegiifolium*, followed in the autumn
by sharp yellow solidago and
Michaelmas daisies.

A well-kept herb garden is
labour-intensive. No herb is long-lived
and all are better for frequent renewal.
Lavender and sage lose their shapeliness
when they are much more than four or
five years old. Herbs are easy to
propagate by division or by cuttings, and

MALLORY COURT HERB PARTERRE

1 *Buxus sempervirens*
2 *Laurus nobilis*
3 *Melissa officinalis*
4 *Mentha suaveolens* and *Mentha ×
    piperita*
5 *Levistichum officinale*
6 *Borago officinalis*
7 Apple tree

8 *Mentha suaveolens*
9 *Allium schoenoprasum*
10 *Thymus serpyllum*
11 *Thymus serpyllum* 'Pink Chintz'
12 *Anthemis nobilis*
13 *Thymus* 'Doone Valley'
14 *Thymus × citriodorus*
15 *Thymus × citriodorus* 'Aureus'

16 *Thymus vulgaris*
17 *Mentha spicata*
18 *Mentha × gracilis* 'Variegata'
19 *Foeniculum vulgare*
    'Purpureum'

those left to run to seed will often produce a superabundance of seedlings. Many of the herbaceous plants (such as mints) are appallingly invasive, running underground in all directions. However, the rewards are great. The attractions of herbs are subtle; few have showy flowers. Their special qualities are the freshness and shape of their leaves or their exquisite scent.

Rooms on the south side of the hotel overlook the parterre – a patchwork of contrasting greens spiked with the occasional purple of thyme. The white-painted Chinoiserie bench at the far end of the central path provides a focal point and the occasional mop-headed standard bay rises up. There are views, too, of the long herbaceous borders on one side and the bed of special vegetables on the other. There is something particularly satisfying in the contrast between the orderliness of the geometric beds and the homeliness of what they contain. It is a modern version of an ancient way of gardening that is both decorative and intensely satisfying.

A PHYSIC GARDEN PLANTED WITH HERBS AND USEFUL PLANTS

In a setting of decorative old farm buildings, a knot garden planted with herbs has a dramatic clipped pear at its centre.

The physic garden shown here is in the form of a knot garden. The knot garden became a common feature of English gardens in the 16th century, gradually transforming itself later on into the far more imposing parterre. At first it consisted of simple beds with low hedges interwoven to resemble the strands of a knot. The spaces between the hedges could be filled with plants or with coloured gravel or chippings.

Physic gardens had their origins in the monastery gardens of the 6th century onwards. They were not intended to be ornamental but were places in which to grow plants for medicinal use.

It is unlikely that the ancient farm which provides the setting for this new garden would ever have had either an ornamental knot garden or a physic garden as such. However, by planting it with medicinal, culinary and useful herbs, many of which are English natives that might very well have been grown here for practical purposes in ancient times, it is given a character of sturdy usefulness while breathing an air of mystery and enchantment.

The setting of the knot garden is an enclosure, roughly square, formed by the old farmhouse, an arcaded former granary and stone walls. At its centre is a silver pear (*Pyrus salicifolia* 'Pendula') clipped into a giant drum – over 10ft/3m in diameter and 13ft/4m high. This beautiful object offends all criteria of sound garden design. It is far too big for its site and, perversely, is fashioned from a plant whose chief natural

attribute – the veil-like sweep of its pendulous foliage – has been obliterated by clipping. Yet, in this context it is completely successful. The pale silver-grey and open texture of the foliage give it an ethereal lightness which playfully contradicts its monumental size. When clipped, it does not form an impenetrable wall of smooth texture – the eye can penetrate the surface to the intricate network of twigs within. Its circular shape sits at the centre of the knot, and the square pattern of beds around it forms a visual base, rooting it to the ground. Lastly, its rounded top closely echoes the arched entrances of the granary that forms the chief architectural ornament of the garden.

The pear sits in a circular bed edged in rough stone and underplanted with silver periwinkle (*Vinca minor* 'Argenteovariegata'). Sandy paths radiate out between beds which together form a square. The shape of the individual beds is attractively intricate, with one side curved to fit around the central bed. They are edged with a form of London Pride (*Saxifraga* 'Elliott's Variety') whose flower stems are a fine tawny red, creating a haze of colour that marks the outlines. All the plants grown within the beds are herbaceous, all have a culinary, useful or medicinal use, and all are English natives.

On either side of the central square, rectangular beds are more artfully composed, with identical planting in each. At either end is a Gallica rose, the

An arcade of openings in an old outhouse overlooks the knot garden. The beds are outlined with *Saxifraga* 'Elliott's Variety' whose stems are tawny red. The weeping pear on the right is underplanted with silver periwinkle (*Vinca minor* 'Argenteovariegata').

168

deep maroon 'Tuscany' and the pale
pink and crimson-striped *Rosa gallica*
'Versicolor' (also known as 'Rosa
Mundi'). These are among the oldest
surviving garden cultivars, dating from
no later than the 16th century. They are
underplanted with the variegated form
of ground elder (*Aegopodium podagraria*
'Variegata') which forms a brimming
mattress, filling the whole area
underneath the roses. In July, when the
roses flower, the ground elder also
flowers, producing a decorative froth of
white. Ground elder, as every gardener
knows, is a horribly invasive plant, and
even this pretty variegated form needs
careful control. Its roots are constricted
to a depth of 16in/40cm by plastic
sheeting, isolating it from the rest of the
garden. Ground elder, or bishop's weed
as it is known in northern England, is
not an English native but it is a
medicinal plant. It was introduced by
monastic communities in the Middle
Ages and was used to treat gout; it is
known in old books as 'herb Gerald'
after the saint whose name was invoked
by gout sufferers. Square beds at the end
of each of these beds of roses have a
single bush of wormwood, either

Artemisia absinthium or *A. abrotanum*,
and all the beds are edged with the
white-flowered form of thrift (*Armeria
maritima* 'Alba'). In beds along the
eastern wall are more roses, cultivars of
the ancient hybrid *Rosa × alba* 'Alba
Maxima', the Jacobite rose – and 'Great
Maiden's Blush' which was known in
gardens in the 15th century. They are
underplanted with a double-flowered
periwinkle (*Vinca minor* 'Multiplex') and
sweetly-scented *Viola odorata*.

The walls of the enclosure are also
embellished. At each end of the granary
is a bush of the Scotch, or Burnet, rose
(*Rosa pimpinellifolia*) in a cultivar with
beautiful pale lilac flowers. The arches
of the granary are garlanded with
honeysuckles, both the early ('Belgica')
and late ('Serotina') cultivars of the
native woodbine (*Lonicera periclymenum*
– whose flowers, steeped in oil, Gerard's
Herball recommended for the treatment
of a body that 'is benummed, and
growne very cold'). A path runs along
the wall of the house, where a little bed
is filled with the fumitory *Corydalis
ochroleuca*, thriving in the relatively
shady position of this east-facing wall.

The arches of the granary are open,
giving a vivid impression of cloisters.
There are benches within and a pair of
mysterious old stone figures rising from
a rug of ivy. I sat there in the cool at six
in the morning on a perfect July day,
disturbed only by the roar of the bees
plundering the flowers in the garden
outside. Straight ahead of me the
clipped pear filled the view, with beds
surrounding it brimming with flowering
herbs. A visitor to the garden once
misunderstood the word 'physic',
thinking it was 'psychic'. It may have
been a mistake but it could equally have
been a perceptive response, for the
spiritual quality is palpable. It comes
from the cloistered calm, the healing
beds, the simple harmony of planting
and design, and the mysterious
monumental totem, surrounded by
flowers, at the garden's centre.

At the centre of the
knot garden a clipped
silver pear (*Pyrus
salicifolia* 'Pendula')
rises up. By high
summer the herbs
have become blowsy,
obscuring the pattern
of beds that contain
them.

HERTERTON PHYSIC GARDEN

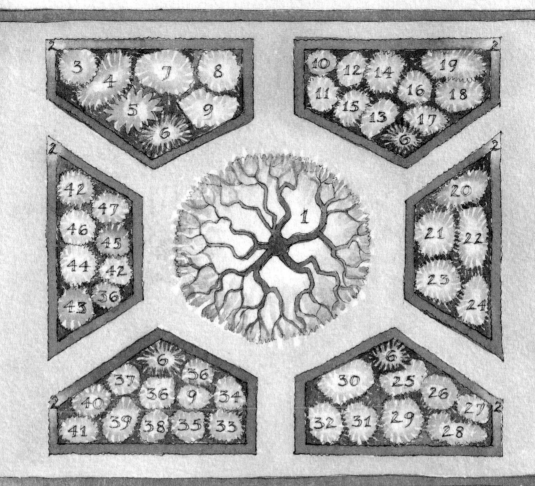

1 *Pyrus salicifolia* 'Pendula'	**17** *Viola tricolor*	**33** *Agrimonia eupatoria*
2 *Saxifraga* 'Elliot's Variety'	**18** *Dictamnus albus*	**34** *Origanum vulgare*
3 *Barbarea vulgaris* 'Variegata'	**19** *Chelidonium majus*	**35** *Lathyrus aureus*
4 *Tragopogon porrifolius*	**20** *Artemisia dracunculus*	**36** *Fragaria vesca* 'Flore Pleno'
5 *Dictamnus albus* 'Purpureus'	**21** *Borago pygmaea*	**37** *Stachys officinalis*
6 *Hyacinthoides hispanica*	**22** *Salvia pratensis* 'Rosea'	**38** *Smilacina stellata*
7 *Geranium macrorrhizum* 'Album'	**23** *Teucrium scorodonia* 'Crispum'	**39** *Echium vulgare*
8 *Convallaria majalis* 'Rosea'	**24** *Asperula tinctoria*	**40** *Alchemilla erythropoda*
9 *Tanacetum vulgare* 'Silver Lace'	**25** *Galega officinalis* 'Alba'	**41** *Teucrium chamaedrys*
10 *Chamaemelum nobile* 'Flore Pleno'	**26** *Aconitum* 'Ivorine'	**42** *Calendula officinalis*
11 *Reseda luteola*	**27** *Sium sisarum*	**43** *Asperula tinctoria*
12 *Melissa officinalis* 'Aurea'	**28** *Hesperis matronalis*	**44** *Meum athamanticum*
13 *Calamintha sylvatica*	**29** *Linum perenne*	**45** *Verbena officinalis*
14 *Salvia sclarea* var. *turkestanica*	**30** *Stachys macrantha*	**46** *Polygonatum verticillatum*
15 *Cynoglossum officinale*	**31** *Lithospermum officinale*	**47** *Tanacetum parthenium*
16 *Filipendula ulmaria* 'Variegata'	**32** *Origanum vulgare* var. *album*	

A MODERN CONSERVATORY ATTACHED TO AN OLD HOUSE

This versatile conservatory provides a room in which to sit or eat, a home for a jungle-like profusion of tender plants, and a link between house and garden.

Conservatories have undergone a great renaissance but few are exploited to their full potential and fewer still fit easily into their surroundings. A properly planned conservatory can be a marvellous adjunct to house and garden, greatly extending the range of plants that may be grown, and with a distinctive atmosphere of its own.

The conservatory shown here is a successful modern addition to a fine 17th-century house, occupying a crucial position in relation to the facade of the house and to the walled garden which it overlooks. Its position is a sensitive one, as the house and garden walls are both built of hand-made bricks dating from the late 17th century. This is no place for a florid Victorian-style conservatory of extravagant design, nor for anything bogusly 'classical'. Conservatories did not exist in the 17th century and it would be absurd to concoct something of hypothetical period character. This one is just about as simple as it could be, with subtle details which allow it to merge with its surroundings. Almost entirely built of glass and white-painted wood, with slender glazing-bars, it rests on a base of low brick walls, only eight courses high, which closely match the old bricks of the house. It is of lean-to construction, the highest point of its roof reaching to just below the window lintels of the first floor. It is devoid of ornament, except for a little pattern of dentilation on the outside, forming a cornice and enclosing the gutter, where the walls meet the roof. Its proportions are good: just over 9ft/2.75m wide by 40ft/11.5m in length.

It is floored in 12in/30cm square quarry tiles which make an attractive and practical surface on which water will inevitably be spilled. Running along the front and back are drainage channels covered in handsome cast-iron panels – cast by a local foundry to a Victorian pattern and costing no more than quarry tiles. There is no built-in heating, but a portable electric heater controlled by a thermostat is put in place for the winter, keeping the interior free of frost but no more. The temperature you choose has an absolute bearing on the range of plants that you can grow, but a merely frost-free conservatory will allow the cultivation of a staggering range of plants which could not survive in the garden. Some conservatory owners make do with no heating at all, but glass is an excellent conductor of cold and affords very little protection by itself. In such conditions, a few nights of severe frost will kill off all but the toughest of plants – plants not needing the protection of a conservatory in the first place.

Excessive temperatures can be just as damaging as very low ones to conservatory plants. Facing west, this conservatory can get very hot indeed, making proper ventilation absolutely essential. Although it has two doors opening into the garden, these alone would be inadequate. All the side panels are hinged at the top, but are often awkward to open because plants get in the way. Vents running the whole length

A stone bust is overhung with the giant leaves of *Sparrmannia africana* and the foreground is fringed with the tender fern *Woodwardia radicans*. Planting outside the conservatory gives the impression of a continuing jungle.

of the roof at its highest point, and controlled by screws and cranks, allow for the best possible ventilation – in conjunction with open doors and windows as necessary. Roller blinds of wooden slats on top of the roof provide shade when it is needed. These blinds, controlled by cords secured to cleats, are much more effective on the *outside*, preventing the glass from heating up and disseminating some of its heat inside.

Striking a proper balance between planting and living space is always difficult in a conservatory. Here, the end nearest the door to the kitchen has a table and chairs, and comfortable wicker chairs are disposed about. All the planting is in pots. This is by no means a disadvantage, for plants in conservatory beds can grow to an embarrassing size. Pots curb the growth and furthermore make it possible to rearrange plants to best effect when they are at their peak – or to move dullards to a less prominent position.

Many conservatories use only a very narrow range of plants, often drawn from the 'conservatory plants' section of the garden centre. The emphasis with these is usually on flower-power, in spite of the fact that foliage and habit make a much more powerful contribution.

However, any plant too tender to grow out-of-doors may be a suitable subject.

Some of the plants in this conservatory grow into huge trees in their native habitat. The Tasmanian blue gum (*Eucalyptus globulus*) will shoot up to heights of well over 170ft/50m in the wild, but it makes a strikingly handsome pot plant with its pale grey bark and glaucous foliage. The South African *Sparrmannia africana* grows in its native country into a large spreading shrub up to 20ft/6m high; in the conservatory its soft pale green leaves, resembling those of a giant grapevine, give precisely the decoratively leafy shade that is needed. The Queensland silver wattle (*Acacia podalyriifolia*) is a shrub or small tree with marvellously ornamental silver-white new growth and foliage. *Homalanthus populifolius*, a distinguished deciduous shrub from the South Pacific, has rounded poplar-like leaves which take on a brilliant red before they fall. The last of the larger plants in this group is an oleander (*Nerium oleander*), a plant familiar in Mediterranean and Californian gardens but which in England needs the protection of a conservatory to flower properly. White-flowered cultivars such as this have the additional attraction of a

SALING HALL CONSERVATORY

1 *Acacia podalyriifolia*
2 *Eucalyptus globulus*
3 *Dodonaea viscosa* 'Purpurea'
4 *Sparrmannia africana*
5 *Woodwardia radicans*
6 *Asplenium nidus*
7 *Homalanthus populifolius*
8 *Nerium oleander*
9 *Strelitzia reginae*
10 *Pelargonium*, unnamed, white
11 *Pelargonium* 'Roi des Balcons'

delicious scent.

Many ferns also flourish in conditions that are just frost-free. The bird's nest fern (*Asplenium nidus*) has pale green glistening leaves rising up handsomely, a good 36in/90cm high, marked with a black central rib. *Woodwardia radicans* is a fern with striking doubly pinnate fronds on arching stems up to 7ft/2m long. The undersides of the leaves carry rhizomes which will root if held down in soil.

Few conservatories succeed as well as this. Because of its careful design, this conservatory does not overpower its surroundings, as many so easily do. Instead, it links house and garden in a subtle way, providing a gardened room that is a passage between the two. With its seats, sculptures and unassuming profusion of plants it has a delightful air of relaxation.

POTTED PLEASURES IN A LONDON ROOF GARDEN

An elaborate roof garden links four Victorian artists' studios and provides attractions all of its own.

The impulse to make gardens in unlikely places is one that is strong enough to overcome almost any inconvenience. To create a roof garden is the logical response to the problems of urban crowding. In doing this, advantages are revealed, as well as a distinct aesthetic which gives this type of garden a special character. A roof garden is not merely a garden moved to the roof, for the peculiarities of the site transform its nature. It imposes all sorts of horticultural discipline but it may result in a kind of garden unlike any other.

The garden shown here came into being in an unusual way. Its owner bought four Victorian artists' studios in the centre of London, linked them together and made them into a large house. The studios had no gardens – only an internal courtyard, which now houses a small glasshouse and provides space for storing and replanting pots. The only other available space at ground-level, of which the owner has made full use, with many pots of shade-loving plants, is a narrow entrance passage leading to what is now the front door of the house.

The roofscape of the house is especially attractive and has been further embellished by the owner. Each of the four studios has a pyramid-like roof with large skylights in the traditional north- and east-facing position. The peak of each roof has been given a charming minaret – made of fibreglass but indistinguishable from stone. These came from Brighton Pavilion, where they had been used as temporary replacements until the final restoration was completed in 1982. The minarets are, of course, much lighter than stone but even so a crane was needed to lift them into position. A roof garden is no place for solemnity and the roofs are further decorated with models of fantailed pigeons, cranes, a cat, squirrels and other prowling creatures. But although the reigning character is one of lightheartedness, the planting is on a grand scale and its detail worked out with great skill.

The main part of the garden lies in the spaces between the roofs and on either side of the narrow walkway that runs down their side. There is no possibility of having beds here, and all the planting is in containers – almost entirely in terracotta pots. This has both limitations and advantages: there is simply not enough room for very large pots, which would in any case be difficult to manoeuvre in a limited space, but pots, of which there are no less than 1,800 in this garden, may be moved and regrouped in all sorts of delightful permutations, so that they become a mobile garden décor. One of the great attractions is the possibility of regrouping pots to make the best of a plant at its peak, and a plant that is past its best may simply be removed – or at very least demoted to a position of less prominence.

Gardening in pots, however, does impose constraints. Terracotta pots dry out very quickly, and on a roof garden, which is airy and exposed to the light, this problem is exacerbated. The pots in this garden need to be watered every day in the summer, and this is best done in

In the roof garden plants in pots are packed together, which gives the appearance of a densely planted border. Here lupins, campanulas, roses and aquilegias jostle together in such profusion as to make the pots almost invisible.

An ornament is made of a small Indonesian carved table, placed upside down with bronze Buddhas balanced on each leg and a further Buddha in a bamboo-roofed temple at the centre. The surrounding planting gives a convincing impression of a miniature tropical jungle.

the morning when less water will be lost through evaporation than would be the case in the heat of the day. It takes at least two hours, although the task has been made a little easier by having taps and hose-pipes positioned at frequent intervals about the roof. Some gardeners line terracotta pots with polythene so that they do not need such frequent watering.

Constant watering also means that nourishment is repeatedly washed out of the soil, so the plants need far more feeding than those in beds would need. The most convenient way of doing this is by a foliar feed which is watered onto the foliage and quickly absorbed into the plant. In the growing season foliar feed is given regularly every two to four weeks, either with a watering can, for spot feeding, or with a hose-pipe to which is attached a reservoir of foliar feed – a very convenient way of coping with large areas.

Frequent watering also causes soil to be washed out through the drainage holes of the pots, so the pots need topping up from time to time. Because of the problem of getting materials up to the roof, and of lack of space in which to do the more mundane gardening work, all compost is recycled and used for

making good any loss of soil in the pots. In late winter every substantial pot is also top-dressed with well-rotted stable manure. A compost made of peat, or more environmentally friendly substances such as coir, is much lighter than earth-based composts which can impose a strain on a roof.

The plants chosen for the pots are exactly those that you would find in a well-planted garden bed. There are a few tender plants – pelargoniums and daturas, for example – but the great majority are hardy garden plants. In the same way, much of the plant grouping is arranged exactly as it would be in a conventional ground-level garden – a golden hop (*Humulus lupulus* 'Aureus'), for example – is found scrambling through a purple-leafed plum (*Prunus cerasifera* 'Pissardii'). The pots are placed in bold groups so that the foliage will often conceal them. More substantial pots containing shrubs and trees are placed at the back, and in these much use is made of underplanting. Very small pots are used to contain such decorative things as violas, cranesbills and primulas. A full-time gardener is employed to maintain this garden, and much of her work lies in the rearrangement of pots and making sure

A LONDON ROOF GARDEN

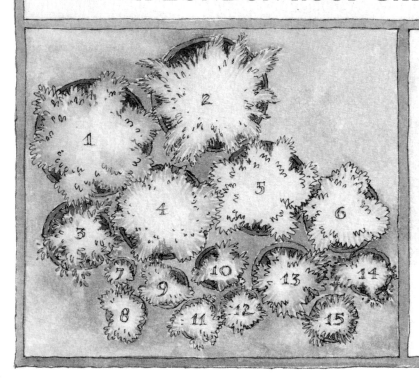

1 *Choisya ternata*
2 *Spiraea* 'Arguta'
3 *Rosa* 'Super Star'
4 *Vernonia peruviana* 'Alba'
5 *Acer palmatum atropurpureum*
6 *Acer negundo* 'Variegatum'
7 *Viola* 'Swanley White'
8 *Senecio cineraria*
9 *Iberis saxatilis*
10 *Aconitum* 'Ivorine'
11 *Campanula persicifolia* 'Gawen'
12 *Thalictrum tuberosum*
13 *Acer palmatum* var. *dissectum*
14 *Cotoneaster*, unnamed
15 *Lupinus* 'Noble Maiden'

that new growth does not obstruct the narrow passages – as well as routine feeding and watering.

One of the great delights of a roof garden in a big city is the charm of the views. Here, apart from the intricate skyline of neighbouring rooftops, there are also fine old trees in adjoining gardens – including a London plane (*Platanus* × *hispanica*) and a huge sycamore (*Acer pseudoplatanus*). It is also easier to find an open sunny sitting place on a roof than it is in gardens on the ground in crowded cities, and on hot summer days the roof garden benefits from delicious refreshing breezes – usually denied to the ground-level garden enclosed by high buildings. This garden, however, is not sufficiently high to be regularly exposed to high winds – which in many roof gardens presents a major problem. Here, only a few of the more substantial and top-heavy plants are discreetly wired to some nearby support. If potted plants are arranged close together they have the advantage of

lending each other support to protect them from buffeting winds.

Everywhere in the garden there are lively and often humorous decorative details. Carved wooden Indonesian tables have been turned upside down, with little bronze figures of Buddha placed on each broad foot. At the centre of each table another Buddha is seated in a Balinese temple with a sweeping roof covered in bamboo shingles, surrounded by a carpet of candytuft. The foliage of the surrounding plants conveys the impression of a jungle – a momentary dislocation of scale. Elsewhere, an enchanting and elaborately detailed miniature conservatory is planted with appropriately miniature plants kept in good heart by a miniature irrigation system. The interior is beautifully furnished with statues, furniture and finely made models of the owner and his wife. Such *jeux d'esprit* are happily accommodated in the lighthearted atmosphere of the place.

PLANT DIRECTORY

Abutilon
A genus of herbaceous and woody mallows.

A. vitifolium
Height: 20ft/6m Zone: 8
Tender but lovely shrub with grey vine-like flowers and, in May, single purple or white flowers. Short-lived but easily propagated by cuttings, it grows fast and may need support. Must have good drainage and a sunny position.

Acacia
A large genus of woody plants, the wattles or mimosas.

A. podalyriifolia
Height: 15ft/4.5m Zone: 8
The Queensland wattle is a graceful open small tree with decorative blue-grey foliage and yellow pompom flowers in spring. Flourishes in a hot dry position. Propagate by seed or cuttings.

Acanthus
A genus of herbaceous perennials propagated by seed or division.

A. spinosus Spinossisimus Group
Height: 42in/1m Zone: 6
Statuesque foliage plant with long narrow leaves, gleaming dark green and finely spined. Good in shade, best in rich soil.

Acer
The maple genus of trees and shrubs.

A. japonicum 'Aconitifolium'
Height: 30ft/9m Zone: 6
A deciduous Japanese maple of spreading form with distinguished leaves with finely pointed and dissected lobes. Magnificent carmine autumn colouring. Best in light shade in a protected place.

Abutilon vitifolium

A. negundo 'Variegatum'
Height: 20ft/6m Zone: 2
The box elder is an elegant deciduous tree forming a spreading crown with leaves broadly variegated with pale cream. Sun or semi-shade.

A. palmatum
Height: 25ft/7.5m Zone: 5
A decorative deciduous Japanese maple with shapely crown and handsome fresh green palm-shaped foliage. A. p. atropurpureum has beautiful deep purple foliage. A. p. var. dissectum has intricately cut leaves giving a most decorative effect.

A. pensylvanicum
Height: 42ft/12m Zone: 3
The moosewood is a snake-bark maple, with beautiful striped markings on the bark. Deciduous with beautiful autumn colouring, a clear butter yellow.

A. pseudoplatanus
Height: 130ft/40m Zone: 5
The European sycamore is a deciduous tree with broadly palm shaped leaves. Old specimens are full of character with striking peeling bark.

Achillea
The yarrows are a genus of herbaceous plants. Propagate by cuttings or division.

A. clypeolata
Height: 30in/75cm Zone: 6
Perennial with fine fern-like foliage and, in June, bold flat corymbs of golden yellow flowers. Best in sun in rich soil.

A. filipendulina
Height: 36in/90cm Zone: 3
A perennial with finely cut foliage and flat corymbs of yellow flowers borne at the tip of long stems. Best in rich soil in a sunny position. A. f. 'Cloth of Gold' is a deep rich yellow. A. f. 'Gold Plate' has rich golden flowers in mounded corymbs.

A. grandifolia
Height: 36in/90cm Zone: 6
The grey, finely dissected foliage of this evergreen yarrow is very ornamental. Flat corymbs of white flowers are produced throughout the season if deadheaded. It is best in a sunny position but flourishes in poor soil.

A. millefolium and hybrids
Height: 24in/60cm Zone: 2
From a mat of ferny dark green leaves the flowering stems carrying in June long-lasting flat corymbs of yellow. The colour is particularly good and will make a telling contribution to many different schemes. It will flower best in a sunny position in fertile soil. It may be propagated by division. A. m. 'Lilac Beauty' has lilac pink flowers. A. 'Apple Blossom' has mottled pink and white flowers. A. 'Coronation Gold' is a good rich yellow. A. 'Forncett Beauty' has lively violet-pink flowers. A. 'Salmon Beauty' (syn. A. 'Lachsschönheit') has deeper pink flowers. A. 'Moonshine' has lemon yellow flowers. A. 'Taygetea' has pale lemon-yellow flowers.

Aconitum

A genus of herbaceous plants.
Propagate by division.

A. carmichaelii 'Barker's Variety'
Height: 7ft/2m Zone: 3
A stately monkshood with spikes
of hooded purple flowers very late
in the season. It may need staking.
Rich soil in part shade.

A. 'Ivorine'
Height: 36in/90cm Zone: 5
Herbaceous perennial with fresh
green palm-shaped leaves and in
June spires of distinguished
creamy-yellow flowers.

A. × maccarum 'Bicolor'
Height: 4ft/1.2m Zone: 4
There are several cultivars of this
hybrid, all with gleaming leaves
and spires of hooded flowers in
summer. *A. × m.* 'Bicolor' has
pretty blue and white flowers.

Actinidia

A genus of climbing plants.
Propagate by layering or cuttings.

A. chinensis see *A. deliciosa*
A. deliciosa
Height: 30ft/10m Zone: 4
The Kiwi fruit or Chinese
gooseberry is a stately, vigorous
deciduous climber with bold
heart-shaped leaves carried on
red-tinged stems. The fruit is
carried only by female plants.

A. kolomikta
Height: 20ft/7m Zone: 4
A curious plant with striking
leathery leaves splashed, as
though by a clumsy decorator,
with white or pale pink. Needs
sun to develop colour.

Aegopodium

A genus of herbaceous plants.

A. podagraria 'Variegata'
Height: 24in/60cm Zone: 4
The pretty variegated version of
the dreadful weed, ground elder.
Pale green leaves edged with
creamy white. Needs careful
watching. Good in shade.
Propagate by division.

Agapanthus

These South African lily-like
plants are herbaceous perennials
whose flowers are often of a
startling and lovely blue.
Propagate by division.

A. campanulatus var. *albidus*
Height: 24in/60cm Zone: 7
The species agapanthus, rarely
seen in gardens, give special
pleasure – narrow leaves and
flowering stems and, in July or
August, graceful white flowers
with narrow curling petals.

A. Headbourne Hybrids
Height: 24–60in/60cm–1.5m
Zone: 7
Among the hardiest agapanthus
with loose umbels of blue flowers
– varying in intensity – in July.

Agastache

A genus of tender herbaceous
perennials.

A. cana 'Cinnabar Rose'
Height: 24in/60cm Zone: 9
Spires of rosy-red flowers in late
summer. Needs well-drained soil
in full sun. Propagate by division.

Agave

A genus of succulents propagated
by offsets or seed. In hot climates
perfect for poor soil in full sun. In
cooler climates needs protection
of glasshouse.

A. americana
Height: 7ft/2m Zone: 9
Succulent with sharply pointed
boldly shaped grey leaves. Yellow
flowers on giant stems (up to
30ft/9m!) produced once only –
the plant subsequently dies. *A. a.*
'Mediopicta' has handsome cream
stripes running along the centre of
the leaves.

A. parryi
Height: 30in/75cm Zone: 9
Striking artichoke-like plant with
overlapping toothed petals, pale
grey-green in colour. Pale yellow
flowers in summer.

Agapanthus Headbourne Hybrid

A. vilmoriniana
Height: 6ft/1.8m Zone: 9
The striking feature is long
curving spined pale grey-green
leaves. Yellow flowers produced
on immense stems in summer.

Agrimonia

A genus of herbaceous perennials.

A. eupatoria
Height: 36in/90cm Zone: 5
Agrimony has hairy rosettes of
leaves with spires of golden-
yellow flowers from June onwards.
Flourishes in a dry, sunny
position. Propagate by seed.

Ailanthus

A genus of trees and shrubs.

A. altissima
Height: 100ft/30m Zone: 6
The tree of heaven is a substantial
tree with graceful fronds of
pinnate foliage. May be stooled to
control size and promote larger
leaves. Propagate by seed.

Alcea

The hollyhock genus of
herbaceous plants.

A. rosea
Height: 10ft/3m Zone: 6
A perennial or biennial, one of the
great cottage garden plants, with
immense stems carrying flat white
or mauve flowers in summer. *A. r.*
'Nigra' has magnificent lustrous
almost black flowers. Needs sun
and rich soil. Propagate by seed.

Allium hollandicum 'Purple Sensation'

A. rugosa
Height: 8ft/2.5m Zone: 3
Magnificent herbaceous summer-flowering perennial with pale yellow open trumpet flowers. Best in dry position in sun, good in poor soil. Propagate by seed.

Alchemilla
A genus of herbaceous perennials.

A. alpina
Height: 6in/10cm Zone: 4
An elegant little foliage plant with fresh green pleated leaves edged in silver. Spires of diminutive yellow-green flowers in spring. Does well in semi-shade, propagate by division.

A. erythropoda
Height: 4in/10cm Zone: 5
This miniature lady's mantle is a pretty little plant with glaucous foliage and diminutive flowers the colour of yellow Chartreuse. Does well in sun or part-shade. Propagate by seed or by division.

A. mollis
Height: 18in/45cm Zone: 4
Marvellous leaves in spring – suede-soft, rounded and lobed, the colour of green Chartreuse, followed by a delicate froth of yellow flowers. Self-seeds with abandon, best to cut off the flowers before seed ripens. Sun or shade and is unfussy as to soil.

Alisma
A group of aquatic or marginal herbaceous plants.

A. plantago-aquatica
Height: 36in/90cm Zone: 6
The foliage is upright, oval and pointed. Clouds of diminutive white flowers in June. Grows in the shade and it must have water at its roots. Propagate by division.

Allium
The onions, a genus with many good garden plants. Propagate by seed or division.

A. aflatunense see *A. hollandicum*

A. christophii
Height: 24in/60cm Zone: 7
Borne on thick fleshy stems, the drumstick flowers of this allium are spectacular in June – 9in/23cm in diameter, with hundreds of starry metallic purple petals. It thrives in shade and will self seed.

A. hollandicum
Height: 24in/60cm Zone: 6
In May the strap-like foliage is surmounted by a tall thin stem bearing a sphere of purple flowerlets. Best in rich soil in a sunny position. *A. h.* 'Purple Sensation' is much taller (36in/90cm) and its flowers are a dazzling rich violet.

A. moly
Height: 9in/23cm Zone: 7
Grey-green foliage is followed in May by umbels of brilliant yellow star-shaped flowers. Sun or semi-shade in rich moist soil.

A. schoenoprasum
Height: 9in/23cm Zone: 5
The culinary chive with grass-like leaves and blue-purple spherical flower heads. It is best in moist soil in sun or part-shade. Propagate by division or seed.

Aloe
A genus of herbaceous and woody plants.

A. vera
Height: 24in/60cm Zone: 9
Spreading succulent with fleshy bright green toothed leaves. Elegant spires of yellow flowers in summer. In tropics relishes dry, hot position. Needs glasshouse protection in cooler climates. Propagate by seed or offsets.

Aloysia
A genus of shrubs.

A. triphylla
Height: 10ft/3m Zone: 8
Lemon verbena is too tender ever to attain its maximum height in temperate climates. Piercing lemon scent of its foliage when crushed. Dull flowers but attractive pale green leaves – but it's the scent that counts. Best in a pot, propagate by cuttings.

Alstroemeria
The alstroemerias are a genus of lily-like perennials, all with corms or tubers. Propagate by division.

A. aurea
Height: 36in/90cm Zone: 7
Flowers of a marvellous colour – a glowing orange with yellow within, starting in July lasting for a long time. Rather floppy and will need support. Needs good drainage, flowers well in dappled shade and in full sun.

A. Ligtu Hybrids
Height: 5ft/1.2m Zone: 8
Trumpet flowers in June varying in colour – white, cream, apricot, pink – above floppy glaucous foliage. Best in rich soil in sun.

Alyogyne
A genus of tender shrubs.

A. hakeifolia
Height: 10ft/3m Zone: 10
Mallow-like fast-growing shrub from Australia with decorative mauve saucer-shaped flowers throughout the summer. Excellent

for pots in the sun. Propagate by cuttings.

Alyssum
A genus of herbaceous and woody plants.

A. murale
Height: 24in/60cm Zone: 7
A herbaceous perennial with rounded grey-green foliage followed in May with corymbs of sprightly yellow flowers. Best in sun. Propagate by seed or division.

Amaranthus
A genus of herbaceous plants.

A. caudatus
Height: 3ft/90cm Zone: 5
Love-lies-bleeding is an annual which produces curious dangling racemes of crimson-purple flowers in summer. Raised by seed and will seed itself. Needs sun but will flourish in poor soil.

Anaphalis
A genus of herbaceous perennials.

A. triplinervis
Height: 12in/30cm Zone: 5
Silver leaves and a profusion of white daisy flowers borne throughout the summer. Needs a sunny position and sharp drainage. Propagate by division.

Anemone
The wind flowers, a genus of herbaceous perennials. Propagate by division.

A. hupehensis var. *japonica*
Height: 24in/60cm Zone: 5
This pink Japanese anemone has beautiful petals with rounded tips and dusty crimson backs. The flower colour varies from a very pale pink to much deeper tones. A particularly good deep-coloured one is *A. h.* var. *j.* 'Hadspen Abundance'.

A. × hybrida
Height: 5ft/1.5m Zone: 5
Handsome foliage with pointed lobes and saucer-shaped warm pink flowers in late summer.

Flowers well in shade and relishes heavy moist soil where it may become embarrassingly invasive. *A. × h.* 'Honorine Jobert' has dark green leaves and dazzling white flowers. *A. × h.* 'Königin Charlotte' ('Queen Charlotte') has semi-double pink-purple flowers. *A. × h.* 'Superba' has larger flowers than the type.

Angelica
A genus of biennial and perennial herbs.

A. archangelica
Height: 8ft/2.5m Zone: 4
Usually a biennial or sometimes short-lived perennial this statuesque plant has magnificent deeply divided leaves borne on a stout hollow stem and huge umbels of pale green flowers in June. Best in rich soil in sun or part shade. Propagate by seed.

Anigozanthos
A genus of herbaceous plants.

A. flavidus
Height: 36in/90cm Zone: 9
The kangaroo paw – a bushy plant with upright flower stems bearing in summer panicles of yellow, red or orange flowers. *A. f.* 'Yellow Gem' is a good golden yellow. Thrives in hot dry position in native land – needs greenhouse protection in cooler climates. Propagate species by seed, cultivars by division.

Anthemis
A genus of herbaceous and small woody plants.

A. punctata sbsp. *cupaniana*
Height: 12in/30cm Zone: 7
Herbaceous perennial with the palest grey leaves of woolly texture. The flowers in May are cheerful white daisies with yellow centres. Needs a sunny position and is propagated by division.

A. tinctoria
Height: 18in/45cm Zone: 4
Beautiful herbaceous perennial

with lemon yellow daisies from June for weeks. Best in sun and rich soil. Propagate by division. *A. t.* 'E.C. Buxton' has soft yellow flowers. *A. t.* 'Sauce Hollandaise' has pale lemon flowers.

Anthericum
A genus of rhizomatous plants. Propagate by division.

A. liliago
Height: 24in/60cm Zone: 7
The St Bernard's lily has airy spires of little white star-shaped flowers in early summer on waving stems. Good in part shade it will flourish in poor soil.

Antirrhinum
A genus of herbaceous plants.

Antirrhinum cultivars
Range in height from 8-36in/20-90cm and all are hardy to Zone 7. Many cultivars derived from hybrids of *A. majus*, grown as annuals and raised from seed. Must have sun and rich soil. *A.* 'Black Prince' (12in/30cm) has deep purple flowers.

Aquilegia
The columbines are a genus of herbaceous plants. Propagate by seed or division.

Anemone hupehensis var. **japonica**

183

A. chrysantha
Height: 42in/1m Zone: 3
Tall American columbine with
yellow flowers sometimes flushed
with pink in summer carried
above elegant fresh green foliage.
Best in sun in rich soil.

A. flabellata
Height: 12in/30cm Zone: 3
Lilac or vaguely white flowers in
spring. Glaucous-grey rounded
leaves. Does well in part-shade. *A.
f. alba* is a crisp white form.

A. vulgaris
Height: 30in/75cm Zone: 5
Easy, self-sowing plant. Emerging
from whorls of glaucous foliage
the flowers in May are carried at
the tips of tall stems – pink,
mauve, purple or white. They are
not invasive and find places for
themselves among other plants.
Flourishes in sun or in semi-
shade, best in rich, moist soil.

Arctotis
African daisies, a genus of tender
herbaceous plants.

A. × hybrida cultivars
These are around 12in/3cm high
and hardy to Zone 9. Flowers well
held above glaucous foliage. *A. ×
h.* 'Flame' produces a profusion of
orange-red flowers. *A. × h.* 'Wine'
is a good red. Propagate by
cuttings. In many gardens used as
a bedding plant. Must have a
warm, sunny position.

Argyranthemum
A genus of tender subshrubs.

Argyranthemum cultivars.
All are around 36in/90cm high
and are hardy to Zone 9. Finely
cut grey-green foliage and a
profusion of daisy flowers. Needs
sun and rich soil to flower well. *A.*
'Jamaica Primrose' is a fine pale
yellow with single flowers.

Armeria
The thrifts are a genus of
herbaceous and woody plants.

A. maritima
Height: 10in/25cm Zone: 6
Sea thrift forms a grassy tuft with
mop-headed sprightly pink
flowers in May. *A. m.* 'Alba' is a
decorative white-flowered
cultivar. Best in sun, good
drainage, propagate by division.

Artemisia
A genus of woody and herbaceous
plants. Woody species are
propagated by cuttings,
herbaceous by division.

A. abrotanum
Height: 36in/90cm Zone: 5
Southernwood is a semi-evergreen
aromatic shrub with very finely
dissected grey-green foliage. Dull
yellow flowers in summer.

A. absinthium
Height: 36in/90cm Zone: 4
Handsome small shrub with fine
pale grey aromatic leaves and
unexciting yellow flowers. Sun
and dry soil.

A. alba 'Canescens'
Height: 12in/30cm Zone: 6
An almost evergreen sub-shrub
with a froth of pewter-grey very
fine leaves. May be gently clipped
to make a decorative shape. One

**Arum italicum sbsp. italicum
'Marmoratum'**

of the tougher artemisias, being
quite hardy and unfussy as to soil.
Good in sun or in partial shade.

A. arborescens
Height: 36in/90cm Zone: 8
The palest silver filigree leaves.
Short-lived and rather tender but
easily propagated by cuttings. Its
youthful foliage is always the most
attractive and older plants in any
case become straggly. *A. a.* 'Faith
Raven' has exceptionally finely
dissected leaves and is hardier
than the type. *A.* 'Powis Castle'
seems indistinguishable.

A. dracunculus
Height: 5ft/1.5m Zone: 3
Herbaceous perennial with
mid-green narrow pointed leaves
and uninteresting yellow flowers.
Flourishes in heavy soil.
Propagate by division. The
delicious herb, tarragon, is the
smaller, much less hardy form *A.
d. dracunculoides* which needs
much sun and sharp drainage.

A. ludoviciana var. *incompta*
Height: 24in/60cm Zone: 5
Herbaceous perennial with
beautiful pewter-grey feathery
leaves which get whiter in
drought. Sun or semi-shade,
relishes moist soil.

A. pontica
Height: 30in/75cm Zone: 4
A herbaceous artemisia, with very
finely dissected leaves of an
attractive pewter grey colour.
Makes a shapely little plant,
excellent as a miniature structural
plant. Yellow flowers in June are
insignificant. Best in a sunny
position with good drainage.

Arum
A genus of herbaceous perennials
propagated by seed or division.

A. italicum sbsp. *italicum*
'Marmoratum'
Height: 18in/45cm Zone: 6
A lovely plant of winter and
spring with gleaming pointed
leaves marbled in pale green. Best
in moist soil in the shade.

Asperula

A genus of herbaceous perennials and shrubs.

A. tinctoria
Height: 30in/75cm Zone: 4
Dyer's woodruff has airy little umbels of white flowers in summer on straggling stems with star-shaped narrow petals. Will grow almost anywhere. Propagate by seed or division.

Asplenium

The spleenworts are one of the largest groups of ferns. Propagate by sowing spores.

A. nidus
Height: 5ft/1.5m Zone: 10
The stately bird's nest fern has glistening undulating pale green leaves. Needs moisture – and the protection of a greenhouse in non-tropical climates.

A. scolopendrium
Height: 12in/30cm Zone: 4
The hart's tongue fern unfurls its lovely strap-like leaves in April, upright, pale green and lustrous. An essential woodland plant it will reproduce itself by spores.

Aster

The daisy tribe, almost entirely herbaceous. All those below are propagated by division.

A. divaricatus
Height: 24in/60cm Zone: 4
A bushy aster covered with white miniature daisies in late summer. A good edging plant in a sunny position.

A. × frikartii
Height: 36in/90cm Zone: 5
A perennial daisy with light blue flowers and a pronounced yellow eye. It needs sun and rich soil.

A. laevis 'Calliope'
Height: 36in/90cm Zone: 4
Bold leafed herbaceous perennial with lavender daisy-like flowers in June. Needs sun and rich soil.

Astrantia major rubra

A. laterifolius 'Horizontalis'
Height: 36in/90cm Zone: 3
This bushy autumn-flowering daisy produces immense numbers of small white daisies with a chocolate centre. Must have a sunny position.

Astilbe

A genus of herbaceous perennials. Propagated by division.

A. × arendsii cultivars
Up to 30in/75cm in height, hardy to Zone 4. These are the most common kinds of astilbe found in gardens. Decorative leaves with pointed lobes and flowers in upright plume-like panicles – white, pink, red and various shades of purple. Best in moist soil, in sun or part shade.

Astrantia

A genus of herbaceous perennials propagated by seed or, in the case of good forms, by division.

A. major
Height: 24in/60cm Zone: 4
A clump of finely cut leaves with tall stems bearing many-pointed cream and green stars. Good in moist soil in semi-shade. *A. m. rubra* has plum-coloured flowers.

A. maxima
Height: 36in/90cm Zone: 6
Palm shaped leaves with deeply cut and finely pointed lobes. Flowers on stiff stems, appearing in May, crisply-formed intricate multi-petalled stars of pale pink

and cream. A cottage garden plant of much charm that will fit easily into almost any scheme. Does well in sun or in part-shade.

Athyrium

A large genus of ferns, many from the tropics.

A. filix-femina
Height: 36in/90cm Zone: 2
The lady fern, with distinguished upright finely pinnate leaves disposed like a shuttlecock. Good in moist soil in the shade. Propagate by spores or division.

A. niponicum var. *pictum*
Height: 12in/30cm Zone: 4
The Japanese painted fern has neatly formed upright triangular leaves suffused with silver and red. Does well in moist soil in the shade. Propagate by division.

Atriplex

Both herbaceous plants, annual and perennial, and shrubs are found in this genus.

A. halimus
Height: 6ft/1.8m Zone: 8
Beautiful semi-evergreen shrub with pale grey foliage making an excellent background. Best in full sun with sharp drainage. Flourishes in poor soil. Propagate by cuttings.

A. hortensis var. *rubra*
Height: 6ft/1./8m Zone: 6
A statuesque hardy annual which throws out handsome red-purple leaves, as large as 6in/10cm in length, oval and pointed. Best in good moist soil, in sun or semi-shade. Its bushiness can be encouraged by pinching out the top growth. Propagate by seed every year, and it may seed itself in congenial conditions.

Aubrieta

A genus of herbaceous perennials.

Aubrieta cultivars
Height around 6in/15cm, hardy to Zone 5. Garden aubrietas form a mound with trailing flower

stems bearing purple flowers in spring. Best in full sun with excellent drainage – flourishes in walls. Propagate by division.

A. deltoidea 'Aureovariegata'
Height: 3in/8cm Zone: 7
Hummock forming herbaceous perennial with pretty straggling veined violet flowers from spring onwards and creamy variegated foliage. Must have sun and good drainage. Propagate by division.

Barbarea
A genus of herbaceous plants.

B. vulgaris
Height: 36in/90cm Zone: 6
Wintercress, a weedy perennial with umbels of small yellow flowers in summer. Sun or semi-shade, moist soil. Propagate by seed.

Begonia
A huge and diverse genus.

Begonia cultivars
Up to 18in/45cm in height, hardy to Zone 10. Exist in a vast range – tuberous and rhizomatous. *Begonia* 'Cleopatra' has dusty pink flowers and delicate foliage.

Bellis
A genus of herbaceous plants.

B. perennis
Height: 1in/2.5cm Zone: 4
The common daisy which lawn perfectionists expend much effort in trying to kill. Several cultivars make pretty spring plants. Propagate by seed or by division. *B. p.* 'Alba Plena' has dazzling white fully double flowers. Much larger than the type, up to 4in/10cm. Needs moisture and does well in shade. Regular division encourages flowering.

Berberis
A genus of shrubs. Propagate by seed or cuttings.

B. × *stenophylla*
Height: 10ft/3m Zone: 5
Substantial shrub with diminutive

Bergenia 'Beethoven'

dark foliage, thorns and a profusion of golden yellow flowers borne along arching branches in late spring. Shining black fruit. Sun or part-shade, flourishes in dry conditions.

B. thunbergii
Height: 6ft/1.8m Zone: 5
Deciduous shrub with little yellow flowers and scarlet fruit. The foliage turns brilliant orange in autumn. The form *B. t. atropurpurea* has rosy purple foliage. *B. t. a.* 'Nana' is a valuable miniature cultivar, rising now more than 24in/60cm. *B. t.* 'Rose Glow' (6ft/1.8m) has plum-coloured leaves prettily splashed with white. All will flourish in sun or in part shade and may be propagated by cuttings.

Bergenia
A small genus of herbaceous perennials. Propagate by division.

Bergenia cultivars
Up to 15in/35cm high, all hardy to Zone 3. Very many cultivars exist. *B.* 'Beethoven' has substantial clusters of white flowers and sprightly red calyces in May or June.

B. ciliata f. *ligulata*
Height: 12in/30cm Zone: 7
Bold rounded leaves and pale pink flowers in early spring borne on fleshy upright stems. Moist soil in semi-shade.

B. cordifolia
Height: 18in/45cm Zone: 3
Rounded, glossy, evergreen foliage forms a permanent ornament with, in late winter, racemes of pink flowers. Does well in moist soil in shade, propagate by division.

Beta
The beet tribe, with some cultivars with strikingly ornamental foliage.

B. vulgaris 'Bull's Blood'
Height: 12in/30cm Zone: 5
A perennial in the wild but, where the fresh young foliage is the desired feature, best grown as an annual or biennial. Upright, fleshy, undulating leaves with a lustrous surface which, in this cultivar, are a dazzling deep purple. Best in rich, heavy soil in partial shade. Propagate by seed.

Betula
The birch genus of trees and shrubs.

B. ermanii
Height: 80ft/25m Zone: 2
Pale peeling bark and shining toothed leaves are the chief beauties of this distinguished Asian tree.

Bidens
This daisy-like genus is known in gardens for the single species described below.

B. ferulifolia
Height: 36in/90cm Zone: 8
Cheerful yellow-flowered perennial of borderline hardiness in all but the mildest gardens. Flowers in June and continuing deep into the autumn. The finely cut foliage, of an attractive grey-green, is also ornamental. Needs a sunny site and sharp drainage. Propagate by cuttings.

Borago

A genus of herbaceous plants.

B. officinalis
Height: 36in/90cm Zone: 7
An annual herb with hairy foliage and pretty blue flowers. Sun or part-shade. Propagate by seed.

B. pygmaea
Height: 24in/60cm Zone: 7
Perennial with pale blue bell-shaped flowers with white centre in summer. Needs sun and moist soil. Propagate by seed or division.

Bougainvillea

A genus of woody plants, some climbers.

Bougainvillea cultivars
Glamorous climber often seen swathing Mediterranean villas. Cultivars are almost all derived from *B. glabra* or *B. × buttiana* and grow up to 50ft/14m and are hardy to Zone 9. Available in many colours – white, purple, red, pink. Propagate by cuttings or layering. Needs rich soil and full sun. *B.* 'San Diego Red' is a beautiful rich blood red.

Brachyglottis

A genus of woody and herbaceous plants.

B. greyi
Height: 4ft/1.2m Zone: 9
Tender shrub with very decorative downy pale grey leaves followed by yellow daisies. Must have sharp drainage and a sunny position. Propagate by cuttings.

Brunnera

A genus of herbaceous perennials, all rhizomes.

B. macrophylla
Height: 18in/45cm Zone: 4
Felty heart-shaped leaves and little forget-me-not blue flowers in April. Flowers well in shade.

Brunnera macrophylla

Buddleja

A varied genus of herbs, shrubs and trees. Woody species are propagated by cuttings.

B. alternifolia 'Argentea'
Height: 10ft/3m Zone: 6
Forms a weeping shrub with a spectacular cascade of honey-scented lilac flowers in May. Slender pale grey leaves. Must have a sunny position.

B. 'Lochinch'
Height: 10ft/3m Zone: 7
A substantial shrub with beautiful pointed grey-green leaves. In July it produces racemes of honey-scented lilac flowers. Needs rich soil and sun.

Buphthalmum

Two species of herbaceous perennials.

B. salicifolium
Height: 36in/90cm Zone: 4
Bushy herbaceous perennial with splender pointed leaves and from June a profusion of sharp yellow star-shaped flowers. Best in sun, does well in poor soil. Propagate by seed or division.

Bupleurum

A genus of herbaceous and woody plants.

B. falcatum
Height: 36in/90cm Zone: 3
A herbaceous perennial with sickle-shaped leaves and fine panicles of diminutive cream flowers in mid summer. Propagate by division.

Buxus

A genus of evergreen woody plants. Propagate by cuttings.

B. microphylla var. *insularis*
Height: 36in/90cm Zone: 6
Spreading low-growing shrub with olive-green bronze-tinged foliage.

B. sempervirens
Height: 20ft/6m Zone: 6
Common box is the most valuable plant for hedges and topiary. Highly ornamental with its shining leaves and compact growth. Clip in late spring and late summer. Grows well in shade. *B. s.* 'Aureovariegata' has foliage marked with creamy-yellow giving a lively, fresh appearance. *B. s.* 'Argenteovariegata' has silver variegated leaves. *B. s.* 'Latifolia Maculata', known as 'the sunshine box', is a good cultivar, naturally forming a domed shape, up to 5ft/1.5m. Foliage a soft yellow when young becoming variegated in the summer and maintaining a golden cast even in winter. *B. s.* 'Suffruticosa', dwarf box, has tiny leaves and will grow very slowly to 36in/90cm but may be severely clipped to form a miniature hedge.

Calamintha

A genus of aromatic herbs. Propagate by division.

C. grandiflora
Height: 1ft/30cm Zone: 6
The leaves of the large-flowered calamint are heart-shaped and toothed, with pale green undersides and a mint-like scent. The flowers in June, lasting for weeks, are rich pink, tubular and hooded, like miniature snapdragons. Flourishes in poor soil in a sunny position. There is a white-flowered form, *C. g.* 'Alba'.

Canna indica 'Purpurea'

C. nepeta sbsp. *nepeta* (syn. *C. nepetoïdes*)
Height: 24in Zone: 6
A compact herbaceous perennial with little oval leaves smelling of mint. Spires of pink flowers appear in June. Needs sun and good drainage.

C. sylvatica
Height: 24in/60cm Zone: 6
The common calamint has mint-scented leaves and dark-spotted lilac tubular flowers in summer. Best in sun with good drainage.

Calendula
The marigolds, a genus of herbaceous plants.

C. officinalis
Height: 24in/60cm Zone: 6
Pot marigold is an annual with cheerful single or double yellow or orange flowers in summer. Many cultivars. Best in rich soil in full sun. Propagate by seed.

Calocephalus
An Australian genus of woody and herbaceous plants.

C. brownii
Height: 18in/45cm Zone: 9
Decorative little shrub with silver-white foliage and insignificant flowers in summer. Needs hot, dry position. Propagate by cuttings.

Caltha
A genus of herbaceous perennials. Propagate by seed or by division.

C. palustris
Height: 12in/30cm Zone: 3
The marsh marigold has fleshy rounded leaves and buttercup-like flowers in the summer of a dazzling golden yellow. Relishes shade and waterlogged soil.

Campanula
A genus of herbaceous plants. Propagate by division or by seed.

C. glomerata 'White Barn'
Height: 12in/30cm Zone: 3
A bellflower with short spikes of lively violet flowers. Needs sun and moist soil.

C. lactiflora
Height: 36in/90cm Zone: 5
Produces a profusion of elongated, bell-shaped blue flowers in the summer. Does well in sun or in semi-shade and is best in rich, moist soil. *C. l.* 'Loddon Anna' has soft pink flowers. *C. l.* 'Prichard's Variety' has violet-blue flowers.

C. latifolia
Height; 4ft/1.2m Zone: 4
Like a larger form of *C. lactiflora* but with purple-blue flowers. It self seeds vigorously. *C. l.* 'Brantwood' has especially fine rich violet flowers.

C. latiloba
Height: 36in/90cm Zone: 4
From a clump of oval basal leaves stiff flower stems are covered in cupped violet flowers in June. *C. l.* 'Highcliffe Variety' is a deeper colour with a pale eye.

C. persicifolia
Height: 36in/90cm Zone: 3
Upright stems of saucer-shaped flowers in June, a good clear violet-blue. *C. p. alba* is a pretty white form. Best in rich soil in a sunny position. *C. p.* 'Gawen' has semi-double flowers. Self seeds easily, cultivars may be divided.

C. rotundifolia var. *albiflora*
Height: 15in/35cm Zone: 3
The northern European harebell has beautiful silver-blue bell-shaped flowers on slender stems from late summer onwards. This is the equally beautiful white-flowered form. Sunny position, good drainage. Propagate by seed.

Canna
A genus of tender herbaceous perennials. Propagate by division.

Canna cultivars
Vary in height from 24in–5ft/60cm–1.5m and are hardy to Zone 8. Statuesque plants with exotically decorative foliage and glamorous flowers in late summer. *C.* 'Erebus' has creamy pink flowers. *C.* 'Louis Cayeux' has excellent pale pink flowers. *C.* 'Striata' has apricot-orange flowers and leaves magnificently striped in pale green and gold. Must have a warm, sunny position and rich soil.

C. indica 'Purpurea'
Height: 7ft/2m Zone: 8
Large canna with stately upright leaves flushed with purple and rich red flowers in late summer. Must have sun and rich soil.

Carex
A genus of grass-like herbaceous perennials.

C. comans bronze
Height: 15in/35cm Zone: 7
Forms dense tufts of wispy rather lax foliage of a distinguished bronze colour. Best in a moist position. Propagate by seed or division.

Ceanothus
A genus of woody plants.
Propagate by cuttings.

C. × delileanus 'Gloire de
Versailles'
Height: 12ft/3.6m Zone: 7
A froth of pale blue flowers,
sweetly scented, in high summer.
Must have sun and protection.
Makes a good wall plant.

C. thyrsiflorus var. *repens*
Height: 36in/90cm Zone: 8
Low-growing evergreen shrub
with small leaves and a profusion
of blue flowers in late spring.
Needs sun and good drainage.

Cedronella
A single species of herbaceous
perennial.

C. canariensis
Height: 5ft/1.5m Zone: 9
Whorls of lilac tubular flowers in
summer borne above cedar-
scented pointed leaves. Must have
sun and good drainage. Propagate
by seeds or cuttings.

Centaurea
A genus of chiefly herbaceous
plants. Propagate by seed or
division.

Centaurea cultivars
Around 24in/60cm high and
hardy to Zone 6. Many cultivars
of cornflowers grown as annuals
raised from seed. Need sun and
rich soil. *Centaurea* 'Black Ball'
has almost black spherical flowers.

C. cyanus
Height: 30in/75cm Zone: 5
The common cornflower is an
annual or biennial with piercing
blue flowers above glaucous
foliage. Best in full sun, needs
good drainage but succeeds in
poor soil. Propagate by seed.

C. hypoleuca 'John Coutts'
Height: 24in/60cm Zone: 5
A herbaceous perennial with very
decorative rich pink daisy-like
flowers. It needs sun and rich soil.

Centranthus ruber

C. montana alba
Height: 24in/60cm
Zone: 3
Perennial cornflower with narrow
leaves crowned in May or June by
crisp white thistle-like flowers.
Best in sun.

C. 'Pulchra Major' see *Leuzea
centauroides*.

Centranthus
A genus of herbaceous perennials.

C. ruber
Height: 36in/90cm Zone: 5
Very ornamental grey-green
foliage. Flowers in early summer
are pink or mauve and
occasionally a fine red. Loves sun
and good drainage where it will
self-seed. *C. r. albus* is a beautiful
white-flowered form.

Cephalaria
A genus of herbaceous plants.

C. gigantea
Height: 7ft/2m Zone: 5
A valuable border plant with
rather coarse toothed foliage and,
in June, pale yellow pincushion
flowers carried at the tips of tall
swaying stems.

Cerastium
A genus of herbaceous plants.

C. tomentosum
Height: 6in/15cm Zone: 4
A mat-forming perennial with fine
silver-grey foliage and quantities
of white single flowers from late
spring. Best in full sun in poor,
well-drained soil. Propagate by
division.

Chaenomeles
A genus of three species, but
many cultivars, of woody plants.

C. × superba 'Crimson and Gold'
Height: 5ft/1.5m Zone: 5
A shrub often trained on walls.
Blood red single flowers with
conspicuous golden anthers in
May. Best in rich soil in a sunny
position. Propagate by cuttings.

Chaerophyllum
A genus of umbellifers.

C. hirsutum 'Roseum'
Height: 36in/90cm Zone: 6
A herbaceous perennial with rosy
stems bearing in late summer
umbels of pink daisy-like flowers
above fine, ferny leaves.
Flourishes in semi-shade in poor
soil. Propagate by seed.

Chamaemelum
A genus of herbaceous plants.

C. nobile 'Flore Pleno'
Height: 12in/30cm Zone: 4
Spreading perennial with aromatic
leaves and button flowers in May,
white with creamy-yellow centre.
Best in sun and good drainage.
Propagate by division.

Chelidonium
A single species of herbaceous
perennial.

C. majus
Height: 24in/60cm Zone: 6
Greater celandine has lemon
yellow flowers in late spring above
decorative rich green leaves with
rounded lobes. Flourishes in
shade. Propagate by seed.

Cistus 'Silver Pink'

Chionodoxa
A genus of bulbs.

C. forbesii 'Pink Giant'
Height: 6in/15cm Zone: 4
March-flowering bulb with
star-shaped flowers in pale pink.
Best in moist soil in sun.
Propagate by division.

Choisya
A genus of shrubs.

C. ternata
Height: 6ft/1.8m Zone: 8
A distinguished evergreen shrub
with shining mid to dark green
aromatic leaves. Flowers from
spring onwards – single, white,
closely resembling orange blossom
but without the scent. Can be
clipped to shape. Sun or
semi-shade. Propagate by cuttings.

Cichorium
A genus of herbaceous plants.

C. intybus
Height: 40in/1m Zone: 3
The culinary chicory – a stately
herbaceous perennial with a
profusion of pale blue daisy-like
flowers in June. Propagate by seed
or division. *C. i. roseum* has chalk
pink flowers.

Cimicifuga
A genus of herbaceous plants.

C. racemosa
Height: 6ft/1.8m Zone: 4
Beautiful large deeply divided
leaves. White flowers, like
bottle-brushes, held high in late
summer. Needs rich moist soil in
part shade. Propagate by division.

Cirsium
A genus of herbaceous plants.

C. rivulare atropurpureum
Height: 5ft/1.5m Zone: 5
A tall thistle with deep crimson
flowers in high summer. Best in
sun, thrives in poor soil.
Propagate by seed or division.

Cistus
A genus of small shrubs.
Propagate by seed or cuttings.

Cistus cultivars
Range in height from
24–48in/60–120cm, hardy to
Zone 8. Flower from early
summer onwards. Must have sun
and sharp drainage, will grow in
poor soil. *C.* 'Doris Hibberson'
(24in/60cm) has pale pink flowers
becoming paler towards the
centre. *C.* 'Silver Pink'
(36in/90cm) has grey foliage and
striking pink-purple single
flowers.

Clematis
Essential climbing and herbaceous
plants. Cultivars propagated by
cuttings or layering, species by
seed.

C. 'Bill Mackenzie'
Height: 25ft/7.5m Zone: 5
Magnificent yellow-flowered
clematis flowering in summer
followed by silvery seed pots. Sun
or part-shade, rich soil.

C. campaniflora
Height: 20ft/6m Zone: 6
A delicate, slightly tender
clematis with pretty violet
hanging flowers in summer.

C. 'Comtesse de Bouchaud'
Height: 10ft/3m Zone: 6
The large mauve-pink flowers of
this clematis appear in early July,
a welcome addition to the late
summer scene. Good in part shade.

C. 'General Sikorski'
Height: 10ft/3m Zone: 6
Large mid-blue flowers with
crinkly margins in May or June.

C. 'Jackmannii Superba'
Height: 10ft/3m Zone: 6
Deep purple single flowers of
velvety texture are produced in
late summer.

C. × *jouiniana*
Height: 10ft/3m Zone: 4
A shrubby clematis with only
limited climbing tendencies.
Produces lavish panicles of mauve
and white flowers in late summer
or autumn. Does well in the shade.

C. 'Kermesina'
Height: 10ft/3m Zone: 6
A viticella clematis with wine-red
flowers in late summer.

C. 'Lasurstern'
Height: 10ft/3m Zone: 5
Large blue single flowers are
borne in May or June. Sun or
semi-shade.

C. 'Little Nell'
Height: 12ft/3.6m Zone: 6
Pale violet-blue flowers with paler
markings in summer. Flowers well
in part shade or in full sun.

C. macropetala
Height: 12ft/3.6m Zone: 5
Very beautiful spring-flowering
clematis with a profusion of
double violet-blue flowers.

C. 'Madame Julia Correvon'
Height: 15ft/4.5m Zone: 5
Beautiful vigorous clematis with
red flowers in high summer. Sun
or semi-shade, rich soil.

C. 'Minuet'
Height: 12ft/3.6m Zone: 5
Vigorous late-flowering clematis
with prettily mottled violet
flowers.

C. montana 'Superba'
Height: 20ft/6m Zone: 5
May-flowering with pink flowers,
sweetly scented. Best on a sunny
wall but will flower in shade.

C. orientalis
Height: 25ft/7.5m Zone: 6
Splendid late-summer hanging
bell-like lemon yellow flowers
followed by decorative seedheads.
Sun or semi-shade.

C. 'Royal Velours'
Height: 12ft/3.6m Zone: 6
Late-summer-flowering clematis
with small velvety very deep
purple flowers. Sun or
semi-shade, rich soil.

C. tangutica
Height: 20ft/6m Zone: 6
Vigorous, with lemon-yellow
flowers in late summer followed
by decorative silver seed heads.
Sun or part shade.

C. 'Victoria'
Height: 10ft/3m Zone: 6
Late-flowering clematis with
pink-purple flowers.

C. viticella
Height: 12ft/3.6m Zone: 5
Summer-flowering with elegant
purple flowers. Flowers well in
semi-shade.

C. 'Vyvyan Pennell'
Height: 10ft/3m Zone: 6
Glamorous large double lilac-blue
flowers in May.

Cleome
A genus of herbaceous plants.

Cleome cultivars
Decorative annuals derived from
the species *C. hassleriana*, rising
to a height of around 5ft/1.5m.
Bushy shape with flowers in a
bold cylindrical head – white,
violet, red or pink. Excellent
gap-fillers for late summer. Needs
sun. Propagate by seed.

Colutea
A genus of deciduous shrubs.

C. × *media*
Height: 10ft/3m Zone: 6
A substantial shrub with delicate
pinnate foliage and tawny or
orange flowers in summer
followed by decorative hanging
bladder-shaped pods. Sun or
semi-shade, good in a dry
position. Propagate by cuttings.

Convallaria
A genus of a single species.

C. majalis
Height: 10in/25cm Zone: 3
Lily-of-the-valley, an essential
plant for which any garden can
find space. Beautiful upright
undulating fleshy leaves and
exquisitely scented little flowers
in May. *C. m.* 'Rosea' has delicate
pale pink flowers. Best in shade in
rich soil. Propagate by division.

Cordyline
A genus of woody plants.

C. australis
Height: 70ft/20m Zone: 10
Tender tree grown in cooler
climates as a decorative pot plant.
Sheaves of sword-like evergreen
leaves. *C. a.* 'Atrosanguinea' has
bronze-tinged leaves. *C. a.*
Purpureus Group has plum-
coloured leaves. Needs full sun
and good drainage. Propagate by
seed or division.

Coreopsis
A genus of herbaceous plants.
Propagate by division.

C. lanceolata
Height: 24in/60cm Zone: 3
Attractive herbaceous perennial
with warm yellow flowers carried
on slender stems. Best in rich soil
in a sunny position.

C. verticillata 'Moonbeam'
Height: 24in/60cm Zone: 6
Herbaceous perennial with
lemon-yellow single daisies in
summer. Needs moist soil in sun.

Corydalis cheilanthifolia

Cornus
The dogwoods, a genus of shrubs
and trees.

C. mas
Height: 25ft/7.5m Zone: 5
The cornelian cherry is a
decorative small deciduous tree
with cheerful yellow flowers in
February. Narrow pointed leaves
take clipping well, sometimes seen
as a hedge. Pretty shining red
fruit in summer and warm yellow
Autumn colour.

Cortaderia
A genus of grasses.

C. selloana 'Aureolineata'
Height: 6ft/1.8m Zone: 5
Stately ornamental grass with
gracefully arching slender leaves
edged in gold followed by feathery
seedheads. Best in sun, any soil.
Propagate by division.

Corydalis
A genus of herbaceous plants.

C. cheilanthifolia
Height: 18in/45cm Zone: 6
Beautiful leaves, ferny and finely
cut forming a mound, with spikes
of yellow flowers in May.
Flourishes in moist soil in sun or
semi-shade. Self-sows with
abandon but not uncontrollably.

C. flexuosa
Height: 6in/15cm Zone: 7
From a hummock of decorative
finely-cut leaves intense blue
flowers emerge in April. *C. f.*

'China Blue' has chalk blue flowers flushed with pink. Best in a shady position in rich, moist soil. Propagate by division.

C. lutea
Height: 10in/25cm Zone: 6
This fumitory forms mounds of fresh pale green foliage with little yellow flowers, from May onwards. Best in moist soil, good in shade, seeds itself gently. May also be propagated by division.

C. ochroleuca
Height: 10in/25cm Zone: 6
Hummocks of finely divided glaucous foliage with creamy-white flowers from spring. Sun or shade, relishes moist soil. Propagate by division or seed.

Corylus
The hazels, trees and shrubs valuable for their nuts.

C. maxima 'Purpurea'
Height: 15ft/4.5m Zone: 5
Filbert cultivar with large rounded leaves of a lustrous deep purple. A big, bold background for spectacular planting. Propagate by cuttings.

Cosmos
A genus of chiefly herbaceous plants, annual and perennial.

C. atrosanguineus
Height: 18in/45cm Zone: 8
A decorative plant with single flowers on wiry stems, an astounding deep chocolate-brown. Far from hardy in northern gardens, needs well-drained soil in a sunny position in warm gardens. Good for pots overwintered in a greenhouse. Propagate by cuttings.

C. 'Purity'
Height: 36in/90cm Zone: 9
Half-hardy annual with dazzling pure white flowers produced over a long period of time. Feathery grey-green foliage is very decorative. Flowers best in a sunny position in rich soil. Propagate by seed.

Cotinus
A genus of woody plants.

C. coggygria
Height: 15ft/4.5m Zone: 5
The smoke-bush is a deciduous shrub with rounded bright green leaves. C. c. 'Royal Purple' has magnificent deep purple foliage, a wonderful background to other planting. Propagate by cuttings.

Cotoneaster
A genus of woody plants.

C. dammeri
Height: 8in/20cm Zone: 6
A creeping shrub whose branches root easily forming handsome groundcover. Pretty red berries in autumn. Sun or semi-shade.

C. horizontalis
Height: 36in/90cm Zone: 4
Deciduous sprawling shrub with curious fishbone-like branches. Dazzling scarlet berries and orange-red autumn colouring. Good in part shade. Propagate by cuttings.

Crataegus
A genus of trees and shrubs.

C. laevigata 'Paul's Scarlet'
Height: 20ft/6m Zone: 6
Hawthorn with especially pretty double deep-red flowers and attractive divided leaves. May be grafted and clipped to make a small decorative garden tree. It will flourish in sun or semi-shade.

Crocosmia
A genus of herbaceous perennials. Propagate by dividing the corms.

Crocosmia cultivars
Range in height from 24in–4ft/60cm–1.2m and are hardy to Zone 7. C. 'Custard Cream' (30in/75cm) has pale yellow flowers in July. C. 'Golden Fleece' (24in/60cm) is pale yellow-flowered, also known as C. 'Citronella'. Flowers in August continuing until the first frosts. C. 'Jackanapes' (24in/60cm) has flowers in August with red and

Crocosmia **'Golden Fleece'**

yellow-orange petals. C. 'Lucifer' (4ft/1.2m) is one of the boldest crocosmias with handsome leaves and brilliant deep scarlet flowers in July. C. 'Star of the East' (36in/90cm) has unusually large and beautifully shaped flowers, carried in sprays much more loosely formed than in most crocosmias – a sumptuous rich apricot-orange in late summer.

C. masoniorum
Height: 36in/90cm Zone: 7
This species still holds its own among all the new cultivars. Flowers in July, for many weeks, are a rich vermilion-orange and neatly formed.

Cuphea
A genus of herbaceous and woody plants.

C. ignea
Height: 36in/90cm Zone: 9
In its native Mexico this is a shrub but in colder gardens it is grown as an annual. Flowers in high summer are dazzling scarlet tubes tipped with a band of dark purple and white. Flowers throughout the season. Needs sun and rich soil.

x Cupressocyparis

A genus of evergreen trees, hybrids of the genera *Cupressus* and *Chamaecyparis*.

× *C. leylandii*
Height: 120ft/36m Zone: 4
A fast growing giant, quickly forming a tall pyramid. In limited space too vigorous for comfort, but takes quite kindly to being hacked about.

Cyclamen

Twenty species of tubers. Propagate by seed.

C. coum
Height: 3in/8cm Zone: 6
Winter- or early spring-flowering plant of great beauty with decorative prettily marked rounded leaves. Flowers a sprightly purple-pink or white. Does well in sun or shade.

C. hederifolium
Height: 3in/8cm Zone: 6
Exquisitely patterned ivy-shaped foliage in winter and beautiful flowers in late summer – sharp pink or white. Loves a shady position in moist soil but will flower in dry shade.

Cydonia

The quince, a single species with a few cultivars.

C. oblonga
Height: 25ft/7.5m Zone: 5
Excellent small ornamental deciduous tree for gardens. Decorative pinkish-white single flowers in April or May. Golden sweetly scented pear-shaped fruit. Needs a sunny open position. Propagate by cuttings. *C. oblonga* 'Portugal' has especially large pink flowers.

Cynoglossum

A genus of herbaceous plants.

C. officinale
Height: 36in/90cm Zone: 6
Handsome biennial with grey-green foliage and, in late spring, pretty deep purple single

Dahlia **'Arabian Night'**

flowers. Best in sun with good drainage. Propagate by seed.

Cyperus

A genus of grass-like plants.

C. papyrus
Height: 10ft/3m Zone: 9
The Egyptian paper reed has tall green stems with umbels of green and brown flowers like loose mops. Needs sun and much moisture – will grow in waterlogged soil. Propagate by seed or division.

Cytisus

A genus of shrubs or trees.

C. battandieri
Height: 15ft/4.5m Zone: 7
A shrub with silver leaves and golden racemes of flowers in May – scented with pineapple. Needs sun and may be trained on a wall in cooler places. Propagate by cuttings.

Dahlia

A genus of herbaceous plants.

Dahlia cultivars
All are hardy to Zone 8. Propagate by dividing the tubers. All flower in late summer and are best in rich soil in a sunny position. *D.* 'Arabian Night' (36in/90cm) is a magnificent deep red, almost black at the centre of its double flowers. *D.* 'Bednall Beauty' (24in/60cm)has semi-double flowers, an excellent rich red. *D.* 'Blaisdon Red' (40in/1m) has rich

scarlet flowers. *D.* 'Bishop of Llandaff' (known in the US as *D.* 'Japanese Bishop') grows to 36in/90cm. Scarlet semi-double flowers with handsome bronze-purple foliage. *D.* 'Chiltern Amber' (30in/75cm) has warm apricot-orange very double flowers. *D.* 'Ellen Houston' (36in/90cm) has large semi-double deep red flowers and finely cut bronze foliage.

Daphne

A small genus of shrubs.

D. acutiloba
Height: 5ft/1.5m Zone: 6
An evergreen shrub with narrow leaves and clusters of white flowers followed by scarlet berries. Sun or semi-shade. Propagate by cuttings.

D. × *burkwoodii* 'Somerset'
Height: 6ft/1.8m Zone: 5
A deciduous or sometimes evergreen shrub with narrow fresh green leaves and pink-flushed white flowers in spring marvellously scented. Best in the sun in a well-drained position. Propagate by cuttings.

Delphinium

A genus of herbaceous plants.

Delphinium cultivars
Up to 7ft/2m high, hardy to Zone 5. These all flower in June and need rich soil and full sun. *D.* 'Alice Artindale' (5ft/1.5m) has rich sky blue flowers in tall narrow spires. *D.* 'Conspicuous' (5ft/1.5m) has semi-double lilac-mauve flowers with dark eyes. *D.* 'Faust' (6ft/1.8m) has semi-double flowers of deep ultramarine overlaid with violet. *D.* Pacific Hybrids (6ft/1.8m) are grown as annuals or biennials, with very large blue, white or cream flowers. *D.* 'Pink Delight' (5ft/1.5m) has pale violet-pink semi-double flowers. *D.* 'Sungleam' (6ft/1.8m) has white and pale yellow flowers.

Dendranthema

A genus of herbaceous plants.

Dendranthema Hybrids
36in/90cm in height, hardy to
Zone 6. *D*. 'Clara Curtis' is a July
flowering single pink flowered
cultivar.

Dianthus

The pinks, carnations and Sweet
Williams are a genus of
herbaceous perennials.

Dianthus cultivars
In height around 4–9in/10–22cm,
hardy to Zone 3. Pinks hybridise
freely and, although some old
cultivar names are preserved, the
most frequently seen are unnamed
seedlings with white, pink or red
flowers, often attractively striped,
and decorative grey-green leaves.
Need good drainage and plenty of
sun. Good kinds can be
propagated by rooting offsets. Or
you can take potluck with seeds.

D. barbatus albus Nigrescens
Group
Height: 18in/45cm Zone: 6
Sweet William, a perennial
commonly grown as an annual.
Deep purple gleaming flowers in
summer. Needs rich soil in sun or
semi-shade. Propagate by seed.

Diascia

A genus of herbaceous perennials.

D. integerrima
Height: 18in/45cm Zone: 8
Slightly tender with pretty spires
of coral pink flowers from June.
Must have sun and good drainage.
propagate by division or seed.

Dicentra

A genus of herbaceous perennials.
Propagate by division.

Dicentra cultivars
Around 10in/25cm high, hardy to
Zone 4. *D*. 'Langtrees' has
feathery leaves and creamy-white
flowers in April or May. *D*.
'Stuart Boothman' has finely cut
glaucous-green foliage and
carmine pink tubular flowers in

Echinops ritro

April or May. Best in moist soil,
sun or part shade.

D. spectabilis
Height: 24in/60cm Zone: 3
From a bold clump of lime green
foliage the cheerful red hanging
flowers – bleeding hearts – appear
in April. Does well in moist soil in
part-shade. Even better is the
white cultivar *D. spectabilis* 'Alba'.

Dictamnus

A genus of a single species.

D. albus
Height: 36in/90cm Zone: 3
Herbaceous perennial with
decorative pinnate foliage and tall
spires of white flowers in May or
June. *D. a*. 'Purpureus' has
plum-pink flowers. Does well in
semi-shade but needs rich soil.
Propagate by division.

Digitalis

The foxglove genus, several
species of herbaceous plants.

D. purpurea
Height: 6ft/1.8m Zone: 6
A statuesque biennial which
produces in May spires of tubular
purple-pink flowers or, in the
form *D. p. albiflora*, a spanking
pure white. It will self-seed and
make a lovely ornament.

Dodonaea

A genus of tropical trees and
shrubs.

D. viscosa 'Purpurea'
Height: 7ft/2m Zone: 9
A distinguished shrub with
rosy-purple foliage and decorative
winged seed-capsules. Outside
tropics needs greenhouse and
plenty of feeding.

Dryopteris

A genus of ferns.

D. affinis 'Pinderi'
Height: 30in/75cm Zone: 6
Elegant evergreen fern with
upright shuttlecock foliage.
Excellent in moist soil in shade.
Propagate by spores or by division.

Echinops

A genus of herbaceous plants.

E. ritro
Height: 4ft/1.2m Zone: 3
Deep blue flowers, like rounded
thistles, held on stiff pale stems,
appearing in July and remaining
decorative for many weeks. It is
best in a sunny position.
Propagate by seed or division.

Echium

A genus of herbaceous and woody
plants.

E. vulgare
Height: 12in/30cm Zone: 7
A biennial with pretty white, pink
or purple flowers over a long
period in the summer. Must have
a sunny position, self seeds.

Elaeagnus

A small genus of woody plants.
Propagate by cuttings.

E. pungens 'Maculata'
Height: 8ft/2.5m Zone: 7
Evergreen shrub with foliage
splashed with golden-yellow. Sun
or semi-shade in rich soil.

E. 'Quicksilver'
Height: 10ft/3m Zone: 5
A dazzling shrub with narrow
silver-grey foliage and

sweetly-scented little yellow flowers in June. Sun or semi-shade, any soil that is not waterlogged.

Epimedium

A genus of herbaceous plants. Propagate species by seed, cultivars by division.

E. grandiflorum
Height: 16in/40cm Zone: 5
Long heart-shaped leaves, edged with bronze-red, overlap to form a wave of decorative foliage. Tiny flowers in summer, white or red. *E. g.* 'Nanum' has good white flowers. Excellent in shade.

E. × rubrum
Height: 12in/30cm Zone: 5
Forms a spreading clump with, in late spring, red and yellow flowers. Good in part shade, moist, rich soil.

Erodium

A genus of herbaceous plants.

E. chrysanthum
Height: 6in/15cm Zone: 7
Forms a handsome cushion of grey-green foliage covered in early summer with the palest yellow papery single flowers. Must have sun and good drainage. Propagate by seed or division.

Eryngium

The sea-hollies, a genus of herbaceous plants. Propagate by seed or by division.

E. alpinum
Height: 24in/60cm Zone: 5
A most beautiful sea-holly with dazzling metallic-blue flowers as intricate as a Renaissance jewel carried above heart-shaped foliage. Best in sun in rich soil.

E. bourgatii
Height: 18in/45cm Zone: 5
The leaves are metallic grey-green, finely mottled, above which rise in June thistle-like violet flowers. Needs sun and well-drained soil. *E. b.* 'Oxford Blue' has deeper blue flowers.

Eryngium giganteum

E. giganteum
Height: 4ft/1.2m Zone: 6
A perennial that flowers once only and then dies – but obligingly scatters its seed. Silver thistle leaves with a dark flower head. Best in sun, with good drainage, but flourishes in poor soil.

E. × tripartitum
Height: 36in/90cm Zone: 5
A wiry perennial with masses of violet thistle-like flowers in summer. Needs sun and good drainage.

E. × zabelii
Height: 18in/45cm Zone: 5
The flowers in June are a thrilling metallic blue with long, narrow, intricately jagged petals borne on blue stems. Best in full sun in well-drained soil.

Erysimum

The wallflower genus of herbaceous plants. Propagated by seed or cuttings.

Erysimum cultivars
To a height of around 24in/60cm, hardy to Zone 6. Perennials but are often grown as biennials. Bushy little plants, sometimes with handsome narrow grey-green leaves. Sun or semi-shade, fertile soil. *E.* 'Bowles' Mauve' has narrow grey-green foliage and warm mauve flowers. *E.* 'Cloth of Gold' has flowers of glowing yellow. *E.* 'Wenlock Beauty' has rich caramel and purple flowers.

E. cheiri
Height: 30in/75cm Zone: 7
A short-lived subshrub with deliciously scented yellow or orange-brown flowers in upright racemes in spring. Flourishes in poor soil, must have sun and sharp drainage. Propagate by seed.

Eschscholzia

A genus of poppies. Propagate by seed.

E. californica
Height: 12in/30cm Zone: 6
Lavish flowers of warm golden yellow or apricot orange in June, best grown as annuals. The leaves are attractive, glaucous green and feathery. Must have sun and will flourish in thin dry soil. *E. californica* 'Alba' is a good creamy-white cultivar.

Eucalyptus

A genus of trees and shrubs. Propagate by seed.

E. globulus
Height: 200ft/60m Zone: 9
One of the grandest of the gums with pale smooth bark and lovely curving glaucous leaves. In cooler places may be grown as conservatory pot plant or bedded out in summer.

E. gunnii
Height: 80ft/25m Zone: 8
A substantial tree with decorative glaucous-grey foliage which, when young, is pierced by the leaf stems. Needs a protected position.

Eucomis

A genus of bulbs.

E. bicolor
Height: 18in/45cm Zone: 8
Broad undulating leaves with a marvellous varnished surface. A fleshy stem produces in late summer a curious pineapple-like pale-green flower, crowned with a tuft of leaves. Needs best-drained sunniest position you can give it. Excellent in pots, where its statuesque character is seen at its

best, or used as a bedding plant.
Propagate by seed or by division.

Eupatorium

A genus of herbaceous plants.
Propagate by division.

E. purpureum
Height: 8ft/2.5m Zone: 4
Joe Pye weed is a giant perennial
with coarse leaves and bold
corymbs of purple-pink flowers on
stiff purple-tinged stems in
summer. Best in alkaline soil, does
well in semi-shade – invasive in
rich, moist soil. *E. p.*
'Atropureum' is a good dark-
flowered cultivar.

E. rugosum
Height: 5ft/1.5m Zone: 6
Perennial with bold upright habit
with large oval pointed leaves. In
late summer the flowers appear,
substantial corymbs of putty-
coloured flowerlets. Best in heavy
soil, in sun or shade.

Euphorbia

A genus of herbaceous and woody
plants.

E. characias sbsp. *wulfenii*
Height: 36in/90cm Zone: 7
Herbaceous perennial with
glaucous foliage and plump yellow
flower heads like giant
bottle-brushes in spring. Sun or
semi-shade, any soil. Self-seeds.

E. cyparissias
Height: 12in/30cm Zone: 4
Lively lime green flowers in
spring. For the wild garden only –
in tamer places, especially in
moist soil, it will take over.

E. dulcis 'Chameleon'
Height: 18in/45cm Zone: 5
A low-growing bushy spurge with
splendid plum-purple foliage. Cut
foliage back in spring for late
summer display. Best in moist soil.

E. griffithii 'Fireglow'
Height: 24in/60cm Zone: 4
The orange-brown flowers emerge
in May, erupting from fleshy
stems and remain for weeks above

Euphorbia griffithii
'**Fireglow**'

pale green foliage. It is handsome
but dreadfully invasive – easily
propagated by division.

E. stricta
Height: 12in/30cm Zone: 6
Biennial with elegant red wiry
stems and red-brown seed
capsules. Easy to please.

Fagus

The beeches, a genus of deciduous
trees.

F. sylvatica
Height: 150ft/48m Zone: 5
The common beech, an ornament
of the landscape, also makes a
superb garden hedge, keeping its
russet foliage through the winter.
F. s. 'Purpurea Pendula' is a
weeping form with glistening
purple foliage. Propagate by
cuttings.

Fallopia

A genus of herbaceous plants.

F. japonica 'Spectabilis'
Height: 6ft/1.8m Zone: 4
The Japanese knotweed, a plant of
thuggish disposition. Jointed
fleshy stems bear creamy-white
flowers. Pink leaves splashed with
yellow. Needs moist soil, best in
semi-shade. Propagate by division.

Ficus

The figs, a genus of woody plants.

F. carica
Height: 25ft/7.5m Zone: 7
The common fruiting fig, with
huge palm-shaped deciduous
leaves. Needs plenty of sun to
ripen fruit, best in alkaline or
neutral soil. Propagate by
cuttings. Most frequently seen in
the cultivar *F. c.* 'Brown Turkey'.

Filipendula

A genus of herbaceous perennials.
Propagate by division.

F. purpurea
Height: 4ft/1.2m Zone: 4
Bold leaves and profuse pink-red
flowers in summer borne in flat
corymbs. Best in moist soil in the
shade.

F. rubra
Height: 7ft/2m Zone: 2
Above deeply cut pointed leaves
immense flower stems rise
crowned in summer with pink
corymbs of flowers. Dramatic but
invasive, especially in moist soil.

F. ulmaria 'Variegata'
Height: 4ft/1.2m Zone: 2
A form of meadow sweet with
yellow variegated foliage.
Sweetly-scented panicles of
creamy-white flowers in summer.
Best in sun in rich soil.

Foeniculum

A genus of a single species.

F. vulgare
Height: 6ft/1.8m Zone: 6
Fennel, a herbaceous perennial
with billowing veils of fine foliage
and delicious scent of aniseed. It
combines statuesque presence
with airy insubstantiality. Highly
invasive, scattering its fertile seed
with abandon. Best in full sun but
will flourish in poor soils. The
bronze-leafed cultivar *F. v.*
'Purpureum' is very pretty.

Fragaria
A genus of herbaceous plants.

F. vesca 'Flore Pleno'
Height: 8in/20cm Zone: 5
The wild strawberry, with fresh
green leaves and, in this form,
pretty double white flowers in late
spring. Sun or part shade, moist
soil. Propagate by runners.

Fuchsia
A large genus of woody plants.
Propagate by cuttings.

F. × colensoi
Height: 6ft/1.8m Zone: 9
Tender New Zealand fuchsia with
lustrous blue-maroon and green
hanging flowers in summer.

F. magellanica
Height: 10ft/3m Zone: 6
A shapely deciduous bush with
hanging red and purple flowers in
summer. Flowers in part shade.

Galactites
A genus of herbaceous plants.

G. tomentosa
Height: 36in/90cm Zone: 5
A plant with spiny stems and
violet thistle-like flowers. It will
seed itself in sunny places.

Galega
A genus of herbaceous perennials.
Propagate by division.

Galega 'Lady Wilson'
Height: 5ft/1.5m Zone: 4
An old cultivar with mauve-pink
flowers in June. Needs sun and
rich soil.

G. officinalis
Height: 4ft/1.2m Zone: 4
Flowers in June, a profusion of
pea-like flowers, lavender or
almost white in colour. *G. o.*
'Alba' has chalk-white flowers.
Needs sun but thrives in poor soil.
May need support.

Geranium
The cranesbills, a genus of mostly
herbaceous plants. Propagate by
division.

Geranium psilostemon

G. 'Ann Folkard'
Height: 36in/90cm Zone: 5
Upright, bushy cranesbill with
dazzling flowers – an intense
magenta with a striking black
centre, starting in May or June
and flowering for weeks. Best in a
sunny site in rich soil.

G. clarkei 'Kashmir White'
Height: 9in/23cm Zone: 7
Handsome leaves, deeply divided
with pointed lobes. The flowers in
May are white, etched with grey
veins held high above the foliage.
Sun or part shade, relishes moist
soil where it will sow itself.

G. endressii
Height: 18in/45cm Zone: 5
Dark green leathery little leaves
form the background to delicately
veined rose-pink flowers in May
and continuing for months. Best
in sun in rich soil.

G. himalayense 'Plenum'
Height: 6in/15cm Zone: 4
The flowers in May or June are
fully double, of a vivid
purple-blue, borne on long
trailing stems. Finely cut leaves.

G. 'Johnson's Blue'
Height: 12in/30cm Zone: 5
The leaves are very finely cut, and
the flowers from May onwards for
months are lavender-blue with a
pale eye. Forms a handsome
billowing cushion of leaves at least
twice as wide as it is tall.

G. macrorrhizum
Height: 9in/23cm Zone: 4
A spreading cranesbill with
curiously pungent smell with
small pale pink flowers in May.
Brilliant autumn colour.
Flourishes in dry shade. *G. m.*
'Album' has white flowers.

G. maculatum
Height: 30in/75cm Zone: 4
Palm-shaped spotted leaves with,
in early summer, little violet
flowers with curved-back petals
carried well above. Good in shade,
relishes rich soil.

G. × magnificum
Height: 24in/60cm Zone: 4
Bold rounded and well-divided
hairy leaves are crowned with rich
purple-blue flowers in May.

G. phaeum
Height: 30in/75cm Zone: 5
Above deeply divided leaves tall
flowering stems carry little
maroon single flowers from May
onwards. The best forms have
very dark flowers. Best in shade
and enjoys heavy moist soil. *G. p.*
'Album' has white flowers.

G. pratense
Height: 48in/120cm Zone: 4
The common European field
cranesbill with boldly divided
foliage and flowers in June, a soft
violet-blue. Many cultivars: *G. p.*
'Mrs Kendall Clark' has flowers of
a ghostly pale colour with silver
veins; *G. p.* 'Plenum Album' has
chalk-white flowers; *G. p.*
'Plenum Violaceum' has fully
double flowers of rich violet.

G. psilostemon
Height: 4ft/1.2m Zone: 6
Finely cut foliage and flowers of
dazzling magenta with black eyes
are the great qualities of this
cranesbill. The flowers start in
June but continue for weeks. Full
sun in rich soil.

G. 'Salome'
Height: 12in/30cm Zone: 6
A brilliant small geranium with
deep violet flowers and a black

central eye. Flowers in June. It must have sun.

G. sanguineum var. *striatum*
Height: 8in/20cm Zone: 5
Neat little cranesbill with finely-lobed foliage of an attractive grey-green. Flowers in May are a beautiful pale silver-pink, laced with darker veins. Self-seeds benignly.

G. sessiliflorum sbsp. *novae-zelandiae*
Height: 10in/25cm Zone: 8
Beautiful brown-green rounded leaves, with little pale pink or almost white flowers in June. In the hybrid *G. s.* sbsp. *n.-z.* 'Nigricans' × *traversii* the leaves are a handsome grey-brown with a silvery overcolour. Needs very sharp drainage and full sun.

G. wallichianum 'Buxton's Variety'
Height: 8in/20cm Zone: 4
Flowers violet blue with a pale, almost white, eye, starting in July but continuing to November, borne on long straggling stems. The felty, slightly mottled leaves are beautiful. Seeds itself but may not come true – its identity can be preserved by division. Flower well in sun or slight shade.

Geum
A genus of herbaceous plants.

Geum cultivars
6in/15cm in height, hardy to Zone 6. The leaves are rounded and lobed, forming a vigorous clump. Flowers in June are carried on tall wiry stems 12in/30cm long. Propagate by division. *G.* 'Mrs J. Bradshaw' has double crimson flowers in the shape of rosettes. *G.* 'Princess Juliana' has vivid orange double flowers.

Gladiolus
A genus of herbaceous perennials.

G. 'The Bride'
Height: 24in/60cm Zone: 8
This coolly beautiful gladiolus has white flowers in late spring or

Helenium 'Moerheim Beauty'

early summer, elegantly shaped trumpets. Needs plenty of sun and good drainage. Good in pots. Propagate by division.

Gunnera
A genus of herbaceous perennials.

G. manicata
Height: 7ft/2m Zone: 7
A spectacular foliage plant with giant rhubarb-like leaves, as wide as 6ft/1.8m across. Flourishes in the shade but needs a protected place and very moist soil. Propagate by division.

Gypsophila
A genus of herbaceous plants.

G. elegans
Height: 18in/45cm Zone: 5
Decorative annual with clouds of profuse little white flowers in early summer. Best in sun, rich soil. Propagate by seed.

G. repens
Height: 8in/20cm Zone: 4
Perennial forming a mound of glaucous leaves with little panicles of pink or white flowers in summer. Needs sharp drainage and sun. Propagate by division.

Hebe
A genus of evergreen shrubs.

H. topiaria
Height: 36in/90cm Zone: 6
Fleshy leaves with small white flowers in summer. Best in sun. Propagate by cuttings.

Hedera
The ivy genus of climbers. Propagate by cuttings or layering.

H. algeriensis 'Gloire de Marengo'
Height: 20ft/6m Zone: 8
A slightly tender ivy with magnificent pale green leaves splashed with cream.

H. colchica 'Dentata Variegata'
Height: 10ft/3m Zone: 6
Vigorous and very decorative ivy with floppy heart-shaped leaves finely edged and splashed with pale cream. Any soil, flourishes and looks very good in semi-shade.

Hedychium
The ginger genus, a small group of tropical rhizomes.

H. flavescens
Height: 10ft/3m Zone: 10
Tender perennial with handsome fleshy leaves and large spikes of yellow flowers in late summer. Must have a warm, sunny position in rich soil. Propagate by division.

Helenium
A genus of herbaceous plants.

Helenium cultivars
All hardy to Zone 5. *H.* 'Moerheim Beauty' (36in/90cm) has orange-russet flowers with chocolate centres; *H.* 'Riverton Beauty' (36in/90cm) has red flowers streaked with yellow; *H.* 'Sunshine' (24in/60cm) has clear yellow flowers; *H.* 'Wyndley' (36in/90cm tall) has deep golden yellow flowers. All best in rich soil in a sunny position. Propagate by division.

Helianthemum
A genus of woody plants.

Helianthemum cultivars
Rockroses are small evergreen shrubs hardy to Zone 7 and up to 36in/90cm in height. Rose-like miniature flowers borne in profusion from early summer onwards – white, yellow, red or orange. Best in full sun with good drainage. Propagate by cuttings.

H. nummularium
Height: 6in/15cm Zone: 6
Mat-forming low-growing shrub
with grey leaves and sharp yellow
flowers from late spring onwards.
Propagate by cuttings.

Helianthus
A genus of herbaceous plants.

H. 'Lemon Queen'
Height: 5ft/1.5m Zone: 3
Lemon yellow perennial
sunflower. Needs heavy soil and
full sun. Propagate by division.

Helichrysum
A genus of herbaceous and woody
plants.

H. italicum
Height: 24in/60cm Zone: 8
An aromatic shrub with curry-like
scent. Very narrow leaves, silver
grey in colour and yellow flowers
in summer. Best in well-drained
soil in the sun. Short-lived but
easily propagated by cuttings.

H. petiolare
Height: 36in/90cm Zone: 10
Tender trailing plant with
rounded grey-green leaves, white
underneath. Needs sun and good
drainage. Propagate by cuttings.

Heliotropium
A genus of herbaceous and woody
plants.

H. arborescens
Height: 7ft/2m Zone: 10
The sweetly-scented cherry pie, a
shrub usually grown as a bedding
annual. Veined leaves and profuse
umbels of pale blue flowers from
June. Best grown in one of
numerous cultivars, especially if
scent is required, and propagated
by cuttings. *H. a.* 'Lord Roberts'
is a fine pale blue cultivar. Needs
rich soil in full sun.

Helleborus
A genus of herbaceous
perennials. Propagate by seed or
by division.

H. foetidus
Height: 36in/90cm Zone: 6
Beautiful palm-like fronds of
toothed leaves. Flowers in late
winter are green-yellow hanging
cups with a red margin. *H. f.*
'Wester Flisk' has beautiful
red-flushed stems. Good in shade
in poor, dry soil.

H. orientalis
Height: 18in/45cm Zone: 4
One of the most beautiful early
flowering plants, appearing in
February or March, with flowers
of creamy white, pink or deep
plum red. Best in rich soil and
will flourish in the shade.

Hemerocallis
The daylilies, a genus of
herbaceous perennials. Propagate
by division.

Hemerocallis cultivars
There is now an immense range of
these with white, yellow, orange,
red or purple flowers of varying
hues. They range in height from
around 8in/20cm to 4ft/1.2m.
They are best in rich soil in the
sun or semi-shade.

H. fulva
Height: 36in/90cm Zone: 4
An old and ornamental garden
plant this species has trumpet-
shaped flowers in July – a fine
rusty-orange with a yellow throat.

Hesperis
A genus of herbaceous perennials.

H. matronalis
Height: 6ft/1.8m Zone: 6
Narrow, pointed leaves and violet
flowers in May with a fabulous,
tropical scent. Best in moist soil
in semi-shade. *H. m. albiflora* is a
beautiful white flowered form.
Propagate by division.

Heuchera
A genus of herbaceous perennials.

H. micrantha
Height: 24in/60cm Zone: 5
The leaves are rounded, vaguely
heart-shaped which form an

Helleborus foetidus

overlapping clump from which the
insignificant white flowers rise. It
flourishes in sun or in part-shade
and should be propagated by
division. *H. m.* 'Pewter Veil' has
beautiful silver-frosted leaves
with red veins. *H. m.* var.
diversifolia 'Palace Purple' has
dark purple-bronze leaves.

Hieracium
A genus of herbaceous plants.

H. sanguinea
Height: 24in/60cm Zone: 4
A herbaceous perennial with
pretty round lobed leaves and
little spires of red flowers from
spring onwards. Good in part
shade. Propagate by division.

H. waldsteinii
Height: 12in/30cm Zone: 6
A perennial with lemon yellow
flowers in summer. Relishes sun
and poor soil. Propagate by seed.

Homalanthus
A genus of tender woody plants.

H. populifolius
Height: 15ft/4.5m Zone: 10
The Queensland poplar has
evergreen rounded poplar-like
leaves flushed with red as they
age. Racemes of yellow flowers in
summer. Good pot plant for the

Propagate by cuttings.

Hosta
A genus of herbaceous perennials.
Propagate by division. All are best
in moist soil and shade or
semi-shade.

Hosta cultivars
Range in height from 12in/30cm
to 48in/1.2m and all are hardy to
Zone 3. *H.* 'Honeybells'
(24in/60cm) has lime green
ribbed foliage with pale violet
flowers in July. *H.* 'Krossa Regal'
(48in/1.2m) has bold vertical
glaucous-green foliage and deep
violet-blue flowers in July.

H. crispula
Height: 30in/75cm Zone: 5
With finely undulating edges to
its long slender leaves, and
exceptionally decorative waving
white margins, this is one of the
most ornamental of hostas.

H. fortunei
Height: 12in/30cm Zone: 5
Pale green undulating leaves,
narrow and pointed, are held in
shapely bunches. *H. f.* var.
albopicta has lime green leaves
striated with paler markings. *H. f.*
var. *aureomarginata* has gold
markings.

H. plantaginea
Height: 24in/60cm Zone: 3
Heart-shaped leaves followed in
late summer by plumes of
sweetly-scented white trumpet
flowers.

H. sieboldiana
Height: 2ft/24in Zone: 3
The striking heart-shaped leaves
of this hosta are curved and finely
ribbed. The flowers, rather
wishy-washy violet, appear in
June. The form *H. s.* var.*elegans*
adds a blueish cast to the foliage.

H. undulata
Height: 18in/45cm Zone: 6
A mound of pointed undulating
leaves, marked with a central area
of creamy white. Unexciting pale
mauve flowers in summer. *H. u.*

Hosta sieboldiana

albomarginata (syn. *H.* 'Thomas
Hogg') has more rounded leaves
with white margins.

Humulus
A genus of two twining plants.

H. lupulus 'Aureus'
Height: 15ft/4.5m Zone: 5
Flamboyant climber with large
lime-green vine-like leaves. Best
in rich soil, sun or semi-shade.
Propagate by division.

Hyacinthoides
Four species of bulbs.

H. hispanica
Height: 18in/45cm Zone: 5
The Spanish bluebell with fleshy
stems and pale or mid-blue bell-
shaped flowers in April. Good in
shade, relishes rich, heavy soil.
Propagate by division.

Hydrangea
A genus of woody plants.
Propagate by cuttings or layering.

H. anomala petiolaris
Height: 36ft/10.8m Zone: 5
A deciduous self-supporting
climber of subdued beauty with
corymbs of green-cream flowers in
April and May. Does well on a
shady wall, and foliage turns a
fine yellow before falling.

H. aspera
Height: 12ft/3.6m Zone: 7
A large and aristocratic deciduous
shrub with magnificent felty
leaves, shapely and pointed. In

late summer the flowers appear,
corymbs of pink-purple. Does
well in part shade.

H. macrophylla
Height: 6ft/1.8m Zone: 6
A deciduous shrub with toothed
pale green leaves and corymbs of
blue or pink. Rich moist soil and
shade. Propagate by cuttings. *H.
m.* 'Brussels Lace' has small,
neatly formed white flowers borne
on open corymbs. *H. m.* 'Veitchii'
has white flowers which become
pink as they age.

H. sargentiana
Height: 10ft/3m Zone: 7
Huge dark leaves, oval and
pointed and up 10in/25cm long,
are the great feature of this stately
shrub. Corymbs of white flowers
in July. Does well in part shade.

Hypericum
A genus of woody and herbaceous
plants.

H. × *inodorum* 'Summer Gold'
Height: 36in/90cm Zone: 8
A deciduous shrub with gold
foliage and tufted yellow flowers
in June followed by red fruit.
Does well in semi-shade.
Propagate by cuttings.

Iberis
A genus of herbaceous plants and
subshrubs.

I. saxatilis
Height: 4in/10cm Zone: 6
Candytuft is a low-growing
subshrub which produces from
late spring onwards a profusion of
white flowers. Best in sun with
sharp drainage. Propagate by
cuttings.

Ilex
The holly genus of woody plants.
Propagated by seed or by cuttings.

I. × *altaclerensis*
Height: 70ft/20m Zone: 6
A group of vigorous evergreen
hybrids with many good cultivars.
I. × *a.* 'Golden King' has
decorative leaves handsomely

edged in rich gold.

I. aquifolium
Height: 50ft/15m Zone: 7
With glossy spined leaves and
scarlet berries common holly is
one of the most decorative of
evergreens. Makes a beautiful
hedge. *I. a.* 'J.C. van Tol' is a
handsome spineless cultivar.

Inula
A genus of herbaceous plants.

I. hookeri
Height: 30in/75cm Zone: 6
A perennial with lemon yellow
flowers with a green tinge.
Relishes heavy rich soil where it
will colonize all too easily.
Propagate by division.

Ipomoea
A genus of herbaceous and woody
plants.

I. lobata (syn. *Mina lobata*)
Height: 15ft/4.5m Zone: 8
Tender trailing perennial with
brilliant little yellow and scarlet
flowers in high summer. Must
have sun and rich soil. Propagate
by seed.

Iris
A genus of herbaceous perennials.
Propagate by seed or by division.

Iris cultivars
Varying in height from 6in/10cm
to 5ft/1.5m, hardy to Zone 5. All
need sun and are propagated by
division. *I.* 'Jane Phillips' is a Tall
Bearded Iris with clear blue
ruffled flowers in April. *I.*
'Superstition' is a Tall Bearded
iris with black-purple flowers in
April. *I.* 'Tropic Night' is an *I.*
sibirica type with deep
plum-coloured flowers.

I. ensata
Height: 36in/90cm Zone: 7
The Japanese water iris is a stately
plant with rich purple flowers. *I.*
e. 'Rose Queen' is pink and frilly.
Excellent in part shade and exists
in countless cultivars.

I. foetidissima
Height: 30in/75cm Zone: 6
The stinking iris has curious
violet-brown flowers in May and
pungent smell when the leaves are
bruised. Handsome scarlet berries
carried into winter on dead stems.

I. orientalis
Height: 5ft/1.5m Zone: 8
This rather tender iris is among
the most beautiful, with
magnificent yellow-tinged white
flowers in June. Striking
sword-like leaves.

I. pseudoacorus
Height: 4ft/1.2m Zone: 5
The water flag has golden yellow
flowers in May half-concealed by
magnificent stiff leaves. *I. p.*
'Varicgata' is edged with silver.

I. sibirica
Height: 24in/60cm Zone: 4
The Siberian iris must have moist
soil. Flowers in May are a deep
rich purple and the slender leaves
are decorative. An essential
water-side plant.

I. tectorum
Height: 12in/30cm Zone: 5
Striking upright sheafs of leaves
are ornamented with crested lilac
flowers in April. Does well in
semi-shade.

Jasminum
A genus of shrubs and climbers.
Propagate by cuttings or layering.

J. humile 'Revolutum'
Height: 7ft/2m Zone: 8
A slightly tender semi-evergreen
shrub with slender leaves and
fragrant yellow flowers in
summer. Needs sun and rich soil.

J. nudiflorum
Height: 10ft/3m Zone: 6
In winter the cheerful yellow
flowers of this jasmine are a lovely
sight. Grow in a sunny position
and cut back after flowering.

J. officinale
Height: 30ft/9m Zone: 7
Twining plant with small white
flowers in high summer of

intense, tropical fragrance. It
must have sun. *J. o.*
'Argenteovariegatum' has white
variegated foliage.

Juniperus
Genus of evergreen trees and
shrubs.

J. procumbens
Height: 30in/75cm Zone: 8
Japanese spreading juniper with
fresh green foliage. Pretty
structural and ground-cover plant.
Good in semi-shade. propagate by
seed or cuttings.

Kirengeshoma
A genus of a single species.

K. palmata
Height: 6ft/1m Zone: 5
The leaves of this handsome
Japanese plant are rounded with
pointed lobes. Late in the summer
it produces beautiful pale yellow
trumpet flowers borne on dark
stems. Must have shade and moist
rich soil. Propagate by division.

Knautia
A genus of herbs.

K. macedonica
Height: 24in/60cm Zone: 6
The flowers are brilliant
pin-cushions of deep purple-red

Iris sibirica

carried on long stems above fine grey foliage. They start in June but continue for months. Needs sun and a well-drained position.

Kniphofia

The red-hot pokers are a genus of rhizomatous perennials. Propagate by division. Need sun and rich soil.

Kniphofia cultivars
Range in height between 24in–6ft/60cm–1.8m and are hardy to Zones 6–8. *K.* 'Erecta' (36in/90cm) has rich coral red flowers. *K.* 'Sunningdale Yellow' (30in/75cvm) is creamy-yellow and flowers from June onwards for a long period.

K. uvaria 'Nobilis'
Height: 6ft/1.8m Zone: 6
Huge and spectacular poker with tomato-red bottle-brush flowers in August continuing for weeks.

Lablab

A single species of herbaceous perennial.

L. purpureus
Height: 20ft/6m Zone: 9
Decorative climbing bean with striking purple or white flowers and deep purple beans. Needs rich soil, good drainage and plenty of sun. Propagate by seed.

Lamium

A genus of herbaceous plants. Propagate by seed or by division.

L. maculatum
Height: 8in/20cm Zone: 4
The leaves are nettle-like, heart-shaped splashed with occasional white stripes. Flowers in spring are pink-purple. Does well in dry shade. *L. m.* 'Beacon Silver' has mauve and silver leaves. *L. m.* 'White Nancy' has silver-grey leaves edged in green. *L. m.* 'Wootton Pink' has frosted foliage with very pale pink flowers.

Lathyrus latifolius

Lathyrus

A genus of herbaceous plants. Propagate by seed or division.

L. aureus
Height: 30in/75cm Zone: 6
Herbaceous perennial with decorative golden-brown flowers in early summer. Best in rich soil in a sunny position.

L. latifolius
Height: 6ft/1.8m Zone: 5
A scrambling perennial with flowers in June lasting for weeks, a lively carmine-pink. Sun or semi-shade, propagate by seed or division. *L. l.* 'White Pearl' has large white flowers.

L. odoratus
Height: 8ft/2.5m Zone: 7
The sweet pea – from which all modern cultivars are derived – has lovely plum and maroon flowers and a marvellous scent. Needs rich feeding and plenty of sun.

Lavandula

The lavender genus of aromatic shrubs. Propagate by cuttings.

L. angustifolia
Height: 24in/60cm Zone: 6
Both the narrow grey leaves and spikes of violet-blue flowers in May or June are deliciously aromatic. Needs well drained soil in the sun, short-lived but easily propagated by cuttings. Makes an admirable informal hedge. *L. a.* 'Hidcote' has paler foliage and deeper violet flowers.

L. × *intermedia* 'Alba'
Height: 30in/75cm Zone: 5
Many old lavenders have been gathered together under this hybrid name. *L.* × *intermedia* 'Alba' Old English Group is vigorous with tall racemes of rich violet flowers.

L. stoechas sbsp. *pedunculata*
Height: 18in/45cm Zone: 8
Tender French lavender with striking long indigo bracts and grey aromatic foliage. Needs sharp drainage and sun.

Laurus

Two species of aromatic shrubs.

L. nobilis
Height: 10ft/3m Zone: 9
A tender shrub with magnificent richly pungent grey-green leaves with crinkled edges. It must have sun and good drainage. It is propagated by cuttings.

Leonotis

A genus of herbaceous plants.

L. nepetifolia
Height: 4ft/1.2m Zone: 8
Annual with toothed heart-shaped leaves and bunches of scarlet tubular flowers in late summer. Fast growing in moist soil in a sunny position. Propagate by seed.

Leucanthemum

A genus of herbaceous plants. Propagated by division or by seed.

L. × *superbum*
Height: 36in/90cm Zone: 5
The shasta daisies flourish in sun or in part shade and are best in rich soil. *L.* × *s.* 'Shaggy' has splendid heavy white mop-heads with spindly twisting petals.

Leuzea

A genus of herbaceous plants.

Leuzea centauroides (formerly *Centaurea* 'Pulchra Major')
Height: 36in/90cm Zone: 7
Glaucous-green leaves with pretty thistle-like flowers in June – pale golden buds turning into

mauve-pink shavingbrushes.
Needs sun and good drainage,
Propagate by seed or division.

Levistichum
A single species.

L. officinale
Height: 6ft/1.8m Zone: 4
A statuesque herbaceous perennial
with decorative divided leaves and
a strong scent of celery. Best in
moist soil, in sun or part shade.
Propagate by seed or division.

Ligularia
A genus of herbaceous perennials.
Propagate by division or by seed.

L. dentata 'Desdemona'
Height: 4ft/1.2m Zone: 5
Heart-shaped cupped leaves with
dramatic red-brown undersides,
fully revealed when they flutter in
a breeze. Mopheads of orange-
yellow, daisy-like flowers on
red-brown stems in late summer.
Best in moist, rich soil where it
will spread gently.

L. 'The Rocket'
Height: 5ft/1.5m Zone: 5
Large handsome leaves, rounded
but with jagged edges. Flowers in
June are slender spires of yellow
borne on dark stems. Flowers well
in shade or in sun and likes moist,
rich soil.

Ligustrum
A genus of woody plants.
Propagate by cuttings.

L. lucidum 'Tricolor'
Height: 15ft/4.5m Zone: 6
Decorative evergreen shrub with
narrow glistening leaves flecked
with gold and pink. Does well in
semi-shade but needs protection.

L. ovalifolium
Height: 12ft/3.6m Zone: 5
Evergreen with shapely little
leaves, clips well and makes good
hedges and topiary. Does well in
shade in poor soil. The
gold-leafed form *L. o.* 'Aureum' is
admirable in small doses.

Lilium
The lilies, a genus of bulbs.

L. candidum
Height: 5ft/1.5m Zone: 6
The Madonna lily has beautiful
white trumpet flowers borne at
the top of upright stems.
Deliciously scented. Flourishes in
full sun in poor soil. Propagate by
scaling bulbs.

L. lancifolium
Height: 7ft/2m Zone: 4
This Japanese tiger lily throws out
tall swaying stems crowned in
June with several Turk's cap
flowers of a lovely orange-red
speckled with chocolate.
Naturalizes well. Best in rich,
moist soil in semi-shade.
Propagate by seed.

L. pardalinum
Height: 6ft/1.8m Zone: 5
Magificent and easy lily with
dazzling Turk's cap orange
flowers borne at the tips of tall
swaying stems in July. Sun or
semi-shade but must have rich
moist soil. Propagate by seed and
naturalizes well.

L. pyrenaicum
Height: 30in/75cm Zone: 3
An easy species lily which
produces yellow Turk's cap
flowers in May. It will flourish in
light shade and naturalize easily.

Linaria
A genus of herbaceous plants.

L. purpurea
Height: 24in/60cm Zone: 6
Toadflax has narrow leaves and
spires of diminutive purple
flowers in early summer. *L. p.*
'Canon Went' has pale pink
flowers. Best in sun and rich soil.
Propagate by division.

Linum
The flaxes, a genus of herbaceous
plants.

L. narbonense
Height: 24in/60cm Zone: 7
Exquisite violet-blue flowers with

Lilium pardalinum

a silvery sheen in June. Slender
leaves a decorative glaucous grey.
Best in sun in well-drained soil.
Propagate by seed or cuttings.

Lobelia
A genus of herbaceous plants.

Lobelia cultivars
Around 36in/90cm high, hardy to
Zone 8. Perennials forming bold
clumps of foliage with dramatic
spires of flowers from July. Needs
a sunny position and moist, rich
soil. Propagate by division. *L.*
'Dark Crusader' has glowing dark
red flowers and leaves suffused
with red. *L.* 'Hadspen Royal
Purple' has rich purple flowers. *L.*
'Queen Victoria' has purple
foliage and scarlet flowers.

L. cardinalis
Height: 36in/90cm Zone: 4
Perennial with purple stems and
foliage and dazzling scarlet
flowers in summer. Needs rich
soil and much sun. Propagate by
seed or cuttings.

Lonicera
A genus of woody plants.

L. hildebrandtiana
Height: 42ft/12m Zone: 9
Magnificent evergreen
honeysuckle with large glistening

leaves and scented cream flowers. Needs much nourishment, possible conservatory plant in cool climates. Propagate by cuttings or layering.

L. × italica
Height: 12ft/3.6m Zone: 6
Beautiful honeysuckle with very attractive sweetly scented pink and cream flowers borne in generous trusses. Flowers in mid summer and continues for weeks. Best in a sunny position.

L. japonica 'Halliana'
Height: 30ft/10m Zone: 4
A climbing honeysuckle with intensely fragrant cream-white flowers in late summer over a long period. Best in sun or part-shade.

L. nitida
Height: 12ft/3.6m Zone: 7
Fast-growing, dense evergreen shrub with diminutive leaves, good for hedging or topiary. Creamy white sweetly scented flowers in summer. Propagate by cuttings. Grows well in shade. L. n. 'Baggesen's Gold' has golden-yellow foliage.

L. periclymenum
Height: 12ft/3.6m Zone: 5
A woodbine with fortissimo honeysuckle scent and creamy-

Lonicera japonica 'Halliana'

yellow flowers in June continuing for weeks. Sun or part shade.

Lunaria
A genus of herbaceous plants.

L. annua 'Alba'
Height: 30in/75cm Zone: 8
Biennial with bold heart-shaped toothed foliage and clusters of white single flowers in early summer. Good in shade and moist soil. Propagate by seed.

Lupinus
A genus of woody and herbaceous plants.

Lupinus cultivars
All are hardy to Zone 3 and flower in May or June. Statuesque herbaceous perennials with striking fan-shaped foliage and flowers in tall spires. L. 'Chandelier' (4ft/1.2m) has creamy yellow flowers. L. 'Noble Maiden' (36in/90cm) has pale cream flowers. Rich soil, sun or part shade.

Lychnis
A genus of herbaceous perennials. Propagate by seed or by division.

L. chalcedonica
Height: 36in/90cm Zone: 4
Vibrant scarlet flowers held at the tip of a tall, slender stem in June. Boldly heart-shaped leaves grouped in a clump. Best in a sunny position. L. c. 'Alba' is a white-flowered cultivar. L. c. 'Flore Pleno' is a striking double-flowered cultivar.

L. coronaria
Height: 36in/90cm Zone: 6
A herbaceous perennial with rosy magenta flowers in June. L. c. Oculata Group has pink and white flowers.

Lysimachia
A genus of herbaceous and woody plants. Those below are herbaceous, propagate by division.

L. ciliata 'Firecracker'
Height: 4ft/1.2m Zone: 4
This is a more refined version of L. punctata but with chocolate-brown foliage to set off the nodding yellow flowers in mid summer. Sun or semi-shade.

L. clethroides
Height: 36in/90cm Zone: 4
A herbaceous perennial with narrow grey-green leaves and airy spires of small grey-white flowers in June. Sun or semi-shade.

L. ephemerum
Height: 5ft/1.5m Zone: 7
A herbaceous perennial which throws out spires of grey-white flowers in June or July above handsome grey foliage. Does well in part shade in fertile soil.

L. punctata
Height: 36in/90cm Zone: 4
Bright and brassy spikes of yellow flowers in summer. Thrives in moist soil in semi-shade. Best for the wild garden.

Lythrum
A genus of herbaceous perennials and shrubs.

L. salicaria
Height: 4ft/1.2m Zone: 3
Purple loosestrife is a coarse but cheerful herbaceous perennial with spires of leafy stems crowned in the summer by whorls of purple flowers. Best in a sunny position in heavy, moist soil. L. s. 'Blush' has soft pink flowers and grows smaller than the type – no more than 30in/90cm tall; L. s. 'Lady Sackville' produces slender spikes of rich purple flowers on a rather bushy plant. L. s. 'Robert' has sharp pink flowers. Propagate by division.

Magnolia
A genus of trees and shrubs.

M. grandiflora
Height: 100ft/30m Zone: 6
An evergreen magnolia with bold leathery leaves and magnificent upright white flowers in late

summer exuding an exotic scent.
Best in rich soil in a sunny
position. Propagate by cuttings.

Mahonia

A genus of woody plants.
Propagate by cuttings.

M. japonica
Height: 6ft/1.8m Zone: 6
Dark green lustrous evergreen
foliage with racemes of sweetly-
scented pale yellow flowers in
winter. Sun or part shade.

M. × media 'Charity'
Height: 10ft/3m Zone: 8
Superb slightly tender evergreen
shrub with stately pinnate leaves
and generous plumes of fragrant
yellow flowers in winter. Needs
protection but thrives in shade.

Malus

The apple genus.

M. domestica cultivars
Up to 20ft/6m in height, hardy to
Zone 5. Culinary apples need rich,
moist soil and plenty of sun in an
open position. Most are grafted
onto dwarf stock today but they
make finer trees on their own
roots. For espaliers they may be
bought ready trained. 'Blenheim
Orange' is a cooker or eater,
golden skinned flushed with red.
'Cox's Orange Pippin' is one of
the most delicious dessert apples,
green-yellow flushed with
orange-red. Will not do in cold
wet soil. 'Ellison's Orange' is a
dessert apple, soft green streaked
with red. 'Laxton's Fortune' is a
dessert variety, lime green
streaked with red. 'Newton
Wonder' is a cooker or eater, lime
green tinged with crimson.

Malva

A genus of herbaceous perennials.

M. moschata
Height: 24in/60cm Zone: 3
The musk mallow is a trailing
plant with pink-mauve flowers in
May or June. Seeds itself or
propagate by division. *M. m. alba*

is a beautiful form is with white
flowers with a hint of pink at the
centre. Flowers well in full sun or
part shade.

Matthiola

A genus of herbaceous and woody
plants.

Matthiola White Perennial
Height: 30in/75cm Zone: 6
A short-lived subshrub with
whorls of fine grey leaves followed
in late spring by white flowers
with a wonderful rich tropical
scent. Propagate by seed. Best in a
sunny position.

Meconopsis

A small genus of poppies.

M. cambrica
Height: 10in/25cm Zone: 6
The Welsh poppy has dazzling
single lemon-yellow flowers from
May onwards. Pretty, pale green
pinnate foliage. Likes moist soil
and flourishes in the shade. Sows
itself with abandon.

Melianthus

A genus of woody plants.

M. major
Height: 8ft/2.5m Zone: 9
Magnificent curved pinnate
fronds, a lovely glaucous green
and finely toothed. In nature a
shrub but in less favoured
climates behaves like a herbaceous
perennial, being cut down to the
ground by frost every year. Best
in rich, moist soil in a really warm
position. The leaves have a
curious, not necessarily pleasing,
smell of warm rubber. Propagate
by division.

Melissa

A genus of herbaceous perennials.

M. officinalis
Height: 30in/75cm Zone: 4
Lemon balm has rounded toothed
fresh green leaves that smell of
lemon when crushed. Insignificant
yellow flowers but forms a
handsome burgeoning bush of

Meconopsis cambrica

foliage. *M. o.* 'Aurea' is a
gold-leafed cultivar. Does well in
part shade, propagate by division.

Mentha

A genus of herbaceous plants.

M. spicata
Height: 24in/60cm
Zone: 5
Spearmint is a creeping perennial
with sweetly aromatic leaves. Best
in moist soil and flourishes in the
shade. Propagate by division.

Mertensia

A genus of herbaceous plants.

M. pulmonarioides (formerly *M.
virginica*)
Height: 30in/75cm Zone: 3
The Virginia cowslip is a
perennial with fresh green leaves
and dazzling blue (or occasionally
white) hanging tubular flowers.
Needs rich soil, good in shade.
Propagate by seed or division.

Mespilus

The medlar, a single species of
tree.

M. germanicus
Height: 15ft/4.5m Zone: 5
A deciduous tree with shapely
sprawling crown, white flowers in
spring and curious russet-brown

fruit in autumn. Best in an open, airy place with plenty of light. Propagate by seed or cuttings.

Meum

A single species of herbaceous perennial.

M. athamanticum
Height: 24in/60cm Zone: 7
Pretty umbels of yellow-white flowers appear from June. Aromatic ferny foliage. Sun and good drainage. Propagate by seed.

Miscanthus

A genus of perennial grasses.

M. sinensis 'Variegatus'
Height: 6ft/1.8m Zone: 4
A magnificent clump-forming grass with arching leaves. *M. s.* 'Gracillimus' has especially slender leaves with white stripes down the centre. *M. s.* 'Variegatus' has leaves striped with cream for their whole length. Needs rich soil and sun or part shade. Propagate by division.

Monarda

A genus of herbaceous plants.

Monarda cultivars
Perennials hardy to Zone 4 and grow to a height of around 36in/90cm. Upright tufted flowers in summer over a long period. Best in rich and moist soil in a sunny position. Propagate by division. *M.* 'Adam' is a lively cherry red. *M.* 'Beauty of Cobham' has pale pink flowers contrasting handsomely with the purple-brown calyces at the base. *M.* 'Cambridge Scarlet' has intense scarlet flowers.

Morina

A genus of herbaceous perennial.

M. longifolia
Height: 36in/90cm
Zone: 6
A sheaf of gleaming toothed leaves is the most striking feature of this morina. Tall stems bear whorls of pale pink flowers in June. Best in

Nectaroscordum siculum

rich soil in a sunny position. Propagate by seed or division.

Morus

A genus of woody plants.

M. alba 'Pendula'
Height: 10ft/3m Zone: 4
The weeping white mulberry is an ornamental miniature tree, with red raspberry-like fruit. Sun or semi-shade. Propagate by grafting.

Muehlenbeckia

A genus of woody plants.

M. axillaris
Height: 10in/25cm Zone: 8
Prostrate spreading shrub with fresh green foliage and little yellow flowers in late summer. Propagate by cuttings.

Musa

The bananas, a genus of herbaceous plants.

M. basjoo
Height: 15ft/4.5m Zone: 8
One of the hardier bananas with spectacular fast-growing leaves up to 7ft/2m long. Needs a warm position, plenty of water and rich soil. Propagate by division.

Myrrhis

A genus of a single species.

M. odorata
Height: 6ft/1.8m Zone: 5
Sweet Cicely is a herbaceous perennial with decorative fern-like leaves and large umbels of diminutive flowers. Aromatic,

smelling of liquorice. Very invasive. Best in moist soil, good in semi-shade. Propagate by seed.

Nectaroscordum

Two species of bulbs closely related to Allium.

N. siculum
Height: 48in/1.2m Zone: 6
Graceful umbels of small hanging flowers in May or June, creamy pink. Pretty, upward pointing seed pods later in season. *N. s.* sbsp. *siculum* has red-brown flowers. Best in moist soil, sun or semi-shade. Self seeds.

Nepeta

A genus of herbaceous perennials. Propagate by division.

N. × *faassenii*
Height: 24in/60cm Zone: 3
A catmint with aromatic grey-green toothed leaves and long spikes of lavender flowers throughout summer.

N. racemosa
Height: 12in/30cm Zone: 4
A pretty catmint with aromatic leaves and whorls of violet-blue flowers in May or June. Needs sun and rich soil.

N. 'Six Hills Giant'
Height: 30in/75cm Zone: 3
Strongly aromatic foliage and trailing stems of lively lavender flowers in summer. Good in poor soil, in sun or light shade.

N. 'Souvenir d'André Chaudron'
Height: 24in/60cm Zone: 5
Aromatic toothed leaves and pale blue flowers. Rampageous in rich soil, good in sun or part shade.

Nerium

A genus of a single species.

N. oleander
Height: 20ft/6m Zone: 9
Spreading shrub with slender pointed leaves and profuse flowers in summer – white, red, yellow, purple – some of which, especially pale colours, are scented. Must

have sun but thrive in poor soil. Good conservatory plant in cool climates. Propagate by cuttings.

Nicotiana
The tobacco plants, a genus of herbaceous and woody plants.

Nicotiana cultivars
Around 24in/60cm in height and are hardy to Zone 7. *N.* 'Lime Green' is a perennial with green-yellow trumpet flowers, usually grown as an annual. Sun and rich soil. Propagate by seed.

N. alata
Height: 48in/1.2m Zone: 7
Herbaceous perennial with deliciously scented lime-green flowers in summer. Needs sun and rich soil. Propagate by seed.

N. langsdorfii
Height: 36in/90cm Zone: 9
An annual with pretty lime-green hanging flowers in profusion from May. Best in rich soil in full sun. Propagate by seed.

N. sylvestris
Height: 6ft/1.8m Zone: 8
Superb annual with hanging white tubular scented flowers from high summer. Needs sun and rich soil. Propagate by seed.

Nigella
The love-in-a-mist genus has a few species of annuals.

N. damascena
Height: 18in/45cm Zone: 6
Intricate sky-blue flowers carried above fine foliage. Starts to flower in May or June and lasts for weeks. Full sun and rich soil. Will self-seed happily.

Nymphaea
The water lilies, a genus of aquatic herbaceous perennials.

Nymphaea cultivars
These grow above the water level to a height of around 24in/60cm and all are hardy to Zone 6. The water lilies, with rounded glistening leaves and glamorous

Nigella damascena

single or double star-shaped flowers – white pink, red or yellow – are handsome ornaments for pools. Propagate by division.

Oenothera
A genus of herbaceous plants, annual and perennial, propagated by seed or by division.

O. missouriensis
Height: 4in/10cm Zone: 5
This evening primrose is a ground-hugging plant with decorative narrow leaves and thrilling yellow single flowers from June onwards. Needs plenty of sun and good drainage.

Omphalodes
A genus of herbaceous plants.

O. verna
Height: 6in/15cm Zone: 6
A perennial with heart-shaped leaves and clear blue flowers in spring carried at the tips of trailing stems. Best in moist shade. Propagate by division.

Onopordum
A genus of biennial herbs.

O. acanthium
Height: 10ft/3m Zone: 6
Immense pale grey thistle leaves of statuesque presence. The small violet thistles in summer are an anticlimax. Best in sun and will usually need support.

Ophiopogon
A genus of herbaceous perennials.

O. planiscapus 'Nigrescens'
Height: 10in/25cm Zone: 6
Grass-like plant with narrow evergreen purple-black leaves. propagate by division. Needs sun and rich soil.

Origanum
A genus of herbs and subshrubs.

O. laevigatum 'Hopleys'
Height: 24in/60cm Zone: 8
Perennial with wiry stems bearing in late summer pink flowers held in purple bracts. Needs full sun in a dry place. Propagate by division.

O. vulgare
Height: 36in/90cm Zone: 5
Common marjoram, a deliciously scented woody perennial with diminutive purple flowers in summer. Best in full sun and does well in poor dry soil. *O. v.* 'Album' has white flowers; *O. v.* 'Aureum' is much lower than the type – no more than 12in/30cm – forming a creeping mat of golden-yellow foliage with mauve flowers. Propagate by division.

Ornithogalum
A genus of bulbs.

O. pyrenaicum
Height: 36in/90cm Zone: 7
Elegant flowers in summer, green-gold borne in tall spires. Rich soil, sunny position. Propagate by seed.

Osmanthus
A genus of woody plants.

O. delavayi
Height: 6ft/1.8m Zone: 7
Evergreen shrub with small, pointed and slightly toothed leaves. Little tubular white flowers in spring are pleasantly scented. Good in sun or semi-shade and takes clipping well. Propagate by cuttings.

Oxalis

A genus of herbaceous and woody plants.

O. vulcanicola
Height: 24in/60cm Zone: 9
A herbaceous perennial with red-flushed leaves and yellow flowers in summer. Must have a sunny position and rich soil. Propagate by division.

Paeonia

The peony genus of herbaceous and woody plants. Propagate by seed; cultivars may be propagated by division or, with woody species, by grafting.

P. lactiflora 'Lord Kitchener'
Height: 36in/90cm Zone: 5
Herbaceous peony with splendid white single flowers with profuse yellow stamens in June. *P. l.* 'Lord Kitchener' is a crimson cultivar. Rich soil and sun.

P. mlokosewitschii
Height: 24in/60cm Zone: 5
Herbaceous peony with exquisite pale yellow single flowers in April. Needs rich soil and sun.

P. officinalis 'Alba'
Height: 24in/60cm Zone: 3
Distinguished divided palmate foliage above which, in the type,

Paeonia mlokosewitschii

blood-red flowers appear in May. The white cultivar is equally fine. Rich soil in sun or semi-shade.

P. suffruticosa sbsp. *rockii*
Height: 5ft/1.5m Zone: 5
A tree peony with beautiful divided foliage and magnificent single white flowers with deep red blotches at the centre in June. Needs rich soil and part shade.

Papaver

A genus of poppies, all herbaceous annuals or perennials, propagated by seed or division.

P. orientale
Height: 36in/90cm Zone: 3
Herbaceous perennial with large papery single flowers in early summer, red, orange-red or pink with deep maroon blotch at base of petals. Best in sun. *P. o.* 'Beauty of Livermere' has blood-red flowers. *P. o.* 'Patty's Plum' has sumptuous deep plum-coloured flowers.

P. somniferum
Height: 4ft/1.2m Zone: 7
Annual opium poppy with glaucous grey foliage and papery flowers – white, mauve, red – single or double, and often with a dark spot at the base of the flower.

Paris

A genus of herbaceous perennials.

P. quadrifolia
Height: 12in/30cm Zone: 6
European herb paris is a curiously elegant plant with a ruff of four leaves and yellowish tufts of flowers in summer. Moist soil in shade. Propagate by division.

Paulownia

A genus of trees.

P. tomentosa
Height: 70ft/20m Zone: 5
Tree with soft, downy leaves. Purple, foxglove-like flowers in early summer. Propagate by seed.

Pelargonium

A genus of woody and herbaceous plants.

Pelargonium cultivars
Shrubs to a height of 6ft/1.8m, all hardy to Zone 10. Overwinter in a frost-free greenhouse and put out of doors when there is no danger of frost. Need a sunny position and plenty of watering and feeding to flower well. Short-lived, propagate by cuttings. *P.* 'Arley Red' is a sprightly cerise pink.

Penstemon

A genus of herbaceous and woody plants.

Penstemons cultivars
24–36in/60–90cm in height they are generally hardy to Zone 5 but must have good drainage – will not survive wet, heavy soil. Long flowering season, from June onwards. Tubular flowers with open lips, like an aristocratic snapdragon. Propagate by division or by cuttings. *P.* 'Andenken an Friedrich Hahn' has rich red flowers. *P.* 'Apple Blossom' has pink and white flowers. *P.* 'Evelyn' makes a bushy plant with pale pink flowers. *P.* 'Garnet' has fine dusty red flowers. *P.* 'Myddelton Gem' is a sprightly pale crimson; *P.* 'Pink Profusion' is a warm pink; *P.* 'Rich Ruby' has velvety flowers of a resonant red. *P.* 'Snow Storm' is pure white. *P.* 'Sour Grapes' has flowers of acidulous violet mottled with white.

Perovskia

A genus of aromatic woody plants.

P. atriplicifolia 'Blue Spire'
Height: 4ft/1.2m Zone: 5
Pale grey toothed foliage, smelling of varnish, with splender spires of hooded blue flowers in late summer. Needs sun and good drainage. Propagate by cuttings.

Phalaris

A genus of grasses.

P. arundinacea var. *picta*
Height: 36in/90cm Zone: 4
Gardener's garters is an invasive
but decorative plant. The chief
virtue of this cultivar is the white
striped foliage. Propagate, if you
need to, by division.

Philadelphus

A group of deciduous woody
plants. Propagate by cuttings.

Philadelphus cultivars
All hardy to Zone 6 and up to
15ft/4.5m in height. *P.* 'Virginal'
(10ft/3m) has particularly large
white double flowers in June with
the sweet, heady scent.

Phlomis

A genus of woody and herbaceous
plants. Propagate herbaceous
species by division or seed, woody
species by cuttings.

P. bovei sbsp. *maroccana*
Height: 5ft/1.2m Zone: 9
A tender herbaceous perennial
with grey foliage and pink-purple
flowers. Needs sunny protected
position and sharp drainage.

P. fruticosa
Height: 6ft/1.8m Zone: 7
The Jerusalem sage is a shrub
with very pale aromatic leaves and
whorls of golden yellow flowers in
May or June. Best in sun. May be
clipped to make a rounded shape.

P. longifolia
Height: 4ft/1.2m Zone: 9
Tender shrub similar to *P.
fruticosa* but with green leaves
with pale woolly undersides.
Whorls of yellow flowers in June.
Needs good drainage and sun.

P. tuberosa
Height: 5ft/1.5m Zone: 6
Herbaceous perennial with bold
spear-shaped leaves and from
June to August pink-purple
flowers on hairy stems.

Phalaris arundinacea var. picta

Phlox

A genus of herbaceous plants.
Propagate by division.

P. maculata
Height: 4ft/1.2m Zone: 5
Big panicles of pink, purple of
white flowers in June. *P. m.*
'Rosalinde' is a good bright pink.

P. paniculata
Height: 4ft/1.2m Zone: 5
Valuable border plants,
floriferous over a long period. *P.
p.* 'Fujiyama' has brilliant white
flowers arranged in bold
cylindrical umbels. *P. p.* 'Iris' has
sumptuous magenta flowers. *P. p.*
'Norah Leigh' has cream
variegated foliage and lilac
flowers. *P. p.* 'White Admiral' has
pure white flowers.

P. subulata
Height: 4in/10cm Zone: 3
A spreading cushion-shaped
alpine phlox with white or
lavender flowers in late spring.
Good drainage, sun or part shade.

Phormium

A genus of herbaceous perennials.

Phormium cultivars
Around 7ft/2m in height, hardy
to Zone 8. New Zealand flax, with
bold upright sheaves of blade-like
leaves. Needs a sunny, protected
position. Propagate by division. *P.*
'Sundowner' has leaves striped in
pink and cream.

Photinia

A genus of woody plants.

P. davidiana 'Palette'
Height: 15ft/4.5m Zone: 8
An evergreen shrub with
pink/white variegated leaves.
Propagate by cuttings.

Physostegia

A genus of herbaceous perennials.

P. virginiana 'Summer Snow'
Height: 36in/90cm Zone: 4
Erect spires of pure white flowers
in June. Best in rich soil in sun or
part shade. Propagate by division.

Picea

The spruces, a genus of conifers.

P. glauca var. *albertiana* 'Conica'
Height: 10ft/3m Zone: 2
Assumes a naturally conical
shape, broad at the base rising to a
a sharp tip. Fresh green foliage.
Does well in sun or shade.
Propagate by cuttings.

Pinus

The pines, a large genus of
evergreen trees and a few shrubs.

P. monticola 'Minima'
Height: 36in/90cm Zone: 4
Dwarf pine forming a
distinguished hummock of glossy
needles. Good in part shade, any
soil. Propagate by cuttings.

Pittosporum

A genus of tender woody plants.

P. tenuifolium
Height: 30ft/9m Zone: 9
A substantial shrub with
gleaming, rounded, undulating
evergreen foliage. *P. t.* 'Tom
Thumb' has dramatic almost black
purple foliage. Needs a protected
site. Propagate by cuttings.

Plantago

A genus of herbaceous plants.

P. major 'Rubrifolia'
Height: 12in/30cm Zone: 5
Rosettes of beetroot-red leaves are
very decorative among red and

Polygonatum × hybridum

purple flowers. Keeps its colour better in a sunny position. Propagate by division.

Platanus

The planes, a genus of trees.

P. × hispanica (syn *P. × acerifolia*)
Height: 160ft/50m Zone: 7
The London plane, a splendid tree with upright rounded crown, large maple-like leaves and, in old age, strikingly mottled bark. Big, beautiful and easy to please. Propagate by cuttings.

Platycodon

A genus of a single species of herbaceous perennial.

P. grandiflorus
Height: 18in/45cm Zone: 4
Intense blue single flowers in July, borne aloft on wiry stems. Best in rich moist soil in sun or semi-shade. Propagate by division.

Plectranthus

A genus of woody plants.

P. argentatus
Height: 36in/90cm Zone: 10
A tender, fleshy shrub with superb heart-shaped leaves of the palest, downy grey. Racemes of blue flowers in late summer. Propagate by cuttings.

Polemonium

A genus of herbaceous plants.

P. foliossisimum var. *flavum*
Height: 30in/75cm Zone: 3
From a bush of pinnate leaves stems bear in summer yellow flowers flushed with tawny-red. Needs rich soil in sun. Propagate by division.

Polygonatum

A genus of herbaceous perennials. Propagate by division.

P. × hybridum
Height: 36in/90cm Zone: 6
Solomon's Seal has magnificent undulating leaves garnished in May or June with hanging creamy-white tubular flowers. An essential plant for a shady place.

P. verticillatum
Height: 30in/75cm Zone: 5
Similar to Solomon's Seal (above) with drooping green-white tubular flowers in spring. Best in rich, moist soil in shade.

Polygonum

A genus of herbaceous plants.

P. amplexicaule
Height: 36in/90cm Zone: 5
A bold foliage plant with heart-shaped leaves and spikes of red flowers from June. Best in sun. Propagate by division.

Polystichum

A genus of ferns.

P. setiferum
Height: 36in/90cm Zone: 7
Beautiful deciduous ferns with spreading intricately pinnate leaves. Best in moist soil in shade. Propagate by spores or by division.

Populus

A genus of deciduous trees.

P. nigra var. *italica*
Height: 100ft/30m Zone: 2
The Lombardy poplar, a tall fast-growing columnar tree with decorative fluttering heart-shaped leaves. Short-lived but marvellous

landscape tree – but not for the small garden. Propagate by cuttings.

Potentilla

A genus of woody and herbaceous plants. Herbaceous plants propagated by division, woody by cuttings.

Potentilla cultivars (herbaceous)
Around 18in/45cm high and hardy to Zone 6. Leafy mounds of decoratively pleated leaves with trailing flowers trail from May onwards. Best in rich soil in a sunny position. *P.* 'Gibson's Scarlet' has brilliant scarlet single flowers. *P.* 'Gloire de Nancy' has orange-red flowers produced throughout the summer. *P.* 'Monsieur Rouillard' has red-brown flowers. *P.* 'William Rollison' has orange-red flowers.

P. aurea
Height: 4in/10cm Zone: 5
A hummock-forming herbaceous perennial with silvery leaves and warm yellow flowers in summer. *P. a.* 'Flore Pleno' has pretty, double flowers. Needs sun and good drainage.

P. fruticosa
Height: 4ft/1.2m Zone: 3
A bushy little shrub with grey-green foliage and decorative little rose-like flowers, yellow or white, in June. Best in full sun. Propagate by cuttings.

P. nepalensis 'Miss Willmott'
Height: 24in Zone: 5
A straggling perennial with rounded leaves and warm pink flowers with a dark eye. Needs rich soil and a sunny position.

P. recta var. *pallida*
Height: 18in/45cm Zone: 4
Perennial with single pale creamy-yellow flowers in summer. Best in sun and well drained soil.

Primula

The primroses, a genus of herbaceous plants propagated by seed or by division.

P. auricula
Height: 8in/20cm Zone: 3
Umbels of scented golden yellow
flowers are borne in spring above
pale green downy leaves. Best in
part shade with good drainage.
Propagate by seed or division.

P. florindae
Height: 24in/60cm Zone: 6
Moisture-loving primula with
magnificent hanging flowers in
May, pale yellow and sweetly
scented. Flowers well in shade.

P. vulgaris
Height: 6in/15cm Zone: 6
The common primrose – pale
yellow flowers single, carried in
the midst of fleshy rounded
leaves. Sun or shade and any soil.
P. 'Devon Cream' is a good very
pale flowered cultivar.

Prunus

A genus of woody plants including
plums, cherries, peaches and
almonds. Propagate by seed or
cuttings.

P. cerasifera
Height: 28ft/8m Zone: 4
A deciduous tree with a
handsomely rounded crown. *P. c.*
'Nigra' (formerly *P.* 'Pissardii
Nigra') has plummy purple foliage
– pink at first but deepening in
colour as the season passes. Makes
an excellent ornamental hedge
needing frequent clipping. *P. c.*
'Pissardii' has red-purple foliage.

P. lusitanica
Height: 45ft/14m Zone: 7
The Portugal laurel is an
evergreen tree with sombre
gleaming pointed leaves. Clips
well and is good in shade.

P. × subhirtella 'Autumnalis Rosea'
Height: 20ft/6m Zone: 5
Deciduous spreading tree with
pink flowers in winter with a scent
of almonds. Does well in
semi–shade.

Pulmonaria

The lungworts, a genus of
herbaceous perennials. Propagate
by division. They all do best in
moist soil and thrive in shade.

P. officinalis
Height: 8in/12cm Zone: 4
The common lungwort has oval,
pointed pale green leaves spotted
with paler colouring. Flowers in
spring are an pink-purple. *P. o.*
'Sissinghurst White' is a dazzling
pure white.

P. rubra
Height: 12in/30cm Zone: 3
Forms a handsome mound of
narrow spotted leaves with vivid
blue flowers in spring.

P. saccharata
Height: 10in/30cm Zone: 4
Pale green leaves, marbled with
paler colouring, are crowned in
April by rosy pink flowers. *P. s.*
Argentea Group has decorative
silver frosting to the leaves.

Pyrus

The pear genus has several trees
and shrubs. Propagate by seed or
cuttings.

P. communis
Height: 50ft/15m Zone: 4
The common pear is rarely seen in
gardens. Old specimens make fine
trees, covered with white blossom
early in the spring.

P. salicifolia 'Pendula'
Height: 15ft/4.5m Zone: 4
The weeping silver-leafed pear
has very narrow, curling leaves of
the palest grey and pure white
flowers in the spring.

P. syriaca
Height: 15ft/4.5m Zone: 7
The Caucasian pear is quite small,
often thorny and bears pretty
little fruit.

Quercus

The oaks, a large genus of trees.

Q. agrifolia
Height: 80ft/25m Zone: 8
The California live oak, an

Primula vulgaris

evergreen with sprawling branches
and fissured bark, full of character
when old. Sun or shade.
Propagate by acorns.

Ranunculus

The buttercups, a genus mostly of
herbaceous plants.

R. acris
Height: 36in/90cm Zone: 5
The meadow buttercup, a pretty
trailing plant with gleaming
yellow single flowers from late
spring. *R. a.* 'Flore Pleno' has
very double flowers. Best in sun
and moist soil. Propagate species
by seed, cultivars by division.

Reseda

A genus of herbaceous plants.

R. luteola
Height: 4ft/120cm Zone: 6
A biennial with a handsome spire
of yellow flowers in late summer.
Flourishes in sun in poor well-
drained soil. Propagate by seed.

Rheum

A genus of herbaceous plants.

R. palmatum 'Atropurpureum'
Height: 6ft/1.8m Zone: 6
Dramatically ornamental leaves up
to 36in/90cm long, palm- shaped
with deeply divided lobes on
gracefully arching stems. Leaves
suffused with red, the bright red
new shoots erupting from the
ground by May. Needs rich, moist
soil in part shade. Propagate by
division.

Rhus

A genus of woody plants.

R. × *pulvinata* Autumn Lace
Group
Height: 10ft/3m Zone: 3
Beautiful shrub with elegant
finely cut pinnate leaves which
turn a marvellous red in autumn.
Upright panicles of cream-green
flowers in July. Propagate by
cuttings.

Ricinus

A single species, described below.

R. communis
Height: 8ft/2.5m Zone: 9
The castor-oil plant has dramatic
splayed leaves, 24in/60cm across
and bright red flowers. A shrub
treated as an annual, raised from
seed each year. Needs rich soil
and a sunny position. *R. c.*
'Carmencita' has marvellous
mahogany leaves. *R. c.* 'Impala' is
similar but more vigorous.

Rosa

The roses, an essential genus of
garden plants. Propagate by
cuttings or, in the case of the
species, by seed. All are best in
sun and flower once only in late
May or June unless otherwise
mentioned.

Rosa 'Comte de Chambord'

R. × *alba*
Height: 8ft/2.5m Zone: 4
The Jacobite rose with lovely
white flowers. *R.* × *a.* 'Alba
Semiplena' is a semi-double
cultivar and *R.* × *a.* 'Alba
Maxima' fully double. All are
sweetly scented and all have the
same grey-green leaves.

R. 'Alister Stella Grey'
Height: 15ft/4.5m Zone: 5
A climbing Noisette rose with
double creamy-white flowers with
a yellow centre and intensely
sweet scent. After the first
flowering further flowers are
produced. It flowers in part shade.

R. 'Altissimo'
Height: 10ft/3m Zone: 5
A modern continuously flowering
rose with splendid deep scarlet
single flowers.

R. 'Ballerina'
Height: 4ft/1.2m Zone: 5
A Hybrid Musk with umbels of
small pink flowers with a white
eye throughout the summer.

R. banksiae 'Lutea'
Height: 7.5m/25ft Zone: 7
The Banksian rose produces its
beautiful little double pale yellow
flowers very early, in May or even
April. Must have a sunny wall.

R. 'Bantry Bay'
Height: 10ft/3m Zone: 5
A modern climbing rose with flat,
semi-double flowers of a warm
pink which appear throughout the
summer. Good in part-shade.

R. 'Blanchefleur'
Height: 5ft/1.5m Zone: 5
An old Centifolia with sumptuous
well scented double pink flowers.

R. 'Bleu Magenta'
Height: 15ft/4.5m Zone: 5
Flowers intermittently throughout
the summer – small, double,
hanging downwards, a deep
purple-red fading to lilac,
wonderfully scented. It does well
in the part-shade of a pergola.

R. 'Buff Beauty'
Height: 5ft/1.5m Zone: 5
A Hybrid Musk rose with
beautiful tawny apricot double
flowers with a marvellous scent.

R. 'Cardinal de Richelieu'
Height: 4ft/1.2m Zone: 5
A Gallica with double flowers of
rich crimson-purple and a deep,
sweet scent. Good in part shade.

R. 'Champney's Pink Cluster'
Height: 15ft/4.5m Zone: 5
A climbing repeat-flowering
noisette with sweetly scented rich
pink double flowers.

R. 'Chanelle'
Height: 36in/90cm Zone: 5
A repeat-flowering Floribunda
with double flowers of a soft
apricot colour.

R. 'Comte de Chambord'
Height: 4ft/1.2m Zone: 4
Fully double flowers in June, deep
pink at the centre, silver pink at
the edges, a marvellous scent.
Intermittent flowers throughout
the season.

R. 'Constance Spry'
Height: 7ft/2m Zone: 5
A lanky modern shrub rose often
trained as a climber. Voluptuous
double pink flowers that have
everything – except scent.

R. 'De Rescht'
Height: 36in/90cm Zone: 4
Valuable Damask for the smaller
garden – a compact bush with
lavish double crimson flowers
with a delicious scent. Repeat-
flowering.

R. 'Dorothy Perkins'
Height: 10ft/3m Zone: 5
A climbing rose with lively pink
flowers, lightly scented.

R. 'Duc de Guiche'
Height: 4ft/1.2m Zone: 5
An old Gallica rose with neatly
shaped double flowers of a rich
violet, very sweetly scented.

R. 'Dusky Maiden'
Height: 4ft/1.2m Zone: 6
A Floribunda rose with large

single flowers of a vibrant scarlet, the texture of velvet. Flowers continuously. It is well scented and good in part shade.

R. 'Easlea's Golden Rambler'
Height: 15ft/4.5m Zone: 5
A rambler of flamboyant character with bold creamy-yellow double flowers with a fine scent. Great impact on a pergola or arbour.

R. eglanteria
Height: 8ft/2.5m Zone: 4
The sweet briar has leaves that smell deliciously of apples. Deep pink single flowers, sweetly scented, and pretty hips. Does well in part-shade.

R. 'The Fairy'
Height: 24in/60cm Zone: 5
A Polyantha rose which flowers intermittently throughout the season. A spreading plant with gleaming toothed leaves and pretty double warm pink flowers.

R. 'Fantin-Latour'
Height: 6ft/1.8m Zone: 5
Magnificent modern shrub rose with old-fashioned character. Large double pale pink flowers with a swoony scent.

R. 'Felicia'
Height: 4ft/1.2m Zone: 5
A Hybrid Musk with deliciously scented double shell-pink flowers. Repeat-flowering.

R. 'Ferdinand Pichard'
Height: 5ft/1.5m Zone: 5
A Hybrid Perpetual with white double flowers splashed with crimson, and with a sweet scent.

R. gallica 'Versicolor'
Height: 36in/90cm Zone: 4
Also known as 'Rosa Mundi', has beautifully striped crimson and pink semi-double flowers with a delicious scent.

R. 'Geranium'
Height: 10ft/3m Zone: 5
Immense rose of wild character with arching stems and single geranium-red flowers. Good hips.

***Rosa* 'Golden Wings'**

R. glauca
Height: 8ft/2.4m Zone: 2
A tall upright bush with grey leaves suffused with red on dusty red stems. The little flowers are cheerful, cerise with white centre. Decorative hips, scarlet and elongated. Seeds itself gently and does well in semi-shade.

R. 'Gloire de Dijon'
Height: 12ft/3.6m Zone: 5
A climber with fully double deliciously scented creamy-buff flowers. Repeat-flowering.

R. 'Golden Wings'
Height: 5ft/1.5m Zone: 4
A modern rose with wild character, with large and lovely lemon-yellow well scented flowers in June. Perpetual flowering.

R. 'Goldfinch'
Height: 8ft/2.5m Zone: 5
A smallish rambler with pretty apricot-yellow semi-double flowers with a light, sweet scent.

R. 'Great Maiden's Blush'
Height: 6ft/1.8m Zone: 4
Ancient garden rose with exquisite double pale pink flowers fabulously scented.

R. 'Gruss an Aachen'
Height: 24in/60cm Zone: 5
A continuous flowering Polyantha with the palest pink double and a sweet scent.One of the best roses for small gardens.

R. 'Handel'
Height: 12ft/3.6m Zone: 5
Modern repeat-flowering climber with white semi-double flowers, petals flushed with crimson.

R. 'Heritage'
Height: 4ft/1.2m Zone: 5
A David Austin 'English Rose' with pale pink double sweetly-scented flowers and gleaming foliage. Good for small gardens.

R. 'Hermosa'
Height: 36in/90cm
Zone: 5
An old China rose with cupped double pink flowers of dazzling charm. Scattering of flowers later in the season.

R. 'Iceberg'
Height: 4ft/1.2m Zone: 5
A repeat-flowering Floribunda (also known as 'Schneewittchen') with good white double flowers. R. 'Iceberg, Climbing' is a good vigorous climbing variety.

R. 'Lady Hillingdon, Climbing'
Height: 15ft/4.5m Zone: 5
A climbing Tea rose with sumptuous pale apricot flowers with an exceptionally delicious scent. Needs a warm, sunny site.

R. 'Len Turner'
Height: 24in/60cm Zone: 5
A repeat-flowering Floribunda with cream flowers suffused with pink. Good scent.

R. 'Leverkusen'
Height: 12ft/3.6m Zone: 5
A leggy rose which may serve as a climber. It has yellow double flowers with a good scent and ornamental lustrous leaves. It flowers well in shade.

R. 'Madame Alfred Carrière'
Height: 15ft/4.5m Zone: 5
A climbing Noisette with double white flowers with hints of cream-pink. Flowers intermittently. Delicious scent and does well in semi-shade.

Rosa 'Sombreuil Climbing'

R. 'Madame Hardy'
Height: 6ft/1.8m Zone: 4
A statuesque Damask rose with
flowers of great beauty – double,
silvery white, sweetly scented.

R. 'Madame Pierre Oger'
Height: 4ft/1.2m Zone: 5
A Bourbon rose with delicate
cupped sweetly scented pink
flowers borne in generous
clusters. Flowers intermittently.

R. 'Maigold'
Height: 12ft/3.6m Zone: 5
A leggy shrub rose often grown as
a climber with huge butter-yellow
semi-double flowers with a good
scent. Flowers intermittently and
does well in part shade.

R. 'Mary Rose'
Height: 4ft/1.2m Zone: 5
A David Austin 'English Rose', a
compact, perpetual-flowering
shrub. Double, pale pink flowers,
sweetly scented. The leaves have a
lustrous surface.

R. 'Mevrouw Nathalie Nypels'
Height: 36in/90cm Zone: 5
A low-growing Floribunda rose
with lively pink flowers,
deliciously scented. Among the
prettiest repeat-flowering roses.

R. moyesii
Height: 10ft/3m Zone: 5
Magnificent species rose of
stunning presence. Huge arched
stems bear brilliant single
blood-red flowers. Beautiful
flask-shaped bright red hips.

R. 'New Dawn'
Height: 10ft/3m Zone: 5
Popular climbing rose with
healthy shining foliage and
profuse pale pink double flowers
with a good scent. Single
flowering only but very attractive.
Does well in part-shade.

R. × odorata 'Viridiflora'
Height: 4ft/1.2m Zone: 7
A curiosity rather than a rose of
great beauty, with odd green
flowers in June.

R. 'Orchard Pearl'
Height: 18in/45cm Zone: 5
Pretty repeat-flowering Patio rose
with creamy-white well-scented
semi-double flowers.

R. 'Parkdirektor Riggers'
Height: 12ft/3.6m Zone: 5
Dark red semi-double flowers,
repeat-flowering. Decorative
gleaming foliage and vigorous
habit. Sun or semi-shade.

R. 'Paul's Lemon Pillar'
Height: 12ft/3.6m Zone: 5
A blowsy climbing Hybrid Tea
with yellow-flushed cream flowers
produced throughout the summer.
Flowers well in part shade.

R. pimpinellifolia
Height: 36in/90cm Zone: 4
Shapely low-growing wild rose
with masses of creamy-white or
pink cupped flowers, fern-like
foliage and spiny stems.

R. 'Prospero'
Height: 24in/60cm Zone: 5
A small David Austin 'English
Rose' with well scented deep red
double flowers. Repeat-flowering.

R. 'Queen Elizabeth'
Height: 5ft/1.5m Zone: 5
A repeat-flowering Floribunda
with sweetly-scented pale pink
double flowers.

R.. 'Roseraie de l'Haÿ'
Height: 6ft/1.8m Zone: 5
A vigorous rugosa rose with
veined foliage and perpetual
crimson-purple semi-double
flowers. Well scented.

R. 'Sadler's Wells'
Height: 4ft/1.2m Zone: 5
A repeat-flowering Hybrid Musk
with semi-double flowers, pale
pink in the centre with richer pink
frilly edge to the petals.

R. 'Sally Holmes'
Height: 4ft/1.2m Zone: 5
A modern repeat-flowering shrub
rose with very pale pink single
flowers fading prettily to white.

R. 'Sanders' White Rambler'
Height: 15ft/4.5m Zone: 5
Rambler with lavish sprays of
double white sweetly-scented
flowers at the beginning of July. It
does well in shade.

R. 'Sombreuil Climbing'
Height: 10ft/3m Zone: 5
Old climbing Tea rose with
magnificent double white flowers
with a creamy pink centre and a
rich scent. Repeat flowering.

R. 'Sunset Song'
Height: 4ft/1.2m Zone: 5
A perpetual-flowering Hybrid Tea
with pale apricot double flowers.

R. 'Super Star'
Height: 4ft/1.2m Zone: 5
Repeat-flowering Hybrid Tea
with silver pink double flowers.

R. 'Tuscany Superb'
Height: 4ft/1.2m Zone: 4
An old Gallica with sumptuous
maroon semi-double flowers with
a spicy scent.

R. 'Variegata di Bologna'
Height: 5ft/1.5m Zone: 5
A Bourbon rose with double
flowers cheerfully striped and
splashed with crimson. Flowers
intermittently.

R. 'Violette'
Height: 12ft/3.6m Zone: 5
Rambling rose with sprays of little
cupped rich purple flowers. It has
attractive shining foliage.

R. 'Wedding Day'
Height: 30ft/9m Zone: 5
Immense rambling rose with
lavish trusses of single white
sweetly-scented flowers.

R. 'White Cockade'
Height: 8ft/2.5m Zone: 5
Repeat-flowering modern rose
with blowsy double white flowers
and glossy foliage.

R. 'White Meidiland'
Height: 24in/60cm Zone: 5
Perpetual-flowering procumbent
rose with old-fashioned white
single flowers and good scent.

R. 'White Popcorn'
Height: 24in/60cm Zone: 5
Low-growing floribunda with
decorative white flowers produced
throughout the growing season.

R. 'Yvonne Rabier'
Height: 36in/90cm Zone: 5
A repeat-flowering Floribunda
rose with double white flowers.

R. 'Zéphirine Drouhin'
Height: 10ft/3m Zone: 5
Beautiful old climbing bourbon
rose with rich silvery-pink loosely
double flowers. Scattered later
flowerings.

Rosmarinus
Two species of shrubs

R. officinalis
Height: 6ft/1.8m Zone: 8
The culinary rosemary forms a
billowing bush with deliciously
scented needle-like leaves and
blue flowers. Needs sun and good
drainage. Propagate by cuttings.

Rudbeckia
A genus of herbaceous plants.
Propagate by division.

R. fulgida
Height: 24in/60cm Zone: 4
Warm yellow daisy-like flowers
with widely spreading petals and a
dark cone at the centre. Starts in
July but continues for many
weeks. *R. f.* var. *sullivanti*
'Goldsturm' has larger flowers (to
4in/10cm across). Needs moist
soil in full sun.

Rumex
A genus of herbaceous plants.
Propagate by seed or division.

Rumex acetosa

R. acetosa
Height: 36in/1m Zone: 5
Culinary sorrel, a perennial with
bold upright leaves with an
attractively bitter taste. Dramatic
plumes of pink-brown flowers in
June.

R. flexuosus
Height: 12in/30cm Zone: 7
Ornamental sorrel with attractive
copper-coloured spear-shaped
leaves and unexciting flowers.

Ruta
A genus of aromatic plants.

R. graveolens
Height: 18in/45cm Zone: 5
Rue, with its pungent scent, is an
attractive herb with glaucous
green foliage and yellow flowers
in summer. Best in full sun.
Propagate by cuttings.

Salix
The willows, a genus of trees and
shrubs.

S. helvetica
Height: 5ft/1.5m Zone: 6
A shrub with beautiful soft silver
silver foliage unfolding from
gleaming caramel-coloured buds.
Often seen as a grafted mop-head
standard. Sun or part shade.
Propagate by cuttings or grafting.

S. 'Onusta'
Height: 36in/90cm Zone: 6
This Japanese willow has pale
grey woolly leaves, oval and
pointed. May be clipped to form a
decorative miniature plant.

Salvia
The sages, a genus of woody and
herbaceous plants.

Salvia cultivars
Up to 4ft/1.2m high, hardy to
Zone 5. Herbaceous perennials
propagated by division. *Salvia*
'Indigo Spires' has tall spikes of
rich blue flowers in June.

S. chamaedryoides
Height: 18in/45cm Zone: 8
Herbaceous perennial with woolly
growth and piercing violet-blue
flowers in summer. Sun and sharp
drainage. Propagate by division.

S. elegans
Height: 6ft/1.8m Zone: 8
Perennial with dramatic scarlet
flowers in late summer. Must have
sun, rich soil and good drainage.
Propagate by division.

S. fulgens
Height: 36in/90cm Zone: 9
Semi-shrub with rich red flowers
in July. Needs sun and good
drainage. Propagate by cuttings.

S. horminum
Height: 18in/45cm Zone: 8
Annual with white, pink or violet
tubular flowers borne throughout
the summer. Must have a sunny
position, where it will self seed.

S. microphylla
Height: 36in/90cm Zone: 9
Semi-shrub with sprightly purple
flowers in late summer. Needs sun
and well drained, rich soil.
Propagate by cuttings.

S. officinalis
Height: 36in/90cm Zone: 5
Culinary sage, an ornamental
shrub with narrow leaves and blue
hooded flowers. Best in sun in a
well drained place. Propagate by
cuttings. *S. o.* 'Icterina' is
variegated with decorative

splashes of gold on its leaves. *S. o.* Purpurascens Group has beautiful plum-purple leaves.

S. pratensis 'Rosea'
Height: 36in/90cm Zone: 3
Perennial with coarse leaves and decorative spires of pink-violet flowers in June. Best in sun with rich soil. Propagate by division.

S. sclarea var. *turkestanica*
Height: 36in/90cm Zone: 5
Biennial with hairy leaves and branching stems of violet tubular flowers in summer. Best in rich soil in a sunny position. Propagate by division.

S. splendens 'Blaze of Fire'
Height: 12in/30cm Zone: 9
A shrub normally grown as a half-hardy annual bedding plant. Dazzling flowers of rich scarlet, through the summer. Raise from seed. Must have rich soil in a sunny position.

S. × superba
Height: 36in/90cm Zone: 5
A herbaceous perennial with striking purple hooded flowers in July and continuing for months. It must have sun and rich soil.

Sedum × rubrotinctum

S. × sylvestris 'Blauhügel'
Height: 24in/60cm Zone: 5
A herbaceous perennial with spires of clear blue flowers in June above toothed foliage. Best in rich soil in a sunny position. Propagate by division.

Santolina
A genus of shrubs.

S. chamaecyparissus
Height: 36in/90cm Zone: 7
A shrub forming a silver dome of finely cut foliage. Needs drainage and a sunny position. Propagate by cuttings.

Saponaria
A genus of herbaceous plants.

S. officinalis 'Rubra Plena'
Height: 12in/30cm Zone: 4
Soapwort is horribly invasive, with pink or white flowers throughout the season. This cultivar has double deep pink flowers. Sun or semi-shade. Propagate by dividing rhizomes.

Sarcococca
A genus of woody plants.

S. hookeriana
Height: 36in/90cm Zone: 6
Slender glistening evergreen foliage and scented flowers in winter. Sun or part shade. Propagate by division. *S. h.* var. *humilis* has pink-flushed flowers.

Satureja
A genus of herbaceous perennials and subshrubs.

S. montana
Height: 18in/45cm Zone: 6
Winter savory, a subshrub with narrow woolly leaves, strongly aromatic. Insignificant white flowers. Propagate by division.

Saxifraga
A very large genus of herbaceous plants propagated by seed or division.

S. 'Bob Hawkins'
Height: 4in/10cm Zone: 4
An alpine saxifrage forming a shapely mound of silver-variegated leaves with yellow-green flowers in summer. Needs good drainage, sun or semi-shade. Propagate by division.

S. 'Elliott's Variety'
Height: 4in/10cm Zone: 4
Rounded leaves and sprays of white flowers carried on fine red-brown stems. Sun or semi-shade. Propagate by division.

S. umbrosa
Height: 10in/25cm Zone: 7
London Pride has rounded leaves and in May or June delicate sprays of little white flowers.

Scrophularia
A genus of aquatic or marginal herbaceous perennials.

S. auriculata 'Variegata'
Height: 12in/30cm Zone: 5
The leaves are decorative, rounded and gleaming with creamy markings. Insignificant flowers. Good in shade. Propagate by division.

Sedum
A large genus, mostly succulents. Propagate by division.

S. 'Herbstfreude' (syn. *S.* 'Autumn Joy')
Height: 24in/60cm Zone: 5
Flat heads of pink flowers in late summer turning red-brown as they age. Ornamental grey-green fleshy leaves. Best in sun.

S. × rubrotinctum
Height: 3in/7.5cm Zone: 9
Creeping stone-crop with very small yellow and red fleshy leaves. Pale yellow flowers in summer. Flourishes in hot dry places.

S. spectabile
Height: 18in/45cm Zone: 5
Glaucous-grey fleshy leaves and a flat corymb of sweetly scented pink flowers in late summer. Grow in poor soil but needs sun.

S. telephium sbsp. *maximum* 'Atropurpureum'
Height: 24in/60cm Zone: 5
Fleshy leaves and umbels of deep purple flowers in summer. Best in sun but thrives in poor soil.

Senecio

A genus of woody and herbaceous plants. Propagate by cuttings or division.

S. cineraria
Height: 18in/45cm Zone: 8
A tender little shrub with dazzling silver white leaves with yellow flowers in summer. Must have sun and good drainage.

S. doronicum
Height: 24in/60cm Zone: 5
Herbaceous perennial with daisy-like yellow or orange flowers in midsummer. Must have sun and good drainage.

Sidalcea

A genus of herbaceous plants. Propagate by division.

Sidalcea cultivars
Up to 36in/90cm, hardy to Zone 5. Spires of flower from June onwards. Best in rich soil in sun. *S.* 'Loveliness' has shell pink flowers. *S.* 'Sussex Beauty' is a soft but lively pink.

S. malviflora
Height: 30in/75cm Zone: 6
Tall racemes of flat flowers, lilac or pink, appear in June. Best in rich soil in the sun.

Silene

A genus of herbaceous plants.

S. dioica 'Flore Pleno'
Height: 18in/45cm Zone: 6
Double-flowered catchfly with sprightly violet-pink flowers in early summer. Sun or semi-shade, any soil. Propagate by division.

Sinacalia

Four species of herbaceous plants.

S. tangutica
Height: 36in/90cm Zone: 5
Perennial with bold oval leaves

Sidalcea 'Sussex Beauty'

and cylindrical racemes of white flowers in summer. Sun or shade, moist soil. Propagate by division.

Sisyrinchium

A genus of herbaceous plants.

S. striatum
Height: 18in/45cm Zone: 8
Grey-green blade-like leaves and pale creamy-yellow flowers in late May. *S. s.* 'Aunt May' (syn. *S. s. variegatum*) has pale yellow stripes on the leaves. Good in part shade or in sun. Propagate by division.

Sium

A genus of herbaceous plants.

S. sisarum
Height: 36in/90cm Zone: 6
Perennial with toothed leaves and umbels of creamy-white flowers in summer. Moist soil, sun or semi-shade. Propagate by seed.

Smilacina

A genus of rhizomatous perennials. Propagate by division.

S. racemosa
Height: 36in/90cm Zone: 4
Furrowed mid-green leaves are crowned in May by frothy spikes of sweetly scented cream flowers. Deep moist soil and shade.

S. stellata
Height: 24in/60cm Zone: 3
Like the above on a miniature scale with much less prominent flowers. Best in shade where, in moist soil, it will be very invasive.

Solidago

A genus of herbaceous perennials. Propagate by seed or by division.

Solidago cultivars
Range in height from 24in/60cm to 5ft/1.5m, all hardy to Zone 4. Many cultivars are available. *S.* 'Crown of Rays' (syn. *S.* 'Strahlenkrone') grows 36in/90cm high with butter yellow flowers. All need sun and rich soil.

S. caesia
Height: 36in/90cm Zone: 4
Slender pointed foliage and clusters of warm yellow flowers in summer. Needs sun and rich soil.

S. canadensis
Height: 5ft/1.5m Zone: 3
A golden rod which flowers in June – feathery golden sprays of diminutive flowers. It needs sun and good drainage.

× Solidaster

A single species, a hybrid between *Solidago* and *Aster*.

× *S. luteus* 'Lemore'
Height: 36in/90cm Zone: 6
Panicles of pale yellow flowers in late summer. Best in sun in rich soil. Propagate by division.

Sparrmannia

Four species of woody plants.

S. africana
Height: 20ft/6m Zone: 10
Evergreen with splendid soft large pale green leaves with umbels of white flowers in summer. Needs rich soil – an excellent conservatory plant in cool climates. Propagate by cuttings.

Sparteum

A genus of a single species.

S. junceum
Height: 10ft/3m Zone: 8
Spanish broom, an upright deciduous shrub with scented yellow flowers in summer. Must have sun and good drainage. Propagated by cuttings or seed.

Spiraea

A genus of deciduous shrubs. Propagate by cuttings.

S. 'Arguta'
Height: 6ft/1.8m Zone: 4
Leavy shrub with corymbs of white flowers in early summer. Well-drained rich soil in sun.

S. japonica
Height: 5ft/1.5m Zone: 5
A twiggy bush with corymbs of pink or white flowers in June. *S. j.* 'Little Princess' is a dwarf cultivar, no more than 24in/60cm in height, with good rosy-pink flowers and red autumn foliage.

S. × *vanhouttei*
Height: 6ft/1.8m Zone: 4
Arching stems with beautiful corymbs of white flowers in summer. Needs rich soil and sun. Propagate by cuttings.

Stachys

A genus of herbaceous plants. Propagate by division.

S. byzantina
Height: 24in/60cm Zone: 5
Perennial with the soft grey, almost white, leaves. Violet-pink flowers in May. Best in a sun but thrives in poor soil. *S. b.* 'Big Ears' has larger leaves and purple flowers. *S. b.* 'Primrose Heron' has golden leaves.

S. macrantha
Height: 24in/60cm Zone: 5
Bold leaves with an undulating surface and pink-violet hooded flowers in June. Needs rich soil and will flourish in part shade.

S. officinalis
Height: 24in/60cm Zone: 5
Spires of purple flowers in summer carried above rosettes of leaves. Sun or semi-shade.

Strelitzia

A genus of herbaceous plants.

S. reginae
Height: 7ft/2m Zone: 9
Glamorous tropical plant with blade-like leaves and dazzling

Stachys macrantha

flowers on stiff stems – orange with blue corollas. Magnificent conservatory plant. Needs warmth and moisture to do well. Propagate by offsets.

Tagetes

The marigolds, a genus of herbaceous plants.

T. patula
Height: 18in/45cm Zone: 9
The French marigold, an annual with dazzling orange, yellow or red single flowers and finely dissected pinnate leaves. Best in sun. Propagate by seed.

Tanacetum

A species of herbaceous or slightly woody plants.

T. vulgare
Height: 48in/1.2m Zone: 4
Aromatic perennial with yellow flowers in flat-topped clusters in late summer. Will grow almost anywhere. *T. v.* 'Silver Lace' has new foliage margined in silver. Propagate by division.

Taxodium

Three species of deciduous trees.

T. distichum
Height: 150ft/45m Zone: 6
The swamp, or bald, cypress, a magnificent tree with a tall conical outline. Autumn colour a fine russet. Sun or shade, damp soil. Propagate by cuttings or seed.

Taxus

The yews, a genus of woody plants.

T. baccata
Height: 70ft/20m Zone: 6
The common yew takes clipping well, producing a smooth surface of a rich, sombre green. Tough, versatile and fast growing – at least 12in/30cm a year. Sun or shade and will grow in most soils except very wet. *T. b.* 'Fastigiata' is the upright Irish yew. Propagate by cuttings or by seed.

Tellima

A genus of a single species

T. grandiflora Rubra Group
Height: 30in/75cm Zone: 6
Heart-shaped leaves flushed with purple. In early summer graceful stems bear elegant pink-fringed little green flowers. Sun or semi-shade, moist soil. Propagate by division.

Tetrapanax

A genus of a single species.

T. papyrifer
Height: 10ft/3m Zone: 8
Decorative large rounded and lobed leaves. Panicles of creamy white flowers in summer. Needs a warm, sunny position and rich soil. Propagate by seed or suckers.

Teucrium

A genus of herbaceous and woody plants.

T. chamaedrys
Height: 18in/45cm Zone: 5
A compact little evergreen shrub with grey-green foliage and little purple flowers in summer. May be clipped to shape, best in well-drained soil in a sunny oposition. Propagate by cuttings.

T. scorodonia
Height: 24in/60cm Zone: 6
Suckering subshrub with downy rounded leaves with wavy margins. Insignificant green-yellow flowers. Particularly decorative cultivars are: *T. s.*

'Crispum' with frilly edges to undulating leaves and *T. s.* 'Crispum Marginatum' with leaves spotted with white variegation. Sun or semi-shade, propagate by division.

Thalictrum

A genus of herbaceous perennials. Propagate by seed or by division.

T. aquilegiifolium
Height: 5ft/1.5m Zone: 6
Tall, airy panicles of flowers in May, mauve or pink-purple, on tall stems. Decorative leaves, a fine glaucous-green and rounded. A white form *T. a.* var. *album* is particularly distinguished. *T. a.* 'Thundercloud' has flowers with rich purple stamens. Best in rich moist soil, full sun or part shade.

T. delavayi 'Album'
Height: 4ft/1.2m Zone: 7
Dark stems with in summer heads of little hanging white flowers with prominent stamens. Best in semi-shade in rich, moist soil.

T. flavum sbsp. *glaucum*
Height: 5ft/1.5m Zone: 6
Handsomely glaucous foliage and stems mark this thalictrum which bears a froth of diminutive yellow flowers in June. Best in a sunny position in rich soil.

T. lucidum
Height: 36in/90cm Zone: 7
Cloudy panicles of creamy-green flowers in summer above glaucous foliage. Best in rich soil in sun.

T. minus
Height: 24in/60cm Zone: 6
Variable plant with finely-cut foliage and panicles of yellow flowers in summer.

T. rochebruneanum
Height: 40in/1m Zone: 8
Lobed leaves and panicles of violet or white flowers in June. Good in part shade, needs rich soil.

Thymus vulgaris aureus

T. tuberosum
Height: 24in/60cm Zone: 8
Elegant foliage and loose corymbs of pale yellow flowers in summer. Needs well drained rich soil and plenty of sun.

Thermopsis

A genus of herbaceous perennials.

T. lanceolata
Height: 36in/90cm Zone: 3
Decorative glaucous leaves and cheerful yellow flowers in May. Best in sun and moist soil. Propagate by division.

Thlaspi

A genus of herbaceous plants.

T. alpinum
Height: 6in/15cm Zone: 3
Perennial forming tufted mats of foliage with little white flowers in spring. Must have good drainage and sun. Propagate by division.

Thuja

A genus of evergreen trees.

T. plicata
Height: 230ft/70m Zone: 6
Fast growing large conifer. Best in heavy soil. Widely used as a hedging material with a shaggy surface. Propagate by seed.

Thymus

A genus of aromatic herbs, woody and herbaceous. Those below are all woody, propagated by cuttings or layering. Flourish in poor soil but need sun and good drainage.

T. × citriodorus
Height: 12in/30cm Zone: 7
Lemon-scented foliage and lilac-coloured flowers throughout the summer. *T. × c.* 'Silver Queen' has pale cream margins to the leaves.

T. polytrichus sbsp. *britannicus*
Height: 2in/5cm Zone: 7
Prostrate thyme with purple flowers.

T. serpyllum
Height: 2½in/6cm Zone: 5
A low-growing shrub which forms a spreading cushion of aromatic leaves with diminutive pink-purple flowers in the summer. *T. s.* 'Aureum' has gold variegated foliage.

T. vulgaris
Height: 12in/30cm Zone: 7
A low spreading shrub with aromatic grey-green foliage. Purple flowers in summer. *T. v. aureus* has gold foliage.

Tiarella

A genus of herbaceous perennials.

T. polyphylla
Height: 15in/35cm Zone: 7
Fresh green, lobed leaves. Pink flowers in upright racemes at the tips of slender stems. Best in moist shade. Propagate by division.

Tilia

The limes or lindens, a genus of deciduous trees.

T. platyphyllos 'Rubra'
Height: 130ft/4cm Zone: 5
The broad-leafed lime, a handsome tree with striking red-tinged shoots. Sun or part shade, grows in most soils. Propagate by cuttings.

Tithonia

A genus of perennials and shrubs.

T. rotundifolia 'Torch'
Height: 6ft/1.8m Zone: 9
Vigorous annual with attractive flowers like a marigold. Must have

plenty of sun and rich soil.
Propagate by seed.

Trachelospermum

A genus of evergreen climbers.

T. jasminoides 'Variegatum'
Height: 15ft/4.5m Zone: 9
Shining leaves with pale, almost
white striations. Sweetly scented
white flowers in high summer.
Needs a hot sunny position.
Propagate by cuttings or layering.

Tradescantia

A genus of herbaceous plants.

T. × andersoniana 'Osprey'
Height: 12in/30cm Zone: 7
Fleshy leaves and stems, white
three-petalled flowers in June.
Best in rich soil and part shade.

Tragopogon

A genus of herbaceous plants.

T. porrifolius
Height: 36in/90cm Zone: 5
Culinary salsify, usually biennial,
with delicious edible roots and
purple thistle-like flowers. Needs
rich well-drained soil and plenty
of light. Propagate by seed.

Trillium

A genus of herbaceous perennials.
Propagate by division.

T. ovatum
Height: 6in/15cm Zone: 5
Beautiful flowers in April, white
flushed with pink above three-
part leaves. Shade and acid soil.

T. sessile
Height: 12in/30cm Zone: 4
Sumptuous deep maroon flowers
in April held at the centre of
beautiful marbled three-part
leaves. Needs a shady position in
humus-rich alkaline soil.

Trollius

A genus of herbaceous perennials.

T. × cultorum
Height: 30in/75cm Zone: 5
Finely cut foliage and glowing
yellow rounded fowers in June.

Best in rich, moist soil, in sun or
partial shade. Propagate by
division. *T. × c.* 'Orange Princess'
has striking orange-yellow
flowers; *T. × c.* 'Superbus' has
much larger flowers than the type.

Tropaeolum

A genus of herbaceous plants.

T. majus
Height: 8in/15cm Zone: 9
The nasturtium, an annual with
trailing shoots up to 10ft/3m long
bearing orange-yellow flowers
with a pleasantly peppery scent.
T. majus 'Hermine Grashoff' has
fully double, deep orange-red
flowers. Flourishes in poor soil
but must have plenty of sun. Raise
from seed each year.

Tulbaghia

A genus of South African bulbs.

T. violacea 'Silver Lace'
Height: 24in/60cm Zone: 8
Slender silver-striped foliage with
beautiful pale chalky violet
flowers rising above in summer.
Must have sun and good drainage.
Propagate by dividing bulbs.

Tulipa

The tulips, essential bulbs, known
mostly in the countless cultivars,

Uvularia grandiflora

remote from their wild origins.
Need fertile soil in sun or semi-
shade. Cultivars do best if lifted
and replanted yearly. Flower
colours and type are noted in
descriptions of tulips in the text.

Ulmus

The elm genus of deciduous trees.

U. minor 'Dampieri Aurea'
Height: 22ft/7m Zone: 5
Fastigiate elm with striking
golden foliage, making a
distinctive structural tree for bold
gardeners. Sun or shade,
propagate by cuttings.

Uncinia

A genus of grasses.

U. rubra
Height: 12in/30cm Zone: 7
Forms a grassy mound with
gleaming red-brown leaves of
distinction. Needs a sheltered
position in rich soil. Propagate by
division.

Uvularia

A genus of herbaceous perennials.

U. grandiflora
Height: 30in/75cm Zone: 4
Elegant glaucous foliage with
lemon-yellow hanging flowers in
March. Best in rich soil in the
shade. Propagate by division.

Verbascum

A genus of herbaceous and woody
plants.

V. bombyciferum
Height: 7ft/2m Zone: 6
Giant biennial with vast felty pale
grey leaves and an astonishing
flower spike covered in yellow
flowers in summer. Best in sun in
rich soil. Propagate by seed.

V. chaixii
Height: 42in/1.2m Zone: 5
Herbaceous perennial with tall
spires of yellow flowers in
summer. Leaves felty, almost
white. Best in rich soil in sun.
Propagate by division. *V. chaixii*
'Mont Blanc' has white flowers.

V. olympicum
Height: 6ft/1.8m Zone: 6
Stately herbaceous perennial or
biennial with silver downy leaves
and tall spires of yellow flowers.
Best in sun. Propagate by seed.

Verbena
A genus of herbaceous plants and
subshrubs.

V. bonariensis
Height: 8ft/2.5m Zone: 8
Annual or perennial with
purple-blue flowers in summer.
Needs sun and sows itself in
suitable conditions.

V. officinalis
Height: 30in/75cm Zone: 4
Common verbena with serrated
leaves and stiff spires of pink-
violet flowers in summer. Full
sun, any soil. Propagate by seed.

V. rigida
Height: 24in/60cm Zone: 8
Perennial with stiff stems carrying
pretty, scented purple throughout
summer. Needs sun and rich soil.
Propagate by division.

Veronica
A genus of herbaceous plants.

V. gentianoides
Height: 12in/30cm Zone: 4
Delicate spires of blue-grey
flowers emerge from gleaming
foliage in spring. Sun or shade,
any soil, Propagate by division.

V. peduncularis
Height: 8in/20cm Zone: 6
An alpine plant with white flowers
veined in pink, in early summer.
Best in well drained position in
the sun. Propagate by division.

Viburnum
A genus of woody plants.
Propagate by cuttings.

V. × bodnantense
Height: 10ft/3m Zone: 6
Stately deciduous shrub of twiggy
growth with intensely scented
pink flowers in the winter. A
sunny position in rich soil.

Viburnum × burkwoodii

V. × burkwoodii
Height: 7ft/2m Zone: 5
Evergreen shrub with deliciously
scented white flowers in May. Sun
or part-shade. *V. × b.* 'Park Farm
Hybrid' has larger, pink flowers.

V. tinus
Height: 10ft/3m Zone: 7
A handsome evergreen shrub with
gleaming dark green oval leaves
and flat corymbs of white flowers
in winter and spring. Excellent in
shade, may be clipped.

Vinca
The periwinkles are a genus of
herbaceous and woody plants.

V. minor 'Argenteovariegata'
Height: 12in/30cm Zone: 4
A trailing evergreen with shining
narrow leaves edged in white and
violet flowers in spring. Best in
moist soil, thrives in shade.
Propagate by division or layering.

Viola
The violets are herbaceous plants,
annual and perennial. Propagate
by seed, division or cuttings.

Viola cultivars
All these are hardy to Zone 5. All
are biennials or short-lived
perennials and should be
propagated regularly by division
or cuttings. *V.* 'Belmont Blue'
(3in/8cm) is a good clear blue,
spring flowering. *V.* 'Foxbrook
Cream' (12in/30cm) is a *V.
cornuta* hybrid with cream

flowers. The flowers of *V.* 'Irish
Molly' (4in/10cm) are golden
coffee colour with a darker brown
centre in summer. *V.* 'Jackanapes'
(6in/15cm) has shapely flowers
that are bi-coloured, sharp yellow
and rusty-brown in early summer.
V. 'Little David' (3in/8cm) is a
summer-flowering violetta with
good creamy-white oval flowers
with frilly edges and the true
vanilla scent of violettas. *V.*
'Swanley White' (3in/8cm) is a
fine creamy white, flowering early
summer. *V.* 'Virginia' (3in/8cm)
has creamy white flowers on tall
stems in June, sweetly scented.

V. cornuta
Height: 12in/30cm Zone: 7
Rich violet-blue flowers open in
May, with backward pointing
'horns'. scrambles decoratively
through other plants. *V. c.* Alba
Group is a dazzling white. Best in
rich but well-drained soil in sun
or part shade. Will seed itself in
good conditions.

V. riviniana Purple Group
Height: 3in/8cm Zone: 4
Bronze rounded foliage and rich
purple flowers from spring
onwards. Any soil, sun or
semi-shade. Invasive in heavy soil.
Propagate by division.

V. tricolor
Height: 2in/5cm Zone: 4
Heartsease, a European wild
pansy with delightful little purple,
white and yellow flowers in
summer. Sun or part shade. Any
soil. Propagate by seed.

Vitex
A genus of trees and shrubs.

V. agnus-castus
Height: 15ft/4.5m Zone: 7
Deciduous shrub with decorative
splayed leaves of soft felty
texture. Racemes of lilac flowers
in summer are sweetly scented.
Needs a sunny position and the
protection of a wall to flower well.
Propagate by cuttings.

Vitis

A genus of vines.

V. vinifera
Height: 10ft/3m Zone: 6
The grapevine, with fine foliage and deeply divided lobes. *V. v.* 'Ciotat' has especially finely divided leaves. *V. v.* 'Purpurea' has very ornamental dusty purple leaves. Any soil, sun or part-shade. Propagate by layering.

Weigela

A genus of woody plants. Propagate by cuttings.

Weigela cultivars
Up to 8ft/2.4m high and hardy to Zone 5. Deciduous shrubs with pink or red flowers and rather coarse foliage. Best in sun. *W.* 'Newport Red' has brick-red flowers.

W. florida 'Aureovariegata'
Height: 8ft/2.4m Zone: 5
A cheerful shrub with pale green leaves edged with cream and a profusion of rosy pink flowers in May or June. Needs sun but flourishes in poor soil.

Wisteria

A genus of twining plants propagated by seed or layering.

W. sinensis
Height: 25ft/7.5m Zone: 5
Chinese wisteria with long hanging racemes of lilac flowers in May. Must have sun and rich soil. *W. s.* 'Alba' has pure white flowers.

Woodwardia

A small genus of ferns.

W. radicans
Height: 6ft/1.8m Zone: 9
Tender fern with magnificent bipinnate feathery fronds. Needs warmth and moisture. Admirable conservatory plant in cool climates. Propagate by spores or by division.

Yucca

A genus of herbaceous and woody plants.

Y. whipplei
Height: 7ft/2m Zone: 8
An amazing sphere of slender stiff silver-grey spined leaves. Cream flowers in summer. Flourishes in sun in dry soil. Propagate by seed.

Vitis vinifera 'Purpurea'

INDEX

NOTE: Picture references are in *italic*. Individual plant species are not indexed; cultivation details are included in the *Plant Directory*, pages 180–222.

adobe 132, *133*
Alberti, Leon Battista 12
annuals 110, 120, 130
Arbour 48, *49*, *157*, 158
Arts and Crafts style 44, 100, 116
Ashtree Cottage *15*, 20–3, 32–5

Beaumont House 56–9
bedding schemes 124–7
beds, raised 152, *153*
Belgium 160
bench 60, *61*, 147
borders 52–5, 60–3, *61*, *61*, 64–7, 65, 68–71, 76–9, *77*, 84–7, 96–8, 104–7, 108–11, 116–9, 128–31, 136–9, 140–3, 144–7, 166; plans *55*, *67*, *71*, *79*, *87*, *107*, *111*, *119*, *131*, *139*, *143*, *147*
'borrowed' landscape and ornaments 83, 86, 90, 146
Bosvigo House *14*, 24–7, 60–3, 120–3, see also The Vean
boundaries, concealing 38
box (*Buxus sempervirens*) 18, 70, 70, 72, *73*, 160, *161*, *165*, 166
Broughton Castle 96–9

California 80–3, 132–5
Carters Cottage 15, 28–31
Chatto, Beth 13, 17, 112–15
Chelsea Flower Show 112
Chenies Manor 124–7
Church, Thomas 11
clematis 22, 66
climbing and wall plants 20–3, 30, 46, 60, 66, 74, 94, 150
Color in my Garden 144
colour 48–51, 66, 68–71, 78, 100–3, 108–11, 120–3, 128–31, 136–9, 144–7
compost 26, 42, 63, 67, 98, 110, 122, 126, 158
conservatory 172–5

drought, plants for 112–15, 132–5
dry gardens 112–15, 132–5
drylands plants 134
dry-stone walls, planting of 84

Education of a Gardener, The 104
entrances 20–31
espalier fruit trees 148
Essex 112

fencing 46
field hedge 17
Firth of Forth 116
flower gardens 68–71, 100–47
formal gardens 24–7, 36, *37*, *39*, 44–7, *45*, *47*, 56–9, *57*, 72–5, *73*, *75*, 124–7, 156–9, *159*, 160–3, *163*, 164–7, *165*, *167*, 168–71
Fox, Martin Lane 106
fruit trees 30, 116, 134, 148, *149*, 150, 160–3; pruning of, *30*, *148*, *161*, 162

garden design, theories of 11–19
Garden House 84–7
Gardens are for People 11
gazebo 64, 65, 104, *105*, 136, 150
Gerard, John 170
gravel garden (Beth Chatto) *16*, 112–15
Great Dixter 100–3
Greene, Isabelle 132

Hadspen Gardens *19*, 128–31
hardiness of plants 115
Hazelby House 104–7
Heale House 15, 148–51
hedges 17–8, 28, 40, 47, 48, 76, 84, 104, 108, 128, 140, 166; clipping 28, 40–2, 58, 108, 140, 166
herb gardens 52–5, *53*, 156–9, 164–7; maintenance of, 54; plans *55*, *159*, *167*
herbaceous borders, *see* borders
Herball (Gerard) 170
Herterton House *13*, 68–71, 168–71
Holdenby House 156–9

Jekyll, Gertrude 54, 66, 110, 136, 144

Kellie Castle 116–9
Kemerton (The Priory) *19*, 108–11
kitchen garden 148–51, 152–5
knot garden 168–71

Lawley, Frank and Marjorie 13, 15
lawns 74, 78, 92
Lloyd, Christopher 13, 100
Lorimer, Hew 116
Lorimer, Robert 13, 116
Lutyens, Sir Edwin 100

Mallory Court 164–7
mixed borders, *see* borders
Mondrian, Piet 68
mulch, uses of 112, 118

naturalistic planting 13, 112
netting, support for herbaceous plants 106, 118, 142
Nicolson, Harold 12
Noel, Anthony 15, 92

orchard *19*, 160–3; plan *163*
organic gardening 118

Page, Russell 104
parterres 44–6, 96, *98*, *99*, 164–7, 168–71
paths 28, 52, 64, 72, 74, 78, 88, *89*, 90, *91*
pavilions *41*, 42
pergola 20–3, *21*, 46, *46*, 134, 150, *150*
period plants 156
Perry, Wendy and Michael 15
physic garden 168–71
Pitmuies, House of 140–3
Pittenweem 116
place, spirit of the 15–17
pool, informal 32–5
Pope, Alexander 132
potager 152–5
pots, plants in 92, 176–9, *173*, 174, 176–9
Priory, The, Kemerton *19*, 108–11
productive gardens 148–71
pruning 28–30, 88

raised beds 152, *153*
Renaissance garden design 12
repetition of plants 114, 140, *142*
raised beds 152
Robinson, William 13, 112
roof garden *11*, 176–9
Roosmalen, Patricia van 19
roses, use of in the garden 20–2, 42, 46, 50, 64, 76, 80, 96, 108, 144

Sackville-West, Vita 12

Saling Hall 18–9, 172–5
scented plants 28, 52–5
Scottish gardening 116
seats 60, *61*, *93*, 162, *162*, 164, *166*
shade, plants for 32–4, 94
Sissinghurst Castle 12
sitting places 48–51, 56–9, *58*, 60–3, *61*, *73*, 74, 162
skyline, importance of 54, 67, *76*, 78, 146, 179
slugs, combatting 26, 34, 122
staking 106
statues 32, 38, *38*
steps 84
Stone House Cottage Garden 76–9
stooling 100
succulents 134
summerhouse 52, *53*, 72–4, *73*, 84,

85, 88, *89*, 156, *157*
Summers, Martin 11
sunken gardens 44–7, 124–7
supports for plants 106, 118, 142
swimming pool 40–3, 82, *82*

terrace 56, *58*, 60, *61*
topiary *13*, 24, 28, *29*, 52, 70, 124, *161*, 148, *149*, 158
town gardens 36–9, 88–91, 92–5
tulip fire 126
tulips, use of in the garden 124–7
tunnel of fruit trees 148–51
turf, *see* lawns

Valentine, Carol 12, 132–5
Vean Garden, The 24–7
Verey, Rosemary 156

Villandry, Château de 152

walled gardens 36–9, 60–3, 72–5, 76–9, 80–3, 92–5, 96–9, 96–9, 128–31, 140–3, 148–51; plans, *75*, *79*, *83*, *95*
walls 80, 92–4
water 32–47
water plants 34, 36
watering, computer controlled 135
watering pots 178
Wild Garden, The 112
Wilder, Louise Beebe 144
Wiley, Keith 17
Wollerton Old Hall 44–7, 64–7, 136–9, 144–7
yew (*Taxus baccata*) 18, 52
York Gate 18, *18*, 52–5